Anemari Jansen

EUGENE DE KOCK

Assassin for the state

Tafelberg

Tafelberg
An imprint of NB Publishers a Division of Media24 Boeke (Pty) Ltd
40 Heerengracht, Cape Town
www.tafelberg.com

Text © Anemari Jansen (2015)
Photo on cover © Jim Hooper
Photos of Eugene de Kock at the TRC (photo section) © Gallo Images/Beeld/Reg
Caldicott

Cover design: Michiel Botha
Book design: Cheymaxim
Editing: Angela Voges
Proofreading: Sean Fraser

Printed and bound in South Africa

ISBN: 978-0-624-07573-8 (Second edition, first impression 2015)
ISBN: 978-0-624-07027-6 (First edition, first impression 2015)
Epub: 978-0-624-07028-3
Mobi: 978-0-624-07029-0

For Rohan, Christian and Carina

Contents

1

The man without spectacles

It is mid-winter and bitterly cold when, on that day in 2011, I first drive into the parking area of the notorious Pretoria Central Prison, the prison known today as Kgosi Mampuru II Correctional Centre. On just the previous weekend, political scientist Piet Croucamp had told a group of mutual friends at the Full Stop Café in Johannesburg of his close bond with Eugene de Kock. He had spoken of his own visits to the prison, of Eugene's razor-sharp intelligence, of thinking it unjust that Eugene was the only person still sitting in jail for doing the apartheid government's dirty work.

To be honest, like most of the people at that crowded table, I hadn't thought about Eugene de Kock for years. To me, he was the man with the spectacles we used to see on TV. I do remember hearing, shortly before his court case in 1995, that he was one of the most highly decorated policemen in the old South African Police (SAP).

Dinner conversation turned to how, as one of the founder members of the notorious police unit, Koevoet, he had survived hundreds of contacts on the Border, to how he had ruled the infamous Vlakplaas unit with an iron fist. Someone speculated that Eugene had been living on borrowed time since his arrest:

1

that, in any other time, he would have been sentenced to death or silenced by one of his own.

Immediately my curiosity was piqued. While the conversation had likely been coincidental, it happened at a personal turning point. That year, I found myself in the no man's land of an unlived life and resolved to challenge myself.

That same evening I decided to muster all of my courage and asked Piet whether I could accompany him to Pretoria Central one Sunday. A one-off visit, I had thought: just to see what a jail looks like inside.

Piet agreed. On the very next Sunday, he met me in the parking lot. He had warned me that I would not even be allowed to take my handbag in. There was row upon row of wooden benches in the reception area, swarms of visitors queueing to fill in visitor forms, and prison warders – men and women – in brown uniforms. The journalist and writer Karin Eloff was with Piet, having visited Eugene a few times before with him.

Piet was in a hurry, so I could not form any clear impressions. I recall the strange experience of being signed in and passing through the inspection point. After being searched, we waited at the back of the reception area for a small bus that transported us some 500 metres to Medium-B. There we waited for another half an hour, and were searched again. Eventually we moved through the final gate into the biting cold of a quadrangle under an awning. More rows of benches. We chose a seat; I couldn't help staring at the clusters of prisoners and their guests, leaning into one another as they spoke.

And suddenly he appeared: the man with the spectacles. Or, to be more precise, the man without any spectacles, who now preferred contact lenses. He walked towards us from the holding area where the prisoners waited for their visitors: a tall, well-built, upright man. He looked different, moved differently, from the prisoners around him. Purposeful. Resolute.

He sat down. Piet quickly introduced him, and off he went. The words poured out of him. There was no chance of interrupting his stream of stories and remarks with questions. He told of events in prison, of Koevoet memories, and remarked on the politics of the day, interspersing everything with his unique humour. Karin touched his arm.

In a blink of an eye, our allotted hour was over. Exhausted and overstimulated, I sank into my car. I recalled virtually nothing of what he had said, but burnt into my memory is how the left corner of his mouth tightened bitterly when he spoke of certain things.

I drove back home to my husband and children, to a safe, warm house, and it hit me like a thunderbolt that I knew nothing about the times and events that had clattered like gunfire from his mouth. Had I been fast asleep in the 1980s and the early 1990s? Born in 1964, I had grown up in apartheid's zenith. Thinking back to my youth, I am surprised and shocked at how uninformed and naïve I was. Did I not want to know why our country was burning, or was I just blind?

Each year, on 16 December (Geloftedag, or Day of the Vow), us children sat in Old Alberton's muggy Voortrekker Hall between people who smelt of talcum powder and silk stockings and tight suits. We were told to pray and thank God: we were His chosen people. I had grown up with an awareness of Afrikaner history – my grandfather had written his doctoral thesis on Blood River and the history of the Republic of Natal.

With most of my friends, I had been committed to the Dutch Reformed Church. At night the streets were safe. Even our garage party gatecrashers were harmless. They'd smoke and drink and do wheelspins on their 50cc motorbikes. During assembly in the Hoërskool Alberton quadrangle, the matric boys would sometimes sing, 'Hey hey hey, he's a wanker.' It took me years to find out what a wanker was.

We had a domestic worker who lived in a maid's room behind our house. Nesta cooked, cleaned, washed and ironed for all the Venters of Fleur Street. It shames me that I can't remember her surname. Samuel looked after the garden. They both drank their coffee from tin mugs and had their own plates and knives, stored under the sink. We called them by their names; they called me and my sister *nonna* Anemari and Annette and my brother *kleinbasie* Hennie. My father and mother's word was law. In 1981 Nesta took to drinking *bloutrein* (methylated spirits), became gravely ill and was admitted to an institution somewhere in northern Natal.

I had no idea my father was a Broederbond member. He worked for Armscor and was overseas for months on end. My mother got a pistol and kept the safe key in her dressing-gown pocket. She attended shooting practise organised by local reservists. At school, we attended Youth Preparedness ('Jeugweerbaarheid') classes. On Fridays, the boys wore cadet uniforms and marched on the rugby field. On occasion us girls also marched: eyes right, forward, march! O South Africa, dear land.

In 1981, our matric Afrikaans class discussed good and evil in the characters of Koki and Raka in Van Wyk Louw's epic work *Raka*. We discussed the outsider personified by Diederik Versfeld in our setwork book *Die son struikel*: 'Iemand het verkeerd gesny – ons geslag is te gou van die moer losgesny ... Ons is nie klaar gebore voor ons in die lewe gelos is nie ...' ('Someone had blundered – our generation had been cut loose from the womb too soon ... We were not yet fully shaped before we were let loose into life ...').[1]

In History class we spent hours discussing European history

and 'natural segregation' that appeared to be a solution for South Africa. Did our naivety ever discourage our teacher? Was he even aware of what was really going on, given the extent to which the National Party government had muzzled the press?

Boys … that was all my friends and I were really interested in. We had endless discussions about relationships, about the party we would attend on the weekend and how meaningful it would be to have a guy 'close dance' with you. We fell in love, kissing on the stands in athletics season and on RAU (Rand Afrikaans University) Island during prefect camps. In matric under the guidance of our cheerleaders we burned the 'old spirit' and we believed we were immortal. God was on our side.

Some of our friends went to the army, called up for two years of national service. When Arthur Froneman and Neville Schoeman died during basic training, death was suddenly among us. In the cemetery right behind the school, we wept in the guard of honour we formed at their funerals.

Eugene de Kock's 1981 was a completely different world. That year he was involved in a number of bloody fights. As one of the founder members of the SAP's covert Operation Koevoet, he had killed more people than he can – or wants to – remember. In 1981 he was reading books like Frederick Forsyth's *The Day of the Jackal*.

By 1982, our group of school friends had scattered far and wide. Some of us went to university. Life got exciting; scholarships were plentiful. There were politically active students, but I did not move in those circles.

Life went on. I got married and, by 1989, I was playing house with my firstborn, a boy. We lived in rural Venda, then in the sleepy backwater of Louis Trichardt (Makhado). I had no political awareness.

In October 1989, Butana Almond Nofomela was on death

row for the murder of a white farmer. He would be hanged. His security police colleagues refused to save his skin, so he decided to speak out about Vlakplaas. The very next month, Dirk Coetzee, a former Vlakplaas commanding officer, dropped the bomb about the Vlakplaas death squads in interviews with the *Vrye Weekblad*'s Jacques Pauw.

A former policeman told me once that at the time the police had distributed a circular stating that Coetzee was diabetic and, consequently, 'not right in the head'. In addition, all police members had to contribute R2 to General Lothar Neethling's legal fund for his court case against the *Vrye Weekblad*. At that stage there were about 134 000 officers in the police force.

My husband is a civil engineer. We moved to Shinyungwe in the Caprivi; the Golden Highway, which links Rundu and Katima Mulilo, was to be upgraded. From 1992 to 1994, a prefabricated structure in a road camp was home for me and my two sons, aged four and one. I was the only woman in a sea of men.

A few years previously, the Border War had still raged there. We had walked on the foundations of what were once the buildings of Fort Doppies, the SADF recce base on the Kwando River. We had no radio or television. That's not an excuse, I know. But I had no political awareness.

We moved again – for the tenth time in as many years – to another rented house. We came back to South Africa just in time for the first democratic election in 1994. In 1995, after the birth of our daughter Carina, we moved yet again – this time to Salt Rock on the KwaZulu-Natal north coast, once the bastion of colonial life. There were good schools for the children, and we lived a safe and privileged life.

Then, the move to Alberton. I became ensnared in suburban monotony, the comfort zone in which the right friends, church groups and activities, and the achievements of your primary-school children, determine your status. I became bored, didn't fit in. For years it felt as if I were in no man's land.

Until the visit to Eugene de Kock in June 2011, when something shifted in my consciousness. Our blood-soaked past punched me in the stomach. I began to wish that I had known, thought, done more. Thirty years later, I want to recoil in shame over my ignorance, my apathy, my blind acceptance of the illusion of normality while a low-intensity war raged in our townships and we fought a full-scale war in what was then South West Africa.

By my fourth visit, I had decided I wanted to learn more about Eugene as a person. I hoped that in the process I would also get to know more about the era in which he had worked as a policeman. We sat in the square near the women's jail, the prison benches reminiscent of garden furniture. Above me, strings of underwear and towels hung out of windows to dry. Behind me, on the first floor, were rows of small windows from which visitors were observed. The warders who moved around everywhere and a few men in orange overalls also kept a keen eye on everybody. Cardboard boxes between the benches served as waste bins. Everything felt slightly dirty.

We drank Coke and shared a KitKat Eugene broke strip by strip. He is an old-fashioned gentleman who always dusted off the dirty bench with his handkerchief before I sat down. His overall was always meticulously ironed, his hair neatly cut. 'Do you see that guy with only one eye?' he said. 'That's the Melville Koppies murderer.'

I looked around. About 20 men in prison overalls sat on benches in groups, chatting to their visitors – parents with plastic carrier bags visiting their sons, and girlfriends and friends. In the bus between the prison entrance and the visiting area, they would strike up conversation. Children in their Sunday best sat on their prisoner-fathers' laps or played on the jungle gym in the sandy square. Christoff Becker, one of the so-called Waterkloof Four, sat to one side with a blonde woman, his hair cut in a mullet and his overall as tight-fitting as a second skin. Later I started recognising others, too: Ferdi Barnard, Clive Derby-Lewis, Janusz Walus.

'What's the story with his eye?' I enquired about the Melville Koppies murderer.

'Gangs.'

Eugene's eyes flashed back and forth. 'I want to ask a favour. I hear that things are not well with the ex-Koevoet policemen who were resettled somewhere in the vicinity of Warmbaths. They are Ovambo and Kavango people ... displaced. Could you please go to Vingerkraal farm where they stay and see how they are doing?'

'Okay,' I said.

The hour-long visits were always intense. One talked quickly, focused acutely, breathed shallowly.

Eugene stood to one side and talked to others while I joined the tuck-shop queue. Two packets of crisps (R4 each), three Cokes (R7 each) and a Tex (R7), handy items for the prison's exchange system. What a different world!

Then it was time to say goodbye again. He stuffed the food into his pockets, gave me a quick hug. I walked out without looking back. The sun made my eyes water as I climbed into the bus.

Who is the real Eugene de Kock? He is a complex individual. It didn't take me long to realise there is more to him than the media's label of 'Prime Evil'. I began to read up on the Bush War and the apartheid era. I collected information from the handwritten notes he had compiled for the psychologists and a criminologist during his trial, and read the diaries he made available to me, the Truth and Reconciliation Commission (TRC) reports, and newspaper clippings. And I listened to family members' and former colleagues' recollections and anecdotes.

Twice a month at visiting time, for three years, I would make notes of our conversations on my arm – paper was prohibited. Back in my car, the first thing I would do, would be to recall our discussion and, using the key words on my arm, write down parts of it.

I am not a psychologist, a historian or a journalist. What I am is a child of apartheid. One who wanted to understand how certain things could have happened. So, I began to travel the country, following in Eugene's footsteps and trying to reconstruct his history, piece by piece. On a quest for greater comprehension.

'All the offender's personal circumstances had to be taken into account. This included his character, his conduct in life and his personality apart from the offences committed. Everything that influenced the commission of the offences had to be taken into account in order to arrive at the correct decision as to the future of that particular individual. In addition to the cold, clinical facts relating to age, factors that influenced the offender in his early years and in later life, experiences, marital status, career, religious and ideological beliefs, previous convictions, educational qualifications, health, and so on, the court further reported that it was necessary to attempt to summarise the individual as a person.'

– QUOTED FROM JUDGE WILLEM VAN DER MERWE'S SENTENCING PROCEEDINGS IN EUGENE DE KOCK'S CRIMINAL TRIAL, 30 OCTOBER 1996.

2

Boy soldier

Midrand's office buildings flash past and, ten minutes later, the Voortrekker Monument looms fatefully ahead. I am on my way to Pretoria Central, Classic FM's volume turned up high. I hum the words of 'Gabriella's Song' from the movie *As it is in Heaven*, the story of an internationally renowned conductor who was bullied as a youngster at school and later returned to his hometown where he had a Damascene experience. The N1 is clear this early on a Sunday.

I laugh when I think back to how naïve I was during my first visits. My ignorance was probably my saving grace. Once, for example, I wanted to give something to Eugene. I thought of a book, but which book? A prison story? I decided on *Shantaram* (where the main character spends a long time in an Indian prison), a packet of biltong and two Lindt chocolates. There must have been an angel on my shoulder that day since I passed through both security checkpoints with the gifts undetected.

Eugene had a support network like very few other prisoners; his affairs were in order. Later, I managed to organise six books and six periodicals that he is allowed to receive monthly and for which he needs a letter of approval from the psychiatrist at Pretoria Central. I also saw to the list of people he wished to see in his allotted visiting hours. We spoke about the books he was inter-ested in and I tried as far as possible to fill his wish list. In between

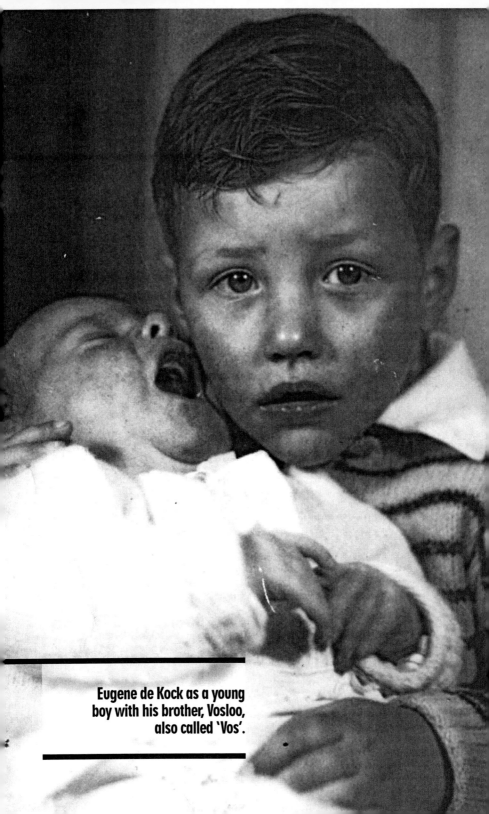

Eugene de Kock as a young
boy with his brother, Vosloo,
also called 'Vos'.

I introduced him to some of my favourites: Cormac McCarthy's epic trilogy (*All the Pretty Horses, The Crossing* and *Cities of the Plain*), Peter Høeg's *Miss Smilla's Feeling for Snow* and the Stieg Larsson trilogy (*The Girl with the Dragon Tattoo, The Girl who Played with Fire* and *The Girl who Kicked the Hornets' Nest*).

I wondered how long it would take before he started trusting me. In my view a true discussion involves two-way communication, a give and take of information and energy. After the umpteenth visit I began to think that, locked up in Pretoria Central, Eugene had simply forgotten how to do this. Even after the seventh, eighth visit, a jumble of stories still poured out in an endless stream, about Koevoet, Vlakplaas, events and contacts, people I didn't know, prison anecdotes – as if his desire to talk was insatiable. While he always told his stories with a twinkle in his eye, he kept the real Eugene carefully hidden.

Then, one Sunday morning, everything changed. 'Today, you will talk and I will listen,' he said. I knew then that we had reached a turning point. From that day I could engage in the kind of conversation with him one would expect in ordinary interaction. No more politics, war stories or hidden agendas. Slowly but surely, piece by piece, Eugene began to share his inner self with me.

Getting to this point was extremely difficult for him, he admitted to me much later. Although he did not want to show it, talking about personal matters was foreign to him.

In time, he arranged for me to meet his brother, Vos, and Rita, Vos's wife, on their plot in Sundra on the East Rand. They would give me more personal background information and I could look through some family photo albums.

'Turn left at the yellow house with the green roof,' said Vos when I phoned him. 'I am at the house next door. I'll wait at the gate.'

At eleven o'clock on a Wednesday morning, Vos was waiting

on the pavement, holding his four-year-old grandson, Alexander, by the hand. 'Get in, son,' he said. 'We're going to have a drink.'

The likeness between Vos and his brother is remarkable. The characteristic De Kock facial features and disposition struck me time and again during the course of that day. As soon as he got into my car, Vos started talking – as intense and committed a storyteller as Eugene. After an eye operation he has virtually no eyesight, but he knows the area and provided precise directions. Even from the back seat he realised when I had taken a wrong turn.

We drove through the dry, white landscape – this was mine and mealie world – to the Grasdak lapa, a restaurant and pub. Everyone there knew Vos. Later, Rita and their youngest daughter arrived. Feet up against the wooden counter, we drank Smirnoff Spins, shooters and whisky. There was much talking and drinking. Despite the conviviality I felt awkward and out of place: I remained an observer.

Here the past is still very much alive – an Afrikaner world from pre-1994. I thought about my own circle of friends and other Afrikaners I knew, and wondered how, almost 20 years after the country's first democratic election, people could be Afrikaners in so many different ways.

Earlier, I had managed to trace Eugene's Grade 3 teacher. She had remembered him as a well-mannered, above-average learner who offered her peanut butter and banana sandwiches at break. I also spoke to his aunt, Naomi van Etten, who regularly visited the De Kocks on weekends. From the accounts she and Vos gave, it seems Eugene was a sensitive and lovable little boy. When Aunt Naomi came to visit it was the greatest treat for the two boys to creep into her bed in the early mornings and curl up next to her. She was like their older sister.

In the 1950s, life for the average Afrikaner boy was simultaneously

Top: The De Kock home on a Sundra small holding on the East Rand.
Bottom: The ten-year-old Eugene (left), with his brother, Vos.

complicated and simple. Boys were taught to be men; they were not allowed to cry and had to master activities like hunting. Afrikaner children (and, for the most part, Afrikaner women) knew not to question authority: the word of the patriarch, the *dominee*, the teacher and the government was law. As Max du Preez puts it, 'God, [the Afrikaner] *volk*, patriarchy and the Broederbond all came together very cosily.'[1]

One of Vos's remarks stood out for me. 'Just before he died my father told the two of us, "The old lion is dead. They are going to come for you cubs." This was a warning to Gene.'

At 00:30 that night we stopped at his gate again. 'Vos, you know what?' I said. 'The roof of the yellow house is red now.'

I drove off with a carload of photos and stories.

To understand Eugene better I first had to get an idea of his origins. I decided to go back in time and try to form a picture of him as a child. For information about his upbringing and formative influences, I turned to his family, but also to his own description of his childhood years, written in a report for a criminologist at the time of his criminal case.[2]

> I should actually have been Josias Alexander de Kock, but my father broke with family tradition. The firstborn son of each generation of De Kocks is supposed to have this name. However, when I was born on 29 January 1949, my father decided to call me Eugene Alexander after the writer, Eugene Marais. Father had great admiration for the works by Marais.
>
> Lourens Vosloo de Kock had a successful career in the Department of Justice. He was a public prosecutor in Springs during my early childhood years when we lived on a plot outside the town. Later he was magistrate, regional

court magistrate in South West Africa and president of
regional courts in Johannesburg.

Mother's name was Jean, but everyone called her Hope.
She was very artistic and she nurtured in me a love of
music – opera and light classical music. My parents had
divergent interests. My mother had always wanted to travel
overseas, but I could never persuade my father to take her.
He was conservative and did not like new things. In later
years they did, however, travel the country.

Father was Afrikaans-speaking and Mother English-
speaking. The children at school[3] sometimes teased me and
my brother, Vossie, who is 18 months younger than me,
about this ... My parents also supported different political
parties – Father voted for the National Party and Mother
for the United Party. Father was also a senior member of
the Broederbond, but he never spoke about it. I was still at
school when he joined this organisation.

Three of my mother's brothers fought in the Second
World War and all returned. My grandfather on my mother's
side was a British soldier who fought against the Boers
and had joined up at fifteen (he added a year to his real
age to qualify) to fight in the old republics against the
Afrikaners. However, after the Anglo-Boer War [1899-
1902] he remained in the country and married an Afrikaner
woman who had been in the Potchefstroom concentra-
tion camp ... My grandfather on my father's side was a
hard-working, honest, straightforward farmer, and my
grandmother came from a very refined Afrikaner family.

Mother was a widow when Father married her and she
was very well off. Her first husband came from an old British
family but he died shortly after their wedding after being

Top: The De Kock family at their home in Commissioner Street in Boksburg. Eugene is second from the left. His mother, Hope, sits to his right. His father, Lourens, is in the foreground. **Bottom:** Eugene and Vos outside the Boksburg house.

stung by a bee. I still have a signet ring, which must be about 200 years old, an heirloom he gave her. It is gold and as heavy as a Kruger rand. After her first husband died, my mother inherited a great deal of money but the De Kocks squandered it. Father's family borrowed money and never returned it … there was this scheme and that scheme. Father bought a car and rolled it, bought a second car and rolled that too – that kind of thing.

While living on the plot, my mother farmed with chickens and made a good living from it. I helped her to slaughter the chickens although I had not even started school yet. It was easy enough to pull the feathers off but when they cut the bird open I realised it was the very chicken we were going to eat that night. Despite my young age, it troubled me that meat or chicken came to the dinner table at a price.

We were raised strictly and with discipline. Father's word was law; in my parental home I learnt never to question authority. My earliest memory of my father is of him giving me a hiding one weekend when I bothered him while he was busy planting seedlings. I pulled out some newly planted seedlings instead of weeds by mistake.

If I had to describe him in a single word, it would be 'domineering'. He could be heartless. There was never any praise or recognition for my or Vossie's good work.

'If you don't work, you are destined to become railway porters,' Father would always warn us. This was his way of teaching us to work hard and to accept adversity. I presume he thought this was the only way in which one could make a success of one's life. Our school holidays, for example, were never real holidays, because we had to work for most of the time. From the age of twelve I spent my holidays helping out on the small piece of land near Boksburg Father rented from a friend of his. We harvested mealies by hand because he had no combine harvester and we had to drag the grain bag along with us. We worked from daybreak to back-break.

My father grew up during the Depression and had a hard life as a child. His parents lost their farm in the Stutterheim-Komga area. It was a massive farm of a few thousand morgen where they farmed cattle and crops. He attended an Afrikaans school up until Standard 8 and then completed Standard 9 and 10 at Dale College in King William's Town, where he was taught in English.

After school my father joined the [extreme nationalist organisation] Ossewabrandwag.[4] He was arrested, and an English magistrate persuaded him to resign from the organisation. He then moved to Benoni to work at the Department of Justice, starting at the bottom as as an interpreter/messenger. He could speak, read and write fluent Xhosa, and English as well – skills few Afrikaners had.

I grew up in an [Afrikaner] nationalist home and we were strongly anti-communist. Father was a member of the Dutch Reformed Church and, in time, even became an elder. When we were little, he donated a large sum of money for the construction of a new church steeple in Sundra. It was about R700 – a huge amount of money at the time. However, while my brother and I were forced to go to Sunday school, our parents were not regular churchgoers. This troubled me a great deal and the obligatory Sunday school attendance made me so rebellious that as an adult I never became a regular churchgoer.

At first my father was a junior and, later, a senior Rapportryer. He was also a member of the Broederbond's executive council but later he resigned from the organisation because they refused to acknowledge the black man as a person. My parents taught us that although there were cultural differences between the different racial groups, black people also had rights.

In my early childhood years our family gave me a solid foundation and a strong sense of family loyalty. There was a congenial and warm atmosphere in our house and I always felt safe.

But one evening everything changed. I was six years old.

Father was often disparaging of Mother. She told me later, for example, that before they went to social events he would warn her not to disgrace him. Once they were at the event he always belittled her publicly. Father smoked heavily and was inclined to drink too much. This was when the arguments began.

I had been aware for some time of the atmosphere that had begun to develop in the house because of their conflict. Initially they only quarrelled late at night and tried to hide it from us, but the fighting became more open. One day, after a terrible fight, my bubble of security was burst. Mother got into the car to drive off, and Father didn't even try to stop her. Vossie and I peered out of the study window to see what was going on outside. He began to cry and was very scared.

I did not cry, but I experienced the extreme anxiety that we were going to be left behind, that my mother was going to desert us. It was a feeling of absolute fear, such as I had never felt before. In later years I would be afraid on numerous occasions, but I never again experienced such

The 1963 Year Book of Voortrekker High School, which Eugene attended, in Boksburg. He was then in Standard 7 (Grade 9).

intense fear – not during the Border War, the political unrest or even when I was involved in hand-to-hand combat with the enemy.

My mother was a dear person, kind-hearted and good to anyone in need. I loved her a great deal and was very protective of her. My father was not a bad man, except for the way he humiliated and broke my mother down … He never lifted his hand to her, not even a finger, but person-ally I would have chosen physical assault over the verbal and psychological abuse he subjected her to. He was an incredibly strong man, but his tongue! He hurt her deeply with his words.

I remember an incident at our home one evening in a fair amount of detail. A group of my father's friends was visiting. At that stage we were struggling financially and my father had a heated argument with the father of a boy

Uniform: This photo of a gymnastrade appeared in the 1963 Year Book of Voortrekker High School.

who was in my class at school. I think Father had invested money with him and it was probably the usual story where he had promised him a greater return than he could eventually pay. The men were all half drunk when Father told me: 'Eugene, go and get the axe.'

I reckoned that, seeing the guy had stolen our money, I had better get the axe. Things could end very badly, but what did I know? I was a child and if your father ordered you to do something, you did it. Luckily the man decided to beat a hasty retreat, but it was an ugly episode during which my mother had gone to hide in the bedroom. Mercifully, Vossie was asleep.

Through hard work, Father also managed to get himself out of that financial pickle.

Despite his domineering attitude, Eugene's father was an important role model. As a young boy he looked up to his father who from a young age had taught him and his brother the basics of hunting. 'He also taught us to swim, fish, catch eels and even how to slaughter poultry and sheep,' writes Eugene. It was his father who taught him to drive at the age of eleven, after which he 'drove for long distances on public and gravel roads, although I could barely see over the steering wheel or reach the clutch'.

Even today, Eugene can clearly remember his first hunt near their house on the Sundra smallholding.

That day I had nothing to do; I only wandered around. I was still too young for a catapult and that sort of thing. The next minute I saw a bird sitting on a branch – it looked at me and I watched it carefully. The bird remained perched on the branch and then it was as if a silence descended. I half looked down and picked up a clod of earth. It lay flat in my hand and, as I threw it, I sensed immediately that it was on course … I hit the bird.

I was scared stiff, but proud because I had hunted. Father always took me with him when he went to shoot the mousebirds that ate his grapes and fruit. I would say from that moment onwards I also felt like a hunter.

I picked up the bird and ran straight to my mother: 'Look, look,' I said.

She looked at me with a pained expression. Today I think it may have been caused by what she realised was my loss of innocence. What I saw in her eyes that day I was destined to see many more times in my adult life in the eyes of parents who had lost their children – the infinite sadness caused by total loss. Mother said nothing except that we should go and bury the bird under the vine pergola.

At six I was given my first *windbuks*, an air rifle, and learnt to shoot. In those years all young boys had an air rifle or a shotgun. Mine was a Falke 70 that was too heavy for me to handle properly, but Father urged both me and Vossie – who had to fire with the rifle rested because he was still so small – to keep practising. He trained us until we could hit a coin from a distance of 15 metres, and we both became dead-accurate shots.

My father was a male role model for us. He was a macho man and a typical Afrikaner.

I was a Voortrekker from Grade 1 to Standard 10 [Grade 12]. Vos and I enjoyed the veld camps a lot. As a result of the Voortrekker camps and my experiences with hunting and fishing, I developed a love of Africa, nature and wildlife.

When I was fifteen, I was allowed to go on a camp to Maun and the Okavango Delta in Botswana.

Our vehicle broke down near Maun on the Makgadikgadi pans. We were a mixed group of about 40 Voortrekkers and Boy Scouts – to improve relations between Boer and Brit. It was 1964 and I was the youngest of the group; the rest were all matric pupils. We were lost for about ten days without any contact with the outside world. Even air searches could not find us.

We had enough food but were short of water; we had to dig to find it. I was the only one in the group who was happy and at home in the veld. It was my natural habitat. Then already I saw how big boys and grown men become panicky and belligerent under pressure. They were frightened, especially at night. But I was a fish in water. I felt no fear at all.

From a young age I had taken refuge in books. At primary school I had already dispensed with Charles Dickens's *A Tale of Two Cities*. I read everything I could lay my hands on: *Die Swart Luiperd, Rooi Jan, Trompie, Fritz Deelman*. I read the *Patrys* series and even my father's *Justitia*[5] journals. At nine I received my first Bible, but I rarely read it. When I turned twelve my parents began to order *Reader's Digest* books for me.

For as long as I can remember the honey badger, or *ratel*, has been my totem. The first book that I read by myself was *Buks*, which was about a honey badger. I can't even remember how old I was. I was fascinated by the story of the honey badger and the otter who had so many problems with each other.

When I went to high school I started reading Heinz

G. Konsalik and in Standard 8 I started on the collected works of [Afrikaans author] CJ Langenhoven. My father owned the entire first edition. I also read all the magazines – *Huisgenoot, Sarie, Brandwag, Femina*. It is probably obvious that I led a protected life as a child.

Yet I knew from an early age that I wanted to be a soldier one day. As a child I read countless books about the Second World War, particularly about the German armed units, their tactics and so on. In History class at school we also learnt about Napoleon – the battle at Borodino fascinated me. I had great respect for the German soldiers' capabilities, their training and their precision.

I have no idea why I wanted to become a soldier; nothing pushed me in that direction. It was almost as if it was in every fibre of my being. It was a feeling I had; this was simply what I was.[6]

The De Kock boys had a strict upbringing. On weekends, Eugene had to do tasks around the house and during the holidays he had to work on farms or do postal deliveries. There was not much visiting or playing with friends. Sometimes he did his homework with one or two friends but there was 'no running around, not during the day or in the evenings':[7]

My father also did not allow us to listen to LM Radio. Look, the 1960s were a different era and anyone who did not listen to *Boeremusiek* was a ducktail. But on Sunday evenings Mother would slip into my room and push a small radio under my pillow. Then it was my chance to listen to LM. I also enjoyed my mother's favourites – Sinatra, Chopin, Caruso (still on old 78s), which we would listen to

Eugene and his brother were both members of the Voortrekker movement. These initiation rituals took place during a Voortrekker camp the boys attended. Photo credit: Vosloo de Kock.

together. This is how my love of classical music developed. My father would not even go to the movies but he would drop my mother and us boys off at movies like *Taxi to Tobruk*, *Polyanna* and all the old Afrikaans movies such as *Die Onderwyseres en die Bosveldboer* and *Groenkoring*.

At that time, women and children were considered to be a man's possessions. My father's word was law and everyone had to dance to his tune … listen to what he wanted to listen to on the radio, do as he said.

The stutter Eugene developed as a young child greatly influenced his school years. His speech impediment was to shape him significantly as a person.

Although I am actually left-handed, at primary school I was forced to write with my right hand. Old Mrs Jankowitz – will I ever forget her name? – smacked my left hand from Grade 1 onwards until I began using my right hand. I don't know whether my speech problem may have started then. In any case, it did me great damage.

We were all so terrified of our teachers. In Grades 1 and 2 the children would rather wet themselves than ask to leave the room. They would also wet themselves when the teachers began to scream at them. As for me, I froze in fear when they became abusive and I couldn't get a single word out.

Today I am right-handed, but I can also shoot left-handed, though not equally well. With my left hand I am good with a pistol and above average with rifles. I also write reasonably well left-handed. However, at school I constantly thought I was doing something wrong. You didn't mention this to your parents – you didn't want to get another hiding at home. When they eventually realised what was going on, it was already too late. While my mom knew I was left-handed, they weren't aware of what was happening at school.

I completed my high-school education at Voortrekker High School in Boksburg and in general I cannot complain about my school days. Aside from my speech impediment – which proved a severe handicap and in reality forced me to avoid people – school was not a bad experience. I never failed a subject and while I was an average scholar, in History I stood head and shoulders above my classmates as it was my favourite subject. Geometry and algebra were not my strong point and frustrated me because I did not understand them. In later years, I looked at geometry again out of interest and found that I could, indeed, master it. Did I lag behind or was our teaching inadequate? I don't know.

What I do know is that the rest was beaten into us, usually with a cane, blackboard compass or a thick plank, sometimes across your back while you were seated. I will never forget how much dust could be raised from a blazer by such a blow.

On occasion I was a class captain – everyone took turns – and later also a prefect. Prefects were elected by all the learners in the school. I presume I was chosen because I treated everyone the same: it made no difference to me which side of the railway tracks you came from (Boksburg North and Boksburg East were separated by the railway line). I was always assigned to the furthest-flung parts of the school grounds where the troublemakers hung out, but never reported any of them.

I had a few very good friends, played rugby and took part in long distance. At home I trained alone by running in the evenings – long distances – and also built a weight-lifting system using materials available to me. I even used containers filled with sand.

My weekends were rather predictable. On Friday afternoons I had to mow the lawn and dig the garden beds. Then I had to do some cleaning and my schoolwork until darkness fell. Vos could not help because of his leg. As a young child he was admitted permanently at the Far East Rand Hospital for a few years with TB, first in one leg and then in the other. Mother told me later that on both occasions the doctors wanted to amputate Vossie's leg, but both times my father had refused – not a son without legs!

Saturdays were nice. There were always rugby matches that lasted until about two o'clock. After that we did homework and then, from about seven to nine o'clock, you could visit your girlfriend. My girlfriend's name was Estelle. She was in Standard 6 and I in Standard 9. She had dark, copper-red hair and a sprinkle of freckles over her nose. She was a bright girl, always first or second in her class, and she excelled in everything she did. Estelle was beautiful. Her family lived a few blocks away from us, but I would have walked to Upington just to see her for those two hours.

When I arrived at her parents' house her father would always be on the front porch busy sharpening his pocket knife.

'Do you know what this pocket knife is for?' he would say when he greeted me.

'No, *Oom*.'

'To cut it off.'

Thereafter he ignored me until about eight-thirty, when he started to cough.

Estelle and I would spend the entire evening talking in the sitting room, sitting on opposite ends of the couch.

No hand-holding was allowed. By about ten to nine I would start paving the way for the farewell kiss at the front door. When we turned away from each other, we were both weak at the knees. I only wish that at the time I had known more about girls, about the female gender. I mean, even when you had a wet dream, you only imagined your girl-friend's face and her body down to about her navel – beyond that, you knew fuck-all.

Estelle and I were a couple for almost eight years and I loved her very much. I planned to marry her, but I didn't want to be poor like so many policemen. I wanted to do things properly and be able to take care of her. At that stage I had to go to Rhodesia [today Zimbabwe] regularly for long periods to serve in the Police Anti-Terrorist Unit (PATU). This meant extra money; I wanted to go one last time to save enough money to buy her an engagement ring.

She said, 'Gene, please don't go.'

I would be away for five months. I went anyway – and, ja well, then I received a 'Dear John' letter. Of course it was my fault; I should not have gone that last time. I really wanted to marry her, but other men hunted her down mercilessly in my absence.

That was one of the greatest tragedies of my life.[8]

Eugene's speech impediment made him an outsider since childhood. He became a young man who swallowed his words and his emotions, who communicated haltingly with the world.

He kept quiet in obedience to his father and had an over-developed sense of responsibility towards his mother.

> We had few discussions at home. We had to perform our duties and carry out our tasks properly or we got a hiding. I was afraid of my father's temper. We could not reason with him at all. Because of this, Vos and I took our problems to my mother. She comforted and tried to protect us.
>
> So, there was poor communication between us boys and Father because he was so domineering, impatient,

'Every Friday we had cadet practice at school. We were taught how to march and shoot with a .22 rifle,' Eugene says. He is second from left (with cap and glasses). The man on the far right is a teacher.

strict and unapproachable. He very often gave us hidings – which sometimes bordered on assault. He was extremely aggressive and he would hit us with a cane until it broke. If we cried he would hit us again. We learnt to suppress our emotions and hide our pain and heartache. I learnt not to cry or look for sympathy.

In my last two years at school my father and mother both became more involved in my school activities. Why, I do not know and at that point it also did not matter to me. Father supported me during rugby matches and gave me advice when I played lock for the first team in Standard 9 and matric – but by then it was too late …

In time, my parents drifted apart. Mother told me about this and discussed it with me. Yet I never hated my father. I was afraid of him and when he was angry or aggressive I usually avoided him. In later years I stayed away from him too, but kept in touch with my mother and sent her money so that she could have things like a microwave oven – which my father would not buy. It was not that he couldn't afford one or was stingy; he simply didn't believe in such things. New innovations did not interest him; he clung to the 'old days'. It was a struggle to persuade him to buy a TV and a titanic battle to persuade him to get M-Net. That was, again, for Mother's benefit and to keep her company. Father only watched sport and the news.

Despite their divergent interests, there was a bond of love between my parents. Or rather, a kind of relationship or friendship that kept them together – a friendship based on mutual respect, trust, understanding, support and the I-am-there-for-you principle. Some of these characteristics naturally flew out of the window when Father drank heavily, but always the relationship would be repaired. While Mother was good-natured, hard-working and solid, she could also be volatile when angered. But she was usually the gentle one. One night in the early 1980s I challenged my father when he again became abusive towards my mother. I told him I would no longer stand for his behaviour. He got aggressive and wanted to start a physical fight. I refused to back down and told him that this was not a father-son issue, that he had to realise my mother was the weaker one. I told him I would no longer tolerate his behaviour, whether directed at my mother or not. That if he raised a finger to her, he would unleash years of pent-up rage in me. Then, we both stepped down.

From that day onwards, my relationship with my father changed dramatically. We developed the kind of bond I had longed for since childhood. From that moment, there was mutual respect and proper communication. This incident still brings tears to my eyes: not the event itself, but the thought of the wasted years that we would never recover.[9]

Professor Anna van der Hoven is a criminologist who, in 1996, drew up an evaluation report for Eugene's criminal court case. In it, she wrote that children can acquire aggressive behaviour patterns through 'family influences, subcultural influence and direct experience'.

She went on to write that 'in the typical Afrikaans culture small boys were taught to be "men", and not to cry. They were taught to suppress emotions such as sadness, empathy, tenderness and so on. However, living out one's aggression was considered accept-able and was encouraged – for example, through contact sports such as rugby.'[10]

According to her, Eugene's father was the 'absolute authority' in the home, an authority that was never questioned or challenged. Furthermore: 'In the typical Afrikaans home children were indoctrinated to respect the government. Whatever the government decided was be accepted as correct. Further indoctrination was brought to bear by the Voortrekker movement and cadets; in which the accused [De Kock] participated until matric. Afrikaans children were taught to obey authority and not to be critical … The result was that the accused accepted orders from an authority such as the police more readily.'

At 35, Eugene had stood up to his father for the first time. At the same time, however, he strove to follow in his father's macho footsteps, because this was the route to praise and recognition.

Hear the mighty rumbling

En hoor jy die magtige dreuning?
oor die veld kom dit wyd aangesweef:
die lied van 'n volk se ontwaking
wat harte laat sidder en beef.
Van Kaapland tot bo in die Noorde
rys dawerend luid die akkoorde
Dit is die LIED van Jong Suid-Afrika.

At high school we all knew the words of Eitemal's 'The Song of Young South Africa' and sang it with fiery patriotism. In 1968 Eugene, too, knew these words. He was nineteen and on the verge of adulthood. Like most boys of that age he was filled with hormones, not afraid to take risks, giving no thought to their consequences – and far more impressionable than he realised.

My own sons are at this age and already spreading their wings. I find the impulsiveness, drive and physical perfection – and, above all, the fearlessness and unshakeable will to live – of boys in this stage of their lives fascinating. I wonder about Eugene's nature, and his experiences, directly after school at a time when national service in the military (or police) was not an option but an order.[1]

Eugene had gone to the Army College in Pretoria in 1967, aiming to study for a BMil degree at Saldanha, but for a variety of

Eugene at the end of 1967, shortly after he left the South African Army College in Pretoria.

reasons things did not work out. Although he enjoyed the training, he was shocked by the junior and non-commissioned officers' behaviour and foul language. Their sole purpose, it seemed to him, was to break the troops' spirit. This left him disillusioned with the defence force.[2]

But what the defence force did succeed in was to reveal his calling. The troops were shown the propagandist 'shockumentary' *Africa Addio (Farewell Africa)*, which portrays the end of the colonial era in Africa. Among other footage, it shows scenes of the aftermath of the Mau-Mau rebellion in Kenya and the revolution in Zanzibar. Internationally, the documentary was heavily criticised as racist in some circles.

However, it upset Eugene deeply. 'For the first time in my life I saw the savagery that one human being could inflict upon another. Not only what black could do to white, but what black could do to black. I don't think I was mature enough to handle the impact [of the film]. In any case, that day I decided that such savagery would never happen in our country – that white people would not be wiped out.'[3]

Then, at nineteen, he made the decision that would change his life: he wanted to fight terrorism. He left the army after a year and joined the South African Police (SAP), believing he could live out this calling there. 'Furthermore, this would save me the trouble of having to communicate with others, and I wouldn't have to humiliate myself any longer. My naivety was blatant. I learnt later that you can run, but you can't hide from your problems. It didn't even occur to me that I would have to do ordinary station work and daily policing and that that would entail communicating with the public.'[4]

The first few times I took the road to Pretoria Central, I asked myself if I would ever really understand anything about Eugene's

Troepleiers — 1968

In June 1968 Eugene (in the middle photo in the third row, third from right) graduated from the Police College in Pretoria West. He was a group leader.

life. I have never been in the police force, I am not married to a policeman, and have never been in a war. I dislike aggressive men and the blood and guts in horror movies. A natural place to start would be to talk to people who were part of Eugene's life and work environment.

When I explained this to Eugene one day he looked at me dead serious. 'Make friends with Larry Hanton. He is like my brother. He can open doors for you if you want a better understanding of things. Take him with you wherever you go. He knows everything and everyone. I'm making him personally responsible for you.'

This was a novelty for me: did I then need someone to look after me?

Larry is a former member of the police's special task force, also called the Takies, and Eugene's long-standing colleague and friend. His nickname was Priester (Pastor). I was apprehensive about our first meeting in a bar in Queen Street in Kensington, Johannesburg. Larry was on his way to the 35-year reunion of the Takies and was dressed up for the event in his only pair of long pants and an open-necked shirt. An unobtrusive man, but one not to be judged by his appearance – beneath the calm exterior is an intelligent man with a capacity for razor-sharp observation. He must be shy, I thought later – the entire evening he never stopped talking. He was anything but a gunslinger.

Larry lives on a yacht in Durban harbour and is at peace with the world. He has a soft heart, a sense of humour and the disposition of a true policeman: he wants to get things done. Like all the former policemen with whom I spoke, the police – the 'Force' – had been his whole life: it had shaped him. Speaking to me often released a flood of memories with him.

With patience and a great willingness to share his nuanced insight, Larry was my guide on my journey along the track of

Eugene's life. For the next three years he took me into an inner circle of former policemen, Koevoet and task-force members, as well as Vlakplaas operators. Larry opened doors for me that as a woman and a civilian I probably never would have passed through.

One of our first visits was to Koos Brits, who was stationed at Benoni where Eugene was sent after his initial training at the Police College. Brits now manages his transport businesses from two lock-up garages in Pomona on the East Rand. The cement floor of the garage was scrubbed clean, his desk was perfectly aligned and an orderly fifteen or so laminated police certificates hung dutifully on the wall, while nature scenes from a calendar decorated another wall. 'You have to make the place liveable,' he explained.

We sat on two chairs and a drum full of oil. Brits is lean, his long beard speckled with grey. How did he remember Eugene as a very young policeman, and what was it like to work for him later?

Brits remembered that first day clearly. 'It was a Saturday morning and a group of newly trained *blougatte* was offloaded at the Benoni police station in Bedford Avenue. I was on duty in the charge office and "received" the group. One youngster stood out. He was well built and wore black glasses with heavy frames. Little did I know that he was destined to walk a long road in the history of the SAP. His stutter also struck me.

'Eugene was allocated to my group; I helped him with his first accident report. Soon he took to the books and wrote exams. It was clear that he had ambition.'

Eugene later became Brits's section sergeant. 'Nobody went off duty until all reports were completed,' he said. 'Gene had a short fuse, though. He got angry quickly and wouldn't take any back-chatting. When he was cross he began to stutter even more and went pale. Then you knew it was best to disappear.'

Yet he was popular and had many friends, Brits said. 'And cocky, I tell you.'

He drew deeply on his cigarette. 'But he was not impossible to persuade. If you did your homework and came to him with a new plan, he would hear you out.'

Later, when I told Eugene about my visit to Brits, it was the remark about his cockiness that got a reaction. 'You know, the SAP guys may have thought that I kept to myself or didn't want to talk to them. But I couldn't talk! Stuttering is hugely stigmatised and I suffered quite badly from it. But I never gave up and simply swallowed my embarrassment.'

In time Eugene was promoted to warrant officer and ordered to form a crime prevention squad. Brits and Larry Hanton were among the members of this squad. 'It was soon clear that you had to do your work properly or you'd be out,' said Brits. 'We were successful under Gene's command. I admired how he gave you credit if you did good work. On many nights, when the station was quiet, we would braai a piece of meat behind the mine dump in Snake Road. Or sometimes on a Saturday, after a successful day, we would get together for a few beers and have a post mortem before going off duty.'

Eugene's experiences as a young policeman on the East Rand prepared him, but also started hardening him. Benoni was, in his own words, 'a hell of a rough place' at that time, but the policemen who worked with him were 'seasoned old dogs and even rougher':

> My first day kicked off with night duty at 22h00, a vehicle inspection and, at 22h10, a hotel fight at which trouble-makers were breaking the place down. I learnt in a few minutes that night that it was all about survival, not about

43

An old *Justitia* magazine (top) and a photo of the Police College (bottom). Eugene was such a bookworm as a child that he even read copies of his father's *Justitias*.

how you won. I could not believe the barbarism of the whites – against fellow whites.

It also occurred to me that my uniform was the trigger, the detonator, for those who were in conflict with one another to join forces against me as a policeman. It is probably wrong of me to think like this, but we never encountered good or decent people – just troublesome ones. That same evening there were father-beating-mother-half-to-death incidents, and child molestation, trespassing, motor accidents, serious injuries, stabbings, drunk driving, housebreaking and any number of other culture shocks.

When I recall it now, it is as if I am looking at a Salvador Dali painting. The veneer of refinement, law-abidingness and good-naturedness was thin.

Yet that night I realised that a successful career in the SAP was something I wanted to – and would – achieve. The East Rand, especially Benoni, was a good training ground, but one incident is burnt into my memory.

In 1969, two or three days after Christmas, Constable Hennie Coetzer and I were called out to a disturbance of the peace complaint, common at this time of year. It was about 02h00 or 03h00 in the morning when we arrived at the house. As the two of us climbed out of the police van we heard a loud crack but did not think it was anything to worry about.

But at the open front door we came upon a bloodied woman in her pyjamas, leaning against the wall. She had been shot in the chest. By that time we had realised the seriousness of the situation and had drawn our weapons. In the dining room we found a man who had just shot himself; his legs were still jerking. He had a head wound and was beyond help. The man had a 9 mm and a .22 pistol with him, and extra rounds.

In the first bedroom we found two small blonde girls, each with a shot to the crown of her head. In the next room, a woman – dead, also bullet wounds – and two little boys, still very small, shot in the head. In the main bedroom we found a policeman who had been shot in his bed. It was Detective Sergeant Corrie Strydom.

And in the sitting room, a Christmas tree with flickering lights and toys. A house filled with corpses, children's bodies at Christmas time … and the start of my sleepless nights and nightmares. There was no reason for them to have died. In those early-morning hours I looked up at the heavens and asked: 'God, are You asleep – why the children?'

A Christmas with a bitter barb. I was barely 20 years old.

Another incident that will always remain with me was a serious motorcar accident that Constable Hennie Coetzer and I came upon in Benoni one Sunday afternoon in 1970 on the Brentwood Park–Kempton Park road. A heavy motorbike had collided head-on with a motorcar.

At the scene we began to follow procedure and took control of the scene, regulated the traffic and made the necessary measurements. I walked to the body of the motorcyclist to make sure he was dead. At first I thought I was hallucinating: from his lower jaw and tongue I could see straight into the gullet. I couldn't breathe; all I could do was stare. My fingertips went ice cold.

When I had pulled myself together, I went in search of the rest of his head. About 10 metres from the body I found the brain. Another 5 metres away I found the crash helmet, but nothing else. The skull was still missing.

Back with Coetzer, I noticed him looking down at my hands. He asked if I had been injured: my hands were covered in blood. Then I looked inside the helmet and saw the top of the deceased's skull lining the inside of it.[5]

Between 1969 and 1974 Eugene completed a total of nine periods of service with the Police Anti-Terrorism Unit (PATU) in Rhodesia. These so-called kitbag squads were so named because their members, most of whom were from the SAP, had to be mobile in the veld and carry all their equipment themselves. For weeks on end they patrolled on foot in the farming and tribal areas of north-eastern Rhodesia, along the Mozambican border. After 1974 the SAP officially withdrew from the conflict, but in talking to former officers I heard that some had secretly stayed behind.

Since I knew very little about our involvement in the Rhodesian conflict I asked Hennie Heymans, a former brigadier, why the SAP had been drawn into a conflict in a neighbouring state. Heymans is the editor of the online police journal *eNongqai* and an expert on the history of the South African Police. 'The reason why SAP members were sent to Rhodesia is simple: sending in army troops could be interpreted as an attack on Britain's rebel colony of Rhodesia,' he explained. 'The police, on the other hand, acted as part of a policing initiative.'

In his report for Professor Anna van der Hoven, Eugene wrote extensively on his experiences in Rhodesia and how they influenced him as a young policeman.

Late in 1968 I was called up for my counter-insurgency course and before Christmas I was sent to the Victoria Falls in Rhodesia, where the border base of the SAP's

A very young Eugene during one of his first periods of service
at the Police Anti-Terrorism Unit (PATU) in the former Rhodesia.

anti-insurgency unit (SAP-TIN) was. This unit also transferred police members for service in PATU.

Although the service period went without incident, a fellow policeman and friend, Constable Cooper from Port Elizabeth, died after falling ill. He died the day after we were supposed to load him onto an air force flight to South Africa. The pilot had refused to transport him, fearing he had an infectious disease such as yellow fever.

The next day we received a message that our friend had died of cerebral malaria. This, after he had complained continually to the doctor at the base that he was sick, and had presented all the symptoms of malaria. But the doctor couldn't care less – he lounged around all day at the Vic Falls hotel, going to the casino and chasing women. Our friend died. There was talk among the older men that they wanted to teach the doctor a lesson, but nothing came of this. He was later transferred.

That was my first experience of the kind of treatment the wounded and sick received from our own people. Today I have no doubt that this treatment led to the death of many young troops and policemen.

The days in the Rhodesian bush were too comfortable, as if terrorism didn't exist. However, with my military background I could identify the gaps in our equipment, formations and numbers should it come down to battle. But it was a case of shut-your-mouth-and-get-on-with-your-work. The everything-is-okay syndrome reigned – for as long as nothing happened.

I learnt a huge amount from the Rhodesian instructors and also, of course, from my own experiences and observations. Every time we went to Rhodesia, we were first sent on a three- to four-week orientation course. We had to learn, or re-learn, basic 'bushwise' principles. New measures against the terrorists were being implemented – and the terrorists were coming in far more sophisticated, better trained, more determined and in greater numbers. These courses were of huge importance later in my life.

Here I encountered the Rhodesian Light Infantry (RLI), who presented some of the courses, but I still felt as if something was missing. On one of the most intensive courses along the Bambeyi River I saw how the Rhodesian African Rifles (RAR) operated. This was the first time I had observed such professional and determined fighting spirit and fighting capacity. For me a black unit such as this, with one or two white members, seemed to be the answer. The white members were very good: less conventional, but still too conventional in the face of the unconventional terrorists they had to confront.

On a subsequent course I encountered Rhodesian Special Air Service (RSAS) officers who were absolutely unconventional and worked in small or large groups, depending on needs and circumstances. But they lacked black members. In my view a combination of the two units – the RAR and the RSAS – would be Africa's answer to terrorism. I was still too young to be taken seriously and, when I mentioned my thoughts to my friends, their answer was: 'Fuck the bush, man – we've only got a few more days to go. We just want to make it back home.'

Two incidents stand out from this time. The first may not have had such a great impact on me because of my youth and ignorance, but showed the cold-bloodedness and murderous intent of the enemy's actions. The second shocked me and made me realise that we weren't dealing with human beings.

The first incident took place in the early 1970s when five SAP members stationed at the Victoria Falls were captured by Zipra/Zanla terrorists while swimming in the Zambezi River.[6] One man was kept alive, but the others were taken a short distance away and were summarily executed. When we went to relieve the unit, local people showed us where they had been murdered. The body of the other policeman was never found. Even during the peace discussions between then prime minister, John Vorster, and the Zambian president, Kenneth Kaunda, no answers were forthcoming. Security information that reached us in bits and pieces indicated that the abductee had been tortured so cruelly that he had died from his injuries, and that those who had been executed had in fact been the lucky ones.

I was under the impression that if you surrendered or put your hands up, you would then be protected according to certain stipulations such as those of the Geneva Convention. This belief was finally shattered in 1974 during my service with PATU. I understood from the Rhodesian police that no convention, of any kind, meant anything to these so-called freedom fighters. I did not have a copy of the convention myself and was not trained in convention protocol; I never found one on any terrorist either. Nothing in the actions of SWAPO, the ANC, PAC or Zipra/Zanla ever indicated that they had been trained in these legalities. All we knew was that we needed to capture terrorists alive for intelligence purposes.

The second incident was really bad. During a second

Top: Here Eugene stands next to a so-called 'pislelie' during one of his periods of service. **Bottom:** PATU members often hunted when they were out in the Rhodesian bush. Eugene is on the far right.

attempt at peace negotiations between Rhodesia and the so-called freedom fighters, with South Africa, Britain and Zambia acting as facilitators, all forces in Rhodesia were told that when the ceasefire came into force, there was to be no firing on any terrorist, even if provoked. The terrorists could also give themselves up and move around freely without weapons.

During this time a group of about seven SAP members and one black British South Africa Police (BSAP) member took two vehicles to Mount Darwin for servicing. On the border, at the Mazoe River, they noticed a group of black men hitchhiking in fatigues. They were members of the Zipra/Zanla forces.

When the front vehicle stopped, one of the men climbed up and held a pistol to the driver's head. The police members riding on the back of the second vehicle were also held at gunpoint. The hitchhikers then hauled AK-47s from the bushes nearby. All the policemen were captured and taken to a nearby shop where they were exhibited as prisoners and humiliated. The terrorists then left with our men.

At the Mazoe River, they began to shoot at them.

The Mazoe was in full flood. When our men tried to escape they came under fire. As far as I know, only two survived. When the message reached us, we immediately wanted to launch a follow-up operation but the terrorists had moved over the Mazoe Bridge to a 'frozen' area to which no other security forces had access. The peace negotiations were still underway and we could not act. The discussions eventually broke down, but by that time it was too late.

This event had an enormous impact on me. I have thought so many times in my life about how our men had no chance. If this was the ideology we were up against, surely we were justified in resisting it with every fibre of our being, using any means? These so-called humanists with their AK-47 rifles were not the democrats they claimed to be. I decided that day to fight against this scum, this rubbish who acted under the banner of justice, with every conceivable means at my disposal.

To rub salt into these raw wounds, about a week later two uniformed SAP colonels turned up at the PATU base and told us that when we returned to South Africa we were not to mention anything about the events at the Mazoe Bridge. I can only hope and pray the events of that day were not orchestrated by the Selous Scouts in an effort to scupper the negotiations. Because I took part in so many covert operations later in my life, I cannot exclude the possibility. I have made many enquiries about this, however, and have found nothing to substantiate my suspicion.

I remember so many incidents as a PATU officer. Our PATU groups were known as 'sticks'. Each stick comprised five men – four white men and a black officer of the Rhodesian BSAP. A stick was the number of heavily equipped members that one Alouette helicopter could transport safely to a specific patrol area or for an operational follow-up.

Our foot patrols were thorough, difficult and exhausting. Patrols could last from a few days to between 14 and 18 days. We reprovisioned in the veld (in other words: 'There's your food, there are your radio batteries, now bugger off back into the veld'). My stick comprised me, two other white members and two black BSAP members.

PATU was sometimes used for enforcing the 'keeps', the

safe settlements established to protect the local population from Zipra/Zanla guerrilla intimidation and influence. Some of these keeps were attacked periodically. We also provided ordinary services such as setting up observation posts and laying ambushes.

PATU was also used as bait. No guerrilla group would ever leave a small group of five men in peace – they would certainly attack us or try to lead us into an ambush. This would give the joint control centre the opportunity to unleash troops and other groups of the security forces on the guerrilla forces. This is not unusual in warfare and is all part of the job. If you didn't like it, you might as well pack up and go home or to a base where you could lie and tan all day.

But PATU paid a high price for these tactics. One day, our stick was waiting for a vehicle to pick us up for re-deployment. The pick-up point was a rural trading store. We watched the vehicle approach. It was 150 metres from the store when a deafening sound hit us and the vehicle disappeared in a fireball and a cloud of black smoke.

The vehicle had detonated a landmine with its right front wheel. Given the force of the explosion and the damage to the vehicle, it must have been more than one landmine or a landmine with additional TNT booster charges. The mine had not been buried – it had simply been laid in a deep pool of water that had collected on the two-track road.

The driver, a Rhodesian, was in a critical condition. These Rhodesians – older reservists were usually used as drivers – were hardened veld people and, like this man, they were volunteers.

His visible injuries were to his feet and his lower legs

The Rhodesian bushveld posed many challenges for soldiers on both sides of the conflict and provided cover for numerous war atrocities.

to just under his knees. That was what we could identify. Internal injuries – back and neck injuries, torn retinas, torn brain membranes and burst eardrums – were not our department. The driver was still breathing, and groaning, and blood was spurting from both his ankles in time with the beating of his heart – which was no longer beating as strongly.

It was horrifying. By then I had witnessed many vehicle and motorcycle accident scenes. While I had been at, and investigated, more gruesome scenes than this one, the wounded were always the paramedics' or ambulance staff's problem.

This man was not a 'problem' – he was one of us. We lifted him out of the vehicle as gently as possible. It was only when he was lying on the ground that the full extent of his injuries struck us. The radio operator had called in the casevac [casualty evacuation] helicopter while the explosion still echoed in the surrounding hills.

No vehicle is landmine-proof. The sandbags in the body of the vehicle and on the floor of the driver's cab had only made a difference up to a certain point. That point was the driver's knees ... Both Achilles tendons had been torn off the bone; all the veins and smaller blood vessels hung like loose threads, and the bone was pulverised to a fine grit. Higher up between his knees, and also between his ankles, a sort of sack of finely ground bone and liquidised tissue, veins, nerves and muscle had formed.

We staunched the bleeding and made him as comfortable as possible, but he was medically unstable. At that moment the first helicopter began to circle like an eagle above us. We heard, later, that he had been flown to a South African hospital and that both his legs had been amputated below the knees. He survived and was sent back home to Rhodesia.

Today I know it was all for nothing.

The landmine had not been in the water for long; the barefoot tracks led to a kraal 200 metres away. Two men, both elderly, were in the kraal. The footsteps led directly to them. They were arrested but would not say anything. The insurgents had probably given them the mine and told them to place it on the road. The men had just placed it in the pool of water and it had worked. Easy, trouble-free, effective.

They would have had no choice: if they refused, they would have been accused of aiding the security forces, of being anti-revolutionary, and would have paid with their lives that same night.

They climbed dejectedly into the helicopter that took them away for further follow-up investigations and interrogation. What more could happen to them where they were going than what would have happened to them that night had they not planted the mine? Neutrality is no option in this kind of war.

Those who defied the freedom fighters – or, rather, the terrorists – often fell victim to the so-called Rhodesian Way. Early one morning I saw an example of this when Rhodesian security branch officers turned up at the PATU base and requested armed accompaniment to investigate a murder committed by the enemy a few kilometres from the base. The victim had been professionally tortured and killed the previous night, then displayed as a 'bush message' to the local black community. What his crime was we will never know, but clearly the rules and legalities of warfare applied only to the security forces and not to the terrorists.

Or were other forces perhaps at work? Was this part of that shadow war so few knew about? I know, now, that covert forces are a widespread phenomenon and that every army or police force involved in a war denies their existence. In all wars there are forces that circumvent the constitution and rules of conventional warfare. Everything is admissable in these forces' unconventional operations. Their reasoning is: We show the enemy how the war against them will and must be fought – we give them a taste of their own medicine.

A few weeks later I thought of the kraal victim again as I stared at the viciously tortured body of another black man – undoubtedly a victim of the liberation forces. Or was he the victim of a pseudo-terrorist team, perhaps?

The victim had been stabbed with the triangular bayonet found on the SKS rifle and the Chinese version of the AK-47. From his toes to the shins, then in the knees, the thighs, the genitals, then the stomach, the chest, the mouth, the face and, later, the eyes. No single wound would have been fatal at the time of the torture, but surely excruciatingly painful. To the point of death, and back again. I don't doubt that the man prayed for the release that only death could bring.

I photographed the body and the scene, then the people who stood and watched the exhumation. I wanted to see what I could read on their faces and in their eyes once the photos were developed. The SB men [the Special Branch of the British South Africa Police] did the usual interrogation, but followed the trail no further. We did not remove the body for an autopsy, took no further steps; we left the victim for the people of the kraal to bury as they saw fit. That was that …

Eugene (left and above, far right) with fellow soldiers in Rhodesia and the PATU insignia (below).

However, my commanding captain, Captain Adriaan de la Rosa, who had been in discussion with the SB men, called me in and asked me to hand over all the film I had used at the time – particularly the roll that was in my camera that morning – and the notebook in which I had recorded my murder scene observations. The SB men explained that I would get them all back once they had developed the rolls of film, but I never saw them again. In any case, the tortured man was another triumphant victory for the 'liberators'.

With this image fresh in my memory I ended my service in Rhodesia. Looking back, I think my emotional blunting began with those early experiences as a young policeman in Rhodesia. The resolution with which I departed was that this kind of monster – that we had seen in action from the Belgian Congo southwards – would never be allowed to take over South Africa.

I completed nine periods in Rhodesia, which spanned three to four months at a time. In 1973, for six or seven months I was part of the state president's guard, but I was very unhappy with my working conditions as they were not what I expected. In 1974 I was transferred back to Benoni and, during that time, I went to Rhodesia again. I was also in South West Africa for two months, where people who murder civilians were hunted down.

In 1975 I wrote my examinations for promotion to lieutenant and passed all my subjects except Statutory Law. I rewrote the subject in 1976 and went on an officer's course that I passed and completed. After the officer's course I wanted to get away from the East Rand. I felt I needed to start training myself in station work. The best option would be a small station where you have to do everything yourself and learn from your mistakes.

At my request I switched places with a fellow officer and became station commander at Ruacana, in the northern part of South West. This brought me closer to my real goal: to become involved in counter-terrorism.[7]

Good and bad, right and wrong, us and them. In Rhodesia Eugene was initiated; he transitioned from boy to man. Two things went almost unnoticed. On one side, his natural leadership came to the fore: Eugene the alpha male awakened. On the other, the principle of 'us versus them', 'me against the enemy', became ingrained.

It was as if everything that had happened to him thus far came together and flowed, liquid, through a funnel to form the essence of the soldier.

Like many boys, Eugene had from a young age believed in the archetypal ideal of the hero-soldier. In the book *Man and his Symbols*, compiled by the psychoanalyst Carl Jung, I read the following description of the myth of the hero: 'Over and over again one hears a tale describing a hero's miraculous but humble birth, his early proof of superhuman strength, his rapid rise to prominence or power, his triumphant struggle with the forces of evil, his fallibility to the sin of pride, and his fall through betrayal or a "heroic" sacrifice that ends in his death.'[8]

Would Eugene's ideal of the heroic soldier ever be reconciled with the real world? For how long can a soldier stay true to his seemingly honourable intentions before he is contaminated – by the violence he must perpetrate, or by his own pride?

In her evaluation report, Professor van der Hoven singles out some of Eugene's important attributes: 'Strong leadership ability … a quick temper … exceptional endurance, which placed the accused in a position to persevere for a long period while operating in a war situation.'

Shortly before Larry and I left Koos Brits' lock-up garage that day, Brits said something that made me realise, again, what a decisive influence one's parents have on one's life.

'I think Gene's entire existence was focused on proving to himself that he was not a softy and could hold his own through thick and thin. The man had difficult childhood years, believe me,' said Brits, looking pointedly at me, 'but let's leave it there.'

Van der Hoven also writes that because of experiences in his childhood years, Eugene learnt to suppress his emotions. 'As a result he comes across as emotionally cold,' she says. 'This also contributed to the heartlessness and determination with which he could pursue and kill the enemy. Because of the long periods he worked in a war situation, emotional blunting gradually occurred.'[9]

After Eugene's departure to South West, Koos Brits had only sporadic contact with him: once at Maleoskop, the police training centre in present-day Mpumalanga where Brits was an instructor, and again in 1982/1983 in Koevoet, where Brits went for classified duty. Brits tells of how Eugene nominated him to join C1 – the covert unit at Vlakplaas – a few years later, but that he did not accept 'mainly because of the opposition of my wife ... and that was just as well.

'I still remember reading Dirk Coetzee's revelations about Vlakplaas, and the series of subsequent arrests, including Gene's, one Sunday on the front page of *Rapport*. Believe me, I was shocked. I knew about some of the operations that the government had ordered, but Gene also crossed the line in some ways. But let's leave it at that ... things happened that were not right and the man received his punishment. The painful thing about this whole episode is how those who gave the orders stabbed him in the back.'

Koos said goodbye with a smoker's cough and a firm handshake.

'Did you ever hunt?' I asked Eugene one day.

'I must have shot a total of three buck in my life. Then I would exchange it for a buck another guy had shot. I can't eat something I have killed.

'I had a bloody rooster that walked around on our plot at the police quarters but once the children gave him a name – it was Red – I said: "Well, you know, we are going to eat Red one of these days".

'Audrey protested: "You can't say that!"

'The eldest shed a little tear and they chased Red around so I couldn't catch him. Then I said: "It's okay, I'll go and buy a chicken for us."'

He looked away. 'You know, once you've hunted people, shooting a buck is never the same again. It sounds bad – but that's how it is.'

The hairs on my neck stood on end.

Eugene left Benoni for northern South West Africa a day or two after Christmas 1976.

'In considering the accused's personal circumstances, the court held that the accused had committed the offences within a particular context and period. He sought to act according to an ideology that had influenced him from his youth and that had been reinforced through the influence and example of other police officers and the accused's superior officers. Both commanding officers and politicians had approved of his actions by giving him awards and commendations, whether he had acted upon instructions or on his own initiative. The accused's religious convictions, patriotism and belief that his actions would prevent the downfall of a civilised system led his actions to contradict norms he would otherwise probably have followed.'

– Quoted from Judge Willem van der Merwe's sentencing proceedings in Eugene de Kock's criminal trial, 30 October 1996.

4

From policeman to soldier

My connection to Eugene de Kock and Larry Hanton meant the police 'family' accepted me with open arms – a 'family' of people who told me about the realities of apartheid South Africa, specifically from a police perspective, and who filled important gaps in my knowledge, took me into their confidence and shared their impressions of, and stories about, Eugene.

Among others, I got to know retired brigadier Hennie Heymans well. Heymans is the editor of the online police periodical *eNongqai*, which caters to police members from the pre-1994 era and focuses on matters from when the current South African Police Service (SAPS) was still the South African Police (SAP). 'He knows SAP history like few others,' Larry said on the drive to meet him.

Heymans welcomed us in the street in front of his spacious double-storey home in Rietondale, Pretoria. He took my hands and had a good look at me, his eyes appraising but warm. With mugs of strong, steaming coffee we made ourselves at home in the twilight of the sitting room. An ageing Labrador settled against the sofa with a sigh and two bantam hens scraped the carpet at out feet. 'Aren't they adorable?' asked Heymans. 'Like children.'

His SAP history knowledge was impressive; he moved fluidly between subjects.

During Eugene's years in South West Africa, first as station commander and later with Koevoet, he was both policeman and soldier – more soldier, perhaps, than anything else. I asked Heymans his thoughts about the concept of a militarised policeman.

He explained how apartheid-era police uniforms illustrated the changing role of the police. 'Our SAP initially wore blue and khaki, but in the early 1980s we became blue and camouflage. These two colours didn't mix. You can't be all things to all people,' he said.

'Policing, by the men in blue, happened at the lowest level, intended to serve the public. But when the interests of the state were involved – in other words, when national security was as stake – policing became the job of the Security Branch. This was when policemen in camouflage began to play a role in border security, unrest control, and so on. Under the previous dispensation, the two uniforms became one and the same.'

Heymans believes strongly that members of the police should not be trained in, or equipped for, warfare. But this training was a requirement in the pre-1994 police force. The low-intensity war that raged in the townships during the late 1970s and early 1980s meant that many policemen like Eugene had to do the work of soldiers. The SAP and its Security Branch were also involved in the Border War: South West Africa was a South African protectorate administered as a fifth province of the Republic.

In time, Heymans asked me to start writing articles for *eNongqai*. This led to a number of interviews and conversations with former members of Unit 6, a riot unit on the East Rand. In these policemen I often detected an urgency to tell their side of the story – that of young boys who had had guns thrust into their hands and had been sent into chaotic unrest-ravaged townships. Or to the border, when some were not even old enough for a driver's licence.

As part of my article research I got hold of a few occurrance books from police stations on the East Rand. I was stunned by the depth and scope of the violence in their pages. In one of the articles, I wrote: 'Wednesday 12 September 1990. Dunnottar riot unit. An ordinary day. The entries in the occurrance book look just like those of other days: filled with corpses, terrorism, manslaughter and angry crowds. Think about it: boys of eighteen, nineteen, who write up these entries every day. Getting into Casspirs, driving into the townships, getting out to search houses, picking up bodies every morning – mutilated, broken, bloody bodies – and taking them to the mortuary.'[1]

They couldn't show that any of this upset them—there was no place for sissies in the police. Now that they have left the police, it is different. In former police members' accounts of those times and the emotions that well up – the trauma only just below the surface – I begin to explore the psyche of the policeman-soldier.

I also met former Takies, members of the police force's elite special task force – a hardened, single-minded group of men. At a Takies reunion in 2012, it was my turn to be initiated: a tandem skydive at the Witbank parachute club. For the task-force members this was nothing, but the jump, and the view from the air, was brand new to me.

On this same occasion I heard Roy Allen's name for the first time, then made e-mail contact with him. For 1968 and 1969 Allen had been transferred to Ruacana. His description of the police station and its surrounds helped me to form an idea of what Eugene was to find ten years later. As Allen put it: 'It was a two-man station with one shared bedroom and an office for administration – with an occurrance book for recording incidents and a radio for contacting Oshakati.'

Very little went on there; it was a restful life for Allen and his successive colleagues. At the time Lafrans, a Windhoek-based construction company, was still busy building the road to Ruacana Falls and the pool below them. For 'entertainment' they would drive a kilometre over the Angolan border to a small Portuguese general dealer that sold flour and other provisions to the local community. At that stage there was only a gate with a cattle grid on the border between South West and Angola, and the gate was not even locked.

'Two middle-aged Portuguese owned the store. We called them Mai and Pai (Ma and Pa). After work we would often ride over for a few ice-cold Cuca beers and, sometimes, a delicious dinner of steak and eggs as only the Portuguese can make.'

When Eugene arrived at Ruacana some ten years later, it was still a dusty little town, but the atmosphere was by no means as tranquil. By the late 1970s the Border War had taken on a different dimension. It increased in intensity after 1974, the year in which Portugal decided to grant independence to Angola. In April of that year the South African Defence Force (SADF) officially took over responsibility for the war from the police.[2]

On 3 January 1977, with the rank of lieutenant, Eugene began working as station commander at Ruacana. In a report he compiled for his criminal trial in 1996 he wrote that on his arrival, the police station and buildings were a 'pig sty'. There was scarcely any stock control and many of the members' uniforms hung off them 'like hessian sacks'. Discipline, pride and good public relations were in very short supply.

> For the year and a half I was there, I tried to master as much station work, and get involved in as many aspects of police administration, as possible. The Border War meant that I had to develop relationships with the South African

Top: The Ruacana waterfall is in the north of Namibia, on the border with Angola. Eugene's first posting in the then South West Africa was as station commander at Ruacana. **Bottom:** According to Eugene, the owner of the only shop in Ruacana was on his way to Onessi when his truck hit a landmine.

Defence Force (SADF), handle the public and, because of the ongoing work on the Ruacana hydroelectric power scheme, deal with a wide variety of foreigners.

I believe I succeeded in making a difference in this small, dynamic town where maintaining harmony between various groups was of cardinal importance. I kept learning on a trial-and-error basis and have many pleasant memories of that time. There were, however, also less-pleasant memories, linked to the actions of the South West Africa People's Union (SWAPO) actions.

In one incident, for example, a friend of mine – a former Angolan policeman who worked at Water Affairs – stepped on a landmine just outside the town. This humble, decent person, who just wanted to support his family, was killed instantly. In Angola he had not simply walked away from his station, but had first put everything in order, typed out his resignation and seen to it that everything was up to date before he had moved south to Ruacana. But the MPLA moved faster than he expected and had caught up with him and his family. He and his two young children had been tied up in a room; he had had to listen while his wife, the mother of his children, was repeatedly raped by 'freedom fighters', the bearers of the hammer and sickle and so-called democracy. He had narrowly escaped, crossing the border with nothing but his wife and children.

I have met many people in my life, but this man's pride without falsehood, his integrity, his compassion for his wife and his children's good manners and behaviour, together with his humility without submissiveness, showed me a side of life rarely seen in any other person I have had anything to do with.

That morning I was one of the first people on the scene, with a warrant officer from the Security Branch. Initially I didn't recognise my friend – his body was burnt black, shattered by the explosion and the shrapnel … This hardened my attitude towards the so-called freedom fighters even more and just convinced me further of their inhumanity.

There were also various incidents around Ruacana of SADF members being shot dead and us doing the judicial investigations. Some were attacked, caught in ambushes, many of them still in their sleeping bags. However, at that stage there were no enemy casualties. In only one case was a terrorist shot dead; in a second incident, the Orange River Regiment attacked Beacon 7 and dealt the MPLA a heavy blow. In another incident the Windhoek Regiment, camped near the Olushandja Dam, was attacked by a large force of SWAPO infiltrators. In our reckoning 150 to 200 PLAN [the People's Liberation Army of Namibia] members took part. The defence force was given a hiding despite its armoured vehicles with 90 mm guns and machine guns.

On the whole, the national servicemen were not at all bushwise. You take a boy of 17, 18 who was in Standard 10 [Grade 12] the previous year, give him a gun and six months' basic training, then throw him into the bush in a country he doesn't know, among people he doesn't understand and an enemy he never sees – it was a heavy responsibility these young men carried thanklessly.

In May 1978 I was transferred to the Security Branch in Oshakati. I was then sent to the division that had brought the Ovambo Home Guard into existence and was still in its infancy, a joint project between the Security Branch of the police and the SADF. It aimed to make things difficult for SWAPO by keeping the human resources they needed out of their hands and serving as a resistance movement against them. While this unit had huge untapped potential, its commanding officer failed, sadly, to achieve its objective.

The failure was due not only to this captain and a certain sergeant's ignorance, but also to their focus on self-enrichment and their desire to build their own little kingdom. SWAPO, meanwhile, went from strength to strength. During my time with the Ovambo Home Guard the captain and sergeant's ideas were in conflict with mine. The sergeant, who had a theory instructor's mentality and no grasp of the practicalities of counter-terrorism, dominated the captain, an inherently good man.

Our effectiveness suffered as a result; I needed to move on, alone. I had the support of the commanding officer of the Security Branch at Oshakati: it was imperative to find new ideas and methods of resisting SWAPO. The fact that SWAPO was difficult to find and did not engage in combat created the perception that they were just a nuisance. This was not the case.

SWAPO insurgents – large groups of them, at that – moved freely in Ovamboland. Guerrilla tactics dictate that you have the initiative, that you decide when you will act and how, and that you do not keep still. You keep moving. But on our side, a conventional warfare mindset prevailed, so the enemy could carry on enforcing its will. They even went as far as declaring liberated zones.

At this stage a new dimension emerged: SWAPO assassination groups that moved around in pairs in Ovamboland and started to murder chiefs and deputy chiefs. I lost two very good members of a group I had trained to resist these assassination groups. I had no success in tracking down any of the assassins.

SWAPO also began to filter southwards to Windhoek and Swakopmund. Bombs started going off in these towns, including one at a bakery in Swakopmund. These murderers never tried to attack military targets: they went for soft targets, where innocent people died. They sowed terror, regardless of the cost.

In contrast, the security forces were bound by the law. You could not pick someone up and torture him until he told you the truth so that you could prevent another explosion. You had to leave him and wait until he planted his next bomb. The terrorists used the very laws that prevented you from harming them to help them cause even more harm. The potential was there to neutralise SWAPO, but I have no doubt that personal considerations and the favouring of certain officers prevented this.

Something I could never understand during my stay in Ovamboland was that virtually every white person in the security forces, with the exception of a few such as Colonel Willem Schoon, the commanding officer of the security forces in Oshakati, completely disregarded the Ovambo people and their culture. So many answers and solutions lay there, but these were never used constructively.[3]

Whenever I read about the Ovambo people, memories of my stay in a road camp in the Caprivi – from 1992 to 1994, shortly after Namibia gained independence – wash over me. Fresh in my memory are the open plains stretching into the distance, the mahangu fields and the huts of the local subsistence farmers and their families, their yards neatly swept beside cattle kraals made of branches. The chief of such a group lives apart, in his own area enclosed by a fence of branches. Cattle skulls are attached to the fences around the huts; the more skulls, the richer and more generous the family.

I try to reconcile my memories of the inhospitable terrain and the defencelessness of the local Kavango and Ovambo people I came to know with the idea of the fit, seemingly unstoppable and sometimes merciless Koevoet[4] members caught in the middle of the war between South Africa and SWAPO.

Unlike his colleagues, Eugene seems to have had a greater awareness that the South African security forces were visitors in a foreign country. But even he, initially, was under the mistaken impression that they were entitled simply to storm in, that victory was guaranteed for the protectors of white civilisation. He would soon learn the truth in the early Border War years.

> Before the end of 1978 a variety of incidents happened that taught me everything I needed to know about SWAPO's tactics in the bush. I realised their strength and how minor the challenge was that we posed to them. I also realised how weak we were as far as attacking them in their own terrain and trying to keep them on the back foot were concerned – not to mention that we had no idea of what was really going on in the bush and that, as far as I knew, SWAPO more or less controlled central Ovamboland. At that stage I did not even know that the situation worsened the further east one went.
>
> SWAPO even distributed pamphlets claiming that central Ovamboland and certain districts of the east and far eastern parts of Ovamboland had been completely liberated.

The security forces treated these claims with disdain and made scornful remarks about them. So did I. I believed the intelligence reports issued by the army, police and national intelligence agency. 'Intelligence' – what a joke!

In time I learnt that SWAPO was not exaggerating. SWAPO ruled, and was busy hammering the true state of affairs into me using everything they had: AK-47s, SKSs, RPG-7s, RPD and PK belt-fed machine guns, anti-tank and anti-personnel rifle grenades, and 60 mm and 82 mm mortars. All these weapons were, at one time or another, aimed at me as a target and ensured my own special, enforced training in the realities of the Border War.

For many months SWAPO's claims proved true, an indication that we would literally have to fight to reclaim and dominate the regions SWAPO regarded as theirs – and that we would have to fight twice as hard to maintain our dominance in those regions.

As time passed, SWAPO's sense of control and power lulled them into a complacency that would prove costly. But we would also pay a price: a very high price for parents who lost loved ones, or for those who were disabled and, in later years, disposed of as political wreckage by their political leaders in the National Party.

But this would only come later. First, my typical underestimation of my enemy's capacity and lack of respect for his background in the bush would teach me my first and most costly lesson.

To this day I bear the heavy burden of the death of the Ovambo Home Guard officer who perished during our first clash with SWAPO. He was one of the most promising young men I had met there – exceptionally courageous. I accepted responsibility for the failed operation, but resolved not to give up and to think of ways of helping to neutralise SWAPO.

This first contact with SWAPO was also my first armed combat … a massive tracking fuck-up. This one-sided fight made me acutely aware of our weak intelligence and SWAPO's domination and capability in the bush.

One morning I went out on patrol with about 12 men (police and Home Guard officers) to find out whether informants' claims – that groups of 100, 150 and even 200 SWAPO infiltrators had come in from Angola and were moving around in the bush – were true. We rejected this information as nonsense but needed to establish the truth. Confirmation [of this information] was critical.

At that moment I thought of the time when, as station commander at Ruacana, I went with the head of the Ruacana Security Branch to a group of Cuca shops at the Olushandja Dam to investigate claims of a massive SWAPO infiltration during the night. A remark by one of the black Security Branch officers has stayed with me. He said: 'They played a soccer game here all night.' There were so many footprints – not the same people's footprints made repeatedly – that the hairs on the back of my neck stood on end. Local residents estimated the number of SWAPO infiltrators at 200 to 300. They were not informing against SWAPO: they were boasting about SWAPO's strength and siding against us.

After getting out of the vehicle, we walked no further than 20 metres into the bush when we came across a SWAPO column's track: about a metre wide and four to five centimetres deep, a small path from north to south in the Onamahoka region's thick bush. The footprints were those of heavily laden people in brand-new boots, no older than four to five hours. Unbeknown to me, about 20 to 30 metres from this trail was a second trail made by an equally large group moving in the same direction, parallel to the trail we were following: one very large group divided into two. I did not reconnoitre the entire area, which was careless of me; I would quickly learn a bitter lesson.

The trackers estimated that the group we were following was 40 to 60 men strong, but could number as many as 80. We had only a short-distance radio and could not contact the police base for reinforcements – either we were outside the reception area or nobody there was listening, the usual story in the war in Ovamboland. We followed the tracks and eventually succeeded in catching up with this group just before midday. Later, I wished that we had never done so …

They had laid a massive L-shaped ambush for us at a kraal. It was not just an ambush: it was Armageddon. We were fucked around properly. It was a total surprise and my group was utterly defeated. Apart from a few mopani trees here and there the area around the kraal had no bush; neither was there any grain in the fields nor veld grass. I managed to fire off one rifle grenade, but when I glanced to the left looking for the rest of my group I realised they had fled. There was no one.

I turned and began to run out of the death-trap. As I ran I saw two rifles, rucksacks, water bottles and cartridge belts, that belonged to my men, lying on the ground. Thrown away. The sand was very thick and SWAPO proceeded to pelt me with every weapon they had. I was the only

Top: At the beginning of the Border War members of Koevoet often tracked SWAPO insurgents on foot during follow-up operations.
Bottom: The Angola-Ruacana power line was sabotaged by SWAPO insurgents in 1977.

person on the run, the only person on the ground in a bare grain field.

Eventually I succeeded in escaping the battlefield and began to walk. I should not have done this. The fucking SWAPO devils began shooting again. As tired as I was, this was encouragement enough and I picked up speed again. SWAPO did their utmost to shoot a 'whitey' as a Roland Ward trophy. So it was that I found myself alone in central Ovamboland with as many as 80 fully armed, fully loaded, mortar-aiming SWAPO members behind me and no sign of any of my own people.

I then moved north, checking my equipment as I walked and making sure I had not been wounded in the ambush. When, at last, I was able to rest for a moment to determine where I was, I destroyed and buried my snake-bite kit. At that stage I had more serious concerns than snakes. The man who had carried the radio had been shot dead; with the radio there was also a map of the area and a compass. (These, along with his body, were recovered later.) Most of the Ovambo Home Guard officers returned to the base that same day, one of them only in his underpants. He had taken no chances, removing all his other clothes to be as lightweight as possible for running.

I moved slowly and carefully and, as far as possible, kept to clumps of thick bush and shadows. I had to double back on my own tracks repeatedly to make sure I was not discovered while I rested. In any case, by that time all of Ovamboland knew we had been seriously fucked up. To see a naked Home Guard member running west at a pace that would make a racehorse eat his dust was a clear enough message.

Very late that afternoon I managed to reach the main road that ran from west to east, parallel with the border. There was no traffic; darkness was already falling. I found a hiding place to spend the night and, after covering and camouflaging myself as best I could, I set up a one-man ambush on my own tracks. It was a very long, sleepless night and I hoped there would be security force vehicles on the road the next day. This soon proved to be a vain hope. It was one of those alternate days on which no army convoy swept the road west or east.

The day before, I had crossed many SWAPO tracks that led in every compass direction. Old and new tracks. Many. Too many. The place swarmed with tracks.

When dawn broke, no fewer than three different goatherds found me. If fucking goats are known for doing one thing, it's going where they shouldn't. They also have an inexplicable instinct for walking to where you are then standing and staring at you. If there is more than one, they stand about 5 metres away in a semicircle around you. Some even kneel on their forelegs, backsides in the air, necks stretched out, and stare balefully at you, leading the goatherd directly to your hiding place. Then the herder rushes back, turbo-powered, to the kraal. As he runs he squeals like a pig, which reverberates like an air-raid siren and announces to everyone within a kilometre's radius what or who his goats have sniffed out. This happened three times; each time, I had to change my position. I was livid.

When it looked as if there'd be no traffic that day and all the locals knew where I was in any case, the fuck-it factor kicked in. I had to move, regardless of the consequences. Being paralysed in an indecisive heap is fatal. I decided to move slowly, carefully, beside the road in a westerly direction and to face whatever fate held for that day.

It may sound dramatic, but in reality it was terrifying. You have to be permanently alert and keep a clear head – SWAPO could surface anywhere, at any time. At last, later that morning, a vehicle approached from the east, a 4x4 that belonged to the Ovambo tribal council. I stopped the vehicle and asked the driver to give me a lift as far as the T-junction to Ondangwa-Onhangwena. He refused; I began to lift my FN rifle, fully intending for him to walk the rest of his journey while I drove to the base.

An elderly tribesman who was also in the vehicle saw what was about to happen and spoke to the driver. They told me to get inside, but I refused and rode on the back of the bakkie. This would at least give me a reasonable chance of shooting or getting away if necessary. I also did not doubt the likelihood of landmines on the road (I heard, later, that earlier that same morning an army vehicle driving east had set one off). I eventually arrived at the base, relieved, naturally, that I had escaped with my life and evaded capture.

I carried the lessons I learnt from this incident with me throughout my term in the bush. Some people thought I was overcautious and even, on occasion, accused me of this. To them, all I wish to say is that SWAPO taught me this lesson properly. After this incident, we – some of us, anyway – began to accept that coming across a group of 200 to 250 SWAPO members who had infiltrated the country would not be unusual. They would initially stay together as an infiltration group, but would break up later and move to their designated areas of operation.

The ambush left two bullet holes in my backpack, and nothing else. This does not mean that SWAPO members were poor shots. Rather, I believe that their training was inadequate. Perhaps it was also their first contact, just as it was mine. In any case, I did not for one moment consider staying out of the bush. Giving up was never an option. Never.

During this time the commander of the Oshakati Security Branch also tried reconciliation between the sergeant of the Ovambo Home Guard, who was such a thorn in my flesh, and me. On one occasion we were together on a follow-up when we were attacked from behind by nine or ten SWAPO members. They were more intent on trying to get away than on wiping us out, however – there were no casualties on either side, as was the case with most fights in Ovamboland at the time.

In the moments just after the fight, when I started getting the formations ready for a follow-up, I saw two small children running. They were on the outside flank of the shooting and were not in danger, but they were terrified. I turned back to my officers and saw the sergeant pick up his R1 and aim at the children. I shouted to him that they were children, but he ignored me. He continued to aim, then shot one child, a girl aged about eight, as she crawled through a fence. I almost shot him on the spur of the moment that day. I was already lifting my rifle when I thought better of it and quickly went to the injured child.

The girl had a bullet wound to her chest; the bullet had exited through her shoulder. I treated her by sealing the worst of the damage with plastic to stabilise the internal pressure and attaching intravenous drips. I sent some

Ovambo people to a nearby kraal to look for transport – the radio worked only intermittently. The child was taken to Windhoek where she recovered fully. Whether she recovered psychologically I do not know.

After this incident I went to see the commander of the Security Branch and told him I never wanted to see the sergeant again. Little did I know that very soon both he and I would be transferred to Operation Koevoet. The commander knew the unit was being planned, but I had to find this out for myself. At that time, I was still an untested member of the Security Branch (whatever the 'test' may be) with very few friends at Oshakati and virtually none in the Security Branch.

I decided to take things as they came, knowing nothing of the difficult times that lay ahead. There were many gossipers and lots of professional jealousy at Oshakati, but I learnt, there, what it took to be in the security context. Later, I saw how some people's careers were made around *braaivleis* fires and drink, while others' were broken. Nepotism in the Security Branch brought promotion for some; *gatkruipery* – currying favour – also ensured promotion if you were willing to stoop low enough.

One of my favourite quotations is by Friedrich Nietzsche: 'The man who fights too long against dragons becomes a dragon himself.'

In late December 1978 I was told I was going to be transferred to another unit that would be formed on 1 January 1979 in Ovamboland. I did not know who would be involved, what the purpose of the unit would be, or what my duties would involve. At the time I was still completely ignorant about security concerns and the basic principles of security work. All I knew was that I was being transferred, and that the new unit was called Operation Koevoet.[5]

Eugene's transformation from policeman to soldier began in Rhodesia and continued during the Border War in South West Africa. Before his 30th birthday, all the experience he would need for covert actions and pseudo-operations had already become an integral part of his make-up.

'If you want to understand soldiering, start with the Vietnam War,' Eugene answered when I approached him about this. 'Read everything you can lay your hands on. There are movies that will teach you everything about modern warfare. *We were Soldiers Once … and Young* is a must. Also *Apocalypse Now*, *Platoon* and *Full Metal Jacket*.'

A book that helped me to get inside the head of a soldier is *What it is Like to Go to War* by Karl Marlantes, a highly decorated former American Marine who published his philosophy of war 40 years after serving. In a graphic study of himself and his fellow soldiers, he analyses every aspect of warfare and its impact on the human psyche.[6]

Explaining how young men and young soldiers' heads work, Marlantes does not beat around the bush: 'Teenage warriors like to fight, drink, screw and rock and roll … [and] indeed combat is like unsafe sex in that it's a major thrill combined with possible horrible consequences.'

He regards battlefield experiences as an extreme, concentrated process of initiation, and explains two initiation processes. The first is social, preparing one to play an adult role in society. The second is spiritual, relating to death and one's awareness of one's own mortality. A young soldier is initiated on both levels simultaneously.

Soldiers are taught to make war – but nobody teaches them how to make peace.

War and soldiering, I realise from all the conversations I have, brings with them an unprecedented sense of power. The force of their attraction never disappears. When you have life and death at your disposal, it's easy to play God.

'The accused's conscience had been blunted and his emotions desensitised through constant exposure to what he had believed to be a full-scale war. To him, what was wrong had become the norm, right and acceptable. He could justify his actions on a subjective level. Some of the offences had been committed at the request of his superiors. The accused's actions had found favour in the eyes of his superiors and the politicians, which increased his self-esteem.

'A rotten system had allowed the accused to commit his crimes and had condoned – or, at least, not condemned – his actions. That very system had also assisted in concealing his crimes and perpetuating his actions.

'The accused believed that he was fighting a war against an enemy in Namibia. This "enemy", he believed, was communist and had targeted his people for destruction; it would have led to the downfall of the dispensation of the time, of everything it stood for and had managed to suppress. This was unacceptable and had given the accused the justification he needed to use any means to fight and destroy his enemy.

'On his return to the Republic, the war had, in the view of the accused, continued here. The only difference was that the enemy was already within the country and had to be fought using methods that would otherwise have been unacceptable.'

– QUOTED FROM JUDGE WILLEM VAN DER MERWE'S SENTENCING PROCEEDINGS IN EUGENE DE KOCK'S CRIMINAL TRIAL, 30 OCTOBER 1996.

5

Zulu Delta

By the late 1970s a solution had to be found to SWAPO's increasing threat in Ovamboland. The South African police responded with a unit similar to the Rhodesian Selous Scouts and so Operation Koevoet was born.

The original plan was for selected members of the SAP's Security Branch to collect information and for members of the newly formed 5 Reconnaissance Regiment (commonly known as 5 Recce) to do the follow-up work. But this arrangement did not work and in time, the founding members of Koevoet devised, and refined, their own operational tactics.

In 1979 Eugene started working for Operation Koevoet at Oshakati under Colonel 'Sterk Hans' Dreyer's command.

To find out more about Koevoet's early years, I spoke with former Koevoet members and writer Jonathan Pittaway, who is compiling a book about the unit called *Koevoet: The Men Speak*. Larry Hanton and I hit the road again – this time to Durban, where Pittaway lives. A product of the upper-crust Michaelhouse school, Pittaway – an auditor by profession – writes and distributes books about combat units in Africa.

Pittaway's Morningside sitting room is filled with antiques and Persian carpets. In true colonial fashion, we drank tea and ate dainty egg-and-ham sandwiches. He made his unpublished manuscript available to me, in which I found the stories

Top: Eugene de Kock's father taught him how to shoot when he was a young boy still. Here he was about 12 years old. **Bottom:** Eugene with his father, Lourens, and his brother, Vosloo ('Vos') on the far right.

Top: Jean 'Hope' de Kock, Eugene's mother, at the family home in Montagu Street in Boksburg East. **Bottom:** Jean and Lourens de Kock.

Top left: Eugene (5) and Vos (4) with their grandfather, Josias Alexander de Kock, who farmed in Komga in the Eastern Cape. **Top right:** Eugene at their home at Van Graan Road in Springs.
Bottom: On this photo of the under-14A rugby team of Voortrekker High School in Springs, Eugene is seated in the middle row, third from the left.

As a teenager, Eugene went on a Voortrekker camp to
Botswana. The group lost their bearings and was missing
for some time before help arrived. According to Eugene,
he wasn't at all unnerved by the experience.

A young Eugene in a relaxed mood with his friends. In the bottom image,
Eugene is in the middle, wearing glasses.

Eugene during one of his periods of service in the former Rhodesia (today Zimbabwe) as a member of the Police Anti-Terrorism Unit (PATU).

Top: Eugene and two unidentified policemen at the border between Rhodesia and Zambia. **Bottom:** The tent in which Eugene lived during one of his periods of service in Rhodesia.

Top: The living quarters at one of the camps in Rhodesia.
Bottom: South African policemen receive training from members of the
Rhodesian army in camouflage gear.

Top: At the end of 1979 Eugene became the commanding officer of Koevoet's Zulu Delta team. Their badge carried the badger as emblem. 'Shi-shi' is the Ovambo word for badger. **Bottom:** With his men from Zulu Delta.

Eugene with his Koevoet comrades Lukas Kilino (left) and Jules (surname unknown) during the training of the first group of Koevoet members at the 5 Recce base.

Top: A newspaper clipping of Eugene and Brigadier Hans Dreyer, commanding officer of Koevoet, after a news conference in Oshakati.
Bottom: A seized 14,5 mm anti-aircraft gun. Eugene is at the back on the far right.

Top: Eugene with a 14,5 mm anti-aircraft gun looted from the army by members of Koevoet. **Bottom:** Koevoet members at a draw well out in the bush. These wells were sometimes sabotaged by Koevoet.

Left: A Swapo fighter taken prisoner by members of Koevoet.

Above: Lukas Kilino of Zulu Delta with another captured Swapo figher.

Top: Eugene and his Koevoet comrade John Adam with whom he also executed the London bombing.
Bottom: The Koevoet stores in Oshakati in which weapons, ammunition, vehicle oil and the like were housed.

Top: At a braai: Eugene is in the middle, wearing a white shirt.
Bottom: Koevoet comrades Attie Hattingh, Rodney Bradley and Fielies Kruger.

Eugene behind a 14,5 mm anti-aircraft gun on the Zulu Delta Casspir during the Border War.

told by former Koevoet member Marius Brand particularly interesting.

'It was the era of the real tough guys,' said Brand. 'The first generation was a handful of hardened Security Branch policemen who set up the unit in Oshakati. All they had was ordinary police equipment. There were no Casspirs. They followed SWAPO terrorists on foot. The SWAPO bases were up to 300 strong in the Eenhana-Okankolo-Nkongo triangle in Ovamboland.'

I gathered from Brand's evidence, and what others had to say, that the first few years of Koevoet's activities were not properly documented. The unit had very few members and many covert operations – 'night work', as Eugene put it – were carried out. Precious little is known about these missions. It appears there were executions of captured SWAPO members at this time, and that local water sources were sometimes made undrinkable.

In the report Eugene wrote for Professor Anna van der Hoven, he says outright that the insurgents arrested by Koevoet never appeared in court. There were only two options for SWAPO prisoners: they could work for Koevoet, or they would be 'let go' (Koevoet members used the Afrikaans expression '*laat ry*', a euphemism for being killed). Was there a specific order to kill SWAPO members? Yes, Eugene told journalist and author Jeremy Gordin in *A Long Night's Damage: Working for the Apartheid State*.[1]

Larry mentioned that in Koevoet, the principle of doing 'body counts', which the American army used in the Vietnam War, was applied: 'Lots of bodies (*koppe*, literally 'heads') on their side, and fewer on your side, meant a contact was successful.'

According to former Koevoet members, the unit gained ground against SWAPO during this time. 'That first Koevoet group tamed Ovamboland,' Brand says in Pittaway's manuscript. 'There were daily contacts due to the large number of SWAPO terrorists in the

Top: Koevoet members at shooting practice with an M79 grenade launcher, also called a 'Snotneus'. Eugene is third from the left. On Mondays, Koevoet members would practise shooting and how to deploy from vehicles.
Bottom: Eugene (in the middle, with hat and glasses) at a kraal in northern South West Africa.

area. By 1983 there were 20 combat groups and about 50 white members. Our SAP budget was very small, the fighting was intense and, with Eugene de Kock around, Oshakati was a dangerous place. Eugene's was the notorious generation. Those guys were the real deal.'[2]

In his book *Covert War: Koevoet Operations Namibia 1979–1989*, Peter Stiff says this of Koevoet's potency: 'Combining their police investigational abilities and skills at getting information, the tracking abilities of their special constables, the landmine protection provided by their Casspirs – with the support of SAAF helicopter gunships – Koevoet emerged as the premier counter-insurgency unit in SWA/Namibia … In its ten-year existence it fought in 1 615 contacts and killed or captured 3 225 PLAN soldiers. But it paid a high price in blood. It lost almost 162 policemen killed in action, with another 949 wounded – more grievous casualties than any other South African fighting unit since World War II.'[3]

Former Koevoet member Dave Baker explains the early structure of the unit: 'The feather in Koevoet's cap was its fighting units, Zulu Delta (Eugene de Kock), Zulu Foxtrot (Frans Conradie), Zulu Sierra (Piet Stassen) and Zulu Whisky (Chris de Witt). The operational officer, Z2, was John Adam, who would later go on a mission to London with Eugene to blow up the ANC headquarters.'[4]

Earlier, Hennie Heymans had told me that Koevoet had reached 'cult status' in the police force. 'Many station commanders sent policemen who were difficult to handle to the Border or the riot units. In Koevoet they flourished because the normal rules of policing did not apply. Although Colonel Hans Dreyer ruled with an iron hand, the men could grow their beards and uniforms were not obligatory.'

According to Eugene, in Oshakati he always wore just a T-shirt, black PT shorts and *velskoene* without socks. Or the same clothes, but with his Hi-Tec boots.

How did the average policeman and *troepie* experience the base at Oshakati in the early 1980s? I found one answer in Anthony Feinstein's book *Battle Scarred: Hidden Costs of the Border War*, in which he describes his experiences as a newly qualified doctor responsible for the psychiatric care of the 'emotionally wounded' at Oshakati. 'We arrive at Oshakati in the late afternoon. The base shimmers under a blazing sun. Thousands of conscripts would rather be elsewhere. They have set up home in a dustbowl, sand as far as the eye can see, their lives coated with layers of sweat and axle grease.'

Feinstein discovered pretty quickly that one thought dominated the men's lives. He describes the metal desk in his office in the sickbay as follows: 'The surface of the desk is badly scratched – florid scatology, phalluses and pudenda are everywhere ... This is the desk they have given to the army psychiatrist, a Rosetta stone of obscene messages, frustrated desires and perverse cravings. Between patients I scrutinise its detail, marvelling at the outpouring of smut and unbridled lust uncontaminated by a clean thought.'[5]

Oshakati: unadulterated, testosterone-soaked world of men.

In 1987, journalist, writer and photographer Jim Hooper moved with Koevoet in the operational area – and was even wounded twice – researching his book *Koevoet! Experiencing South Africa's Deadly Bush War*. Hooper met Eugene that year at Oshakati. 'He was already commander of Vlakplaas – which I'd never heard of – and was passing through Oshakati "on business". Even though I had no idea who he was, my curiosity was piqued by dedicated soldiers' awed references to his legendary status. He gave me his business card and invited me to contact him when I was in Pretoria.'

Hooper did so and the two got together one day and started

talking about Koevoet's early years, becoming good friends in the process. I asked him to tell me about the psyche of a soldier.

'Few people understand the difference between a soldier and a professional combatant. The most difficult thing is understanding why certain men become addicted to warfare. Most of the young guys who went to the Border hated every minute of being away from their girlfriends and their moms' cooking. But then there was the small group who found their *raison d'être* in war and volunteered for high-risk units such as Koevoet, 32 Battalion, the Parabats and the Recces.

'These men share an above-average IQ and a specific biochemistry – a genetic predisposition – for risk. It is particularly evident in those with an elongated DRD4 gene, which rewards near-death experiences with dopamine, a hormone as addictive as cocaine or methamphetamine.'

Hooper describes Eugene as 'one of the most impressive people' he had ever met. 'A brilliant tactician and strategist, a lateral thinker, mercilessly effective against the enemy, a loyal friend, enigmatic. Even when he knew his arrest was inevitable, he phoned me to apologise for the visit the police would probably pay me because of our friendship. That his former commanders worked with the old and incoming regimes to demonise him was immoral, cowardly and criminal.'

I thought again of one of the first remarks Jonathan Pittaway had made about Eugene. He said Eugene had a certain magnetism, that when he walked into the room he brought with him an unmistakeable aura of power.

Eugene is busy writing his own manuscript about his time in Koevoet. The following piece is compiled from this and his report for Van der Hoven.

The policemen who were to launch Koevoet were sought out in the Republic. Initially we were eight men with a few vehicles. We also received six .38 revolvers with 600 soft-nosed bullets. For executions. Assassinations ... night work.

Soft-nosed bullets, which can mutilate a person horrifically, are used to make ballistic identification impossible. The same .38 Special revolvers would be given much later, in 1989, to the unit at Vlakplaas for further use. However, within a week the weapons were withdrawn to be destroyed. No ammunition came back to Vlakplaas with them.

The idea was initially for the police to source information and conduct interrogations, and for the reconnaissance commando to be responsible for pseudo-operations. In Ovamboland a force would be raised as a so-called freedom movement against SWAPO and that could operate inland. SWAPO's networks in Ovamboland and further south had to be wiped out as soon as possible. The total destruction of the intelligence, espionage and sabotage groups in the white south was an immediate priority.

A second group would operate on the same principles as the Selous Scouts. Among other things, this involved infiltrating the freedom movement's territories and periodically attacking the enemy. The group would also establish the enemy's positions and send them through to air and ground combat units for actions, poison their food and clothes – in other words, do anything to kill or compromise the enemy ...

It was a challenge to gather information; for three or four months we had no breakthroughs against SWAPO's assassination gangs. But in April or May 1979, the Security Branch at Oshakati made an arrest and members of Operation Koevoet did the interrogation. This was our first breakthrough in terms of SWAPO's intelligence network in Ovamboland – a turning point. We started reeling the entire network in, delivering it a blow from which SWAPO never really recovered.

Many of the SWAPO members Koevoet arrested started working for the unit. In time, some of these people started disappearing. On the grounds of discussions I had with our members, there is no doubt in my mind that a considerable number of them are now in the hereafter. On three occasions I made people disappear myself; there might have been more, but I can't remember.

In the winter months of May and June 1979 the SWAPO infiltration from Angola through Ovamboland to the farming district of Tsumeb took place. Koevoet members, including those trained by 5 Recce, were sent south to counter it. In one incident a group of SWAPO terrorists attacked a farmhouse in the Tsumeb district and murdered a grandmother with a little girl and boy. These 'brave heroes' shot the elderly woman and the small girl dead, and beat the boy to death against the wheel hub of a tractor or some other vehicle. Any form of empathy or sympathy from my side took another hit.

The SWAPO members then started moving north to exfiltrate. A group was sent on a follow-up under the same sergeant with whom I did not get along. Within a few hours Colonel Dreyer loaded me and the rest of the 'freedom movement' into helicopters with orders to stop the SWAPO group that was on its way back to Angola.

When we arrived at the airstrip at Ondangwa, a group of

about 30 black members waited on us. Dreyer gave me two maps of the area we were heading for, but they were inadequate. He assured me that the group that would accompany me was heavily armed, fighting fit and operational. I still wanted to go through their equipment, but he said we had no time to waste. This was my first experience of follow-up operations in the south.

I had my own long-distance and ground-to-air radios, a medical kit and food for two days. My radio equipment was the best that was issued to the SADF troops at the time. I had to steal it from the SADF. The police still used the rubbish we had been issued in Rhodesia, handed out to you even though it never worked. Standing orders said you had to have a radio – but didn't say it had to work. In the end, all the Koevoet units had to steal SADF radios – lives depended on it, and the SADF had surplus.

If it wasn't for the stolen radios, I don't know whether we would have survived that excursion. Dreyer neglected to tell me that the group was poorly equipped and inadequately trained. They had not been issued with food, water bottles or ammunition. Dreyer gave me a set of radio frequencies for reporting and logistics. There was not even time to make sure they were correct.

We were taken to Oongodi in the far eastern part of Ovamboland, landing in unfamilar, densely wooded terrain with few locals and even fewer water sources. Only God, the helicopter pilots and I knew where we were: not another soul, except the SWAPO guerrillas who were waiting for us.

Once we had offloaded, I started going through the black members' equipment. They had no radios or medical supplies and food for only two days. Checking their weapons, I realised we would be in serious trouble if we ran into SWAPO. Most of our men had too few magazines – on the belts of their machine guns were sections of loops with only eight or ten rounds in them. I alone had a medical kit, hand grenades, smoke grenades, etc. We would ultimately be in the veld for six days, with food for only two.

We had been told we were merely a stopper group, that there would be no SWAPO insurgents in the area. I learnt very quickly that there was no place in Ovamboland of which one could say there were no SWAPO insurgents. Guerrilla warfare has no frontlines; SWAPO was everywhere.

The operators jokingly described such actions by Dreyer as the HPS method: *hoes, poep en storm* (cough, fart and storm). It was pure luck that we lost virtually no lives in

Koevoet members were issued with meat, which they would often eat semi-raw, when out on operations. Sometimes, when they were out in the bush, they would also hunt game.

these unplanned, impromptu operations that were given no professional deliberation.

A group of SWAPO insurgents lay in wait for us at the waterhole nearest to our drop-off spot. The insurgents were 15 to 20 strong. Immediately after the helicopters departed we formed a perimeter defence. I sent a search party to the nearest kraal to assess the situation. It walked straight into the ambush SWAPO had set up at the waterhole. A short, extremely intense firefight followed, which the search party won.

The next morning at six o'clock we encountered a group of five terrorists in very thick bush, so dense we had to drag our equipment behind us. We attacked this group from behind. One was wounded and got away, but some useful equipment was left behind. On the evening of the second day we realised that although we were on the trail and regularly crossed new trails, we were being followed by a group of SWAPO terrorists. That night we dug ourselves in and lay in wait.

On the third day we did not move at all. That afternoon, about 20 SWAPO terrorists passed in front of us, completely relaxed, rifles slung over their shoulders. Without waiting for the enemy to walk properly into our ambush, a black member jumped up and opened fire wildly. The whole group escaped unscathed, leaving only equipment behind. Our ammunition was practically finished; the next day a helicopter dropped off some SADF troops with extra ammunition.

Our survival over the next five or six days was thanks to good radio communication and strategy on my part as well as the black members' bushcraft. All but one of the 30 black members were unknown to me. As in Rhodesia, I saw that combat teams made up of black and white soldiers – who were properly trained, were confidant in the bush and had the latest technology – could be a winning recipe against SWAPO.

I explained these ideas to Dreyer, and thereafter we started planning. The classic Koevoet fighting unit emerged from this deployment. The unit's foundation was laid on that day.

The sergeant wanted to continue with his 'freedom movement' and I could ultimately only get hold of two or three members of his group, all former FNLA members from Angola. We then went on a recruitment campaign, enlisting 60 black members. They, along with a white officer and myself, were sent to Fort Doppies, the reconnaissance commando's training base in the Caprivi, for a month's intensive training. While the training was not new to me (it was a repeat of the courses I had done in Rhodesia), it transformed the black Koevoet members from cads into one of the best fighting units in the SAP at that stage. The group was later split in two, starting a second group under the other white officer's command. In time the 'freedom movement' was also disbanded.[6]

Early one morning at the end of October 1979, just after completing our training at Fort Doppies, we were deployed to eastern Ovamboland by 5 Reconnaissance (5 Recce). At that stage SWAPO, not the security forces, controlled the area. SWAPO was doing whatever they wanted there.

The first patrol was with the new group, Zulu Delta. We moved in battle formation as we had been taught, adapting it immediately to the terrain without orders. Everyone knew what to do. I was the only white member in the group – on deployment day, the other white officer suddenly didn't feel well enough to go into the bush.

About three kilometres into the patrol, we noticed some movement near a group of kraals and the central waterhole that served them. They were definitely SWAPO. Heads clearly visible, they peered at us over the high fence of branches around the waterhole. They didn't give a damn that we saw them. They taunted us, actually – sticking their heads out, pulling them back down, sticking them out again.

It was clear they had no fear of, or respect for, us, this lone whitey and a group of armed black soldiers. The Ovambo members began to laugh softly. They were looking for trouble after the merciless, murderous training session at Fort Doppies. They wanted a fight. I had seen a similar expression only in one other instance and that was on the faces of troops from the South African parachute battalion.

Fifteen minutes later, SWAPO's opinion of the approaching group was to change. We reached the fence and started to determine the direction in which the enemy had moved, using the trail, so we could start the follow-up. The footsteps led directly to the waterhole, but were indistinct from there onwards.

I took four members with me, climbed over the fence and moved towards the waterhole to see if some of them were there and, if they weren't, to determine where the trail would take us. Halfway to the waterhole, where there wasn't a single blade of grass or tree for cover, the SWAPO group opened fire with AK-47s, a PK machine gun, RPG-7 rockets and a 60 mm mortar. The dust kicked up by the firing gave us cover and the mortars fell behind us. Our only chance was to run into the firing line and make straight for the waterhole to shelter.

Meanwhile our black group leader, Lukas Kilino, divided the group into two, threw the equipment to one side, and left six men to guard it and to cover the rearguard in the event of an attack from behind. The two groups then moved along the kraal fence towards the firefight, parallel to each another.

The SWAPO fighters didn't see this one coming – the next minute the two flanks of Zulu Delta were upon them. The heavy fire at the waterhole eased off; we were able to move forward until we were parallel with our two flanks and could join them to form one line. Control over formations is an absolute priority – we would, otherwise, shoot one another in the back.

When we reached SWAPO's line of defence, we realised they had had a fuck-you attitude from the outset. Their trench had been dug the previous night and they had clearly just been waiting on someone who they could give a beating.

In the trench one of their men lay dead. One of our 60 mm mortars had landed about three metres from him; some shrapnel must have struck his head. It had surgically removed a piece of his scalp and his skull. Although the hole in his skull was relatively small, there was nothing inside it. His head was hollow. Other than that, there was not a mark on the man. At first I thought I was hallucinating and asked the others to come and look. They stared with the same disbelief at the empty skull. One of the members then called me and pointed to something lying in the veld about four metres away.

We went to look. It was his brain, still in its cerebral membrane, without a scratch. I could hardly believe my eyes – I would never be able to get the brain back into the skull through the small hole, never mind how hard I tried.

Since we operated under 5 Recce, they immediately sent a helicopter. All clothing, jewellery, hairstyles or emblems on the insurgents clothing were replicated for pseudo-operations. Their equipment would also be used in such operations.

But I had a problem – what to do with the brain? I called the group together only to have 40 tough, heavily armed men dig in their heels and say not a fuck are we touching that brain. The *shirumbu* – that would be me – would have to handle it.

That was one thing about black Koevoet members – they never touched a dead body. Neither would I, as a rule, but the Puma helicopter had already made its first pass. The reconnaissance regiment was incomparably professional: they removed the body and equipment, replacing our spent ammunition, rifle grenades and mortars too. We picked up the SWAPO trail again and were ready to move on.

In his final radio transmission to relay the direction of the follow-up, the pilot asked, 'Where is the fucking man's brain?'

'Look in the cardboard box next to the body,' I said.

'Why the fuck did you put the brain in there?' he wanted to know.

'What the fuck else was I supposed to do with it?' I countered. The brain was in a ration pack.

Some time later, after I had completed an explosives course (I was sent on it to get some rest), I worked out for myself that when a mortar detonates it briefly creates a vacuum on explosion. The man's brain was probably sucked out of his skull through the hole the shrapnel had made.

Even today I don't know if I'm right about this. The whole thing of the brain on the ground was strange … the two lobes and the ridges looked like the inside of a pecan nut you have carefully opened. It also made me think back to the day in 1970 when I came upon a motorbike accident in Benoni and the rider's brain had also 'disappeared'.

A few days later, in another skirmish in northern Namibia, one of the enemy was shot in the head, causing his brain to hang out of the side of his head. It looked like oatmeal. On that day, as on the day of the motorbike accident in 1970, I knew that nothing would ever be the same again.[7]

Former Koevoet member Rodney Bradley was in Eugene's Zulu Delta group from 1980 to 1982. I met him in Durban in December 2012 and I asked him how he remembered his former commander.

'One image stands out,' he recalled. 'He had the habit of twisting his hair with his right hand when he was thinking. I will always remember the picture of his right arm sticking out in front of me in the Casspir and him twisting his hair around and around with his finger.

'Gene is a fantastic leader. I would work with him any day. If he asked me to work with him again I would in a flash. Look, he was explosive, but he was a wonderful leader.'[8]

Eugene's explosiveness comes up regularly. In an unpublished manuscript, former Koevoet member Dawid (Attie) Hattingh also refers to it: 'He had a very short fuse and could become volatile in seconds. He had an unpredictable temperament and was inclined towards excessive mood swings. From early childhood Eugene stuttered and this was exacerbated during operations when he was fed up [or the adrenalin started pumping]. Then all you could hear on the radio was "fok, fok, fok" – which led to his nickname, Fok-fok de Kock.

'Naturally no one would dare call him by his nickname. But then, we were all overly aggressive. We were expected to be. Eugene became our role model, the hard-working, drinking fighter-operator with a take-no-shit attitude.'[9]

According to Hattingh, Eugene was a charismatic, dynamic leader who demanded enormous respect 'through his example and professional conduct in the bush'. Hattingh says Eugene regarded anyone who was not involved in the heat of the battle as 'jam-stelers' (jam thieves, literally translated). 'The majority of the administrative personnel fell into this category. This caused a gradual rift between factions in the operational and administrative staff, which would lead, eventually, to Eugene's departure from the unit.'

Hattingh also told of the regular bar fights that broke out between Koevoet members and the SADF at the International Guesthouse and the Blou Klub at Oshakati. The owner would usually phone Colonel Dreyer and inform him that Koevoet members were going to be barred from the guesthouse. The guilty ones were then paraded before Dreyer, with the most senior in rank – usually Eugene – heading up the parade. According to Hattingh the highly annoyed Dreyer would then ask, in colourful language, exactly what had happened – but the uitkakparade, or 'disciplinary parade', would not last long.

It would calmly be explained to Dreyer that the Koevoet members had been provoked to a point at which they could no longer ignore the insults and consequently had to retaliate to protect their reputation and honour. Then Dreyer would usually start to relax. He would ask, 'Gene, who won?'

'We did, colonel,' was usually the answer.

Dreyer would then smile mischievously and say, 'Right, now

fuck off. I will fucking chase away the next *bliksem* who gets into a fight.'[10]

From the very beginning Dreyer played an important role in Eugene's life, becoming something of a father figure for him.

I got the feeling that throughout his life Eugene yearned for a father figure and for approval from such a figure. When I asked him about their relationship, Eugene admitted that it was fatherly in nature. 'He was my mentor.'

Under Dreyer, Eugene had the chance to fully develop his combat skills, vision and expertise in the bush. In Koevoet, he became deadly.

However, it is also clear that Eugene was a loose cannon during his time on the Border. Dreyer put up with a great deal – Eugene's temper, the cursing and the after-hours punch-ups.

What is the psyche of the archetypal soldier? I asked Eugene on one of my visits. What motivated you?

As was often the case when he wore his glasses, his eyes became unreadable. 'I'll have to think about that … Generally, you're a soldier, or you're not. There isn't a profile. You're a protector to the very end, or you're not. Nothing is too much to ask or to give. It's never about you, but about others and their wellbeing.'

Soldiers have the power of life and death – a role usually ascribed to God, I read in a book by Karl Marlantes called *What it is Like to Go to War*. As Marlantes puts it: 'What is this thing in young men? We were beyond ourselves, beyond politics, beyond good and evil. This was transcendence.'[11]

But there is another aspect – an important one I have not found in the psychological reports and post-traumatic stress disorder (PTSD) diagnoses and newspaper articles about Eugene. It is one that cannot be ignored: the space in which many former soldiers find themselves. The world of a former Koevoet member on the frontline, for example, differs vastly from the world of ordinary people who live in normal society. The two have no touchpoints. Their world is – and remains – the testosterone-saturated domain of the soldier, where warfare and firefights bring on high levels of adrenalin and where the rules are laid down by the brotherhood.

Men who have been there know this. Veteran soldiers and pilots who felt the heat of that bush war tell of an addiction. The *godgevoel*, the feeling of godlike omnipotence, where the urge to live throbs at its strongest, as a soldier once explained it. During battle, explains journalist and writer Jim Hooper, the conscious and the unconscious are acutely focused on survival.

'It felt good to shoot someone, that's all,' said a former Koevoet member when we talked about the Border War. 'I can't explain it any other way. It gives you a kick. If you don't shoot him first, he shoots you.'

To be god.

'In considering the purposes of punishment, the court
found that the crimes germinated in a particular milieu
and era. The accused has been removed from those
circumstances and will probably never return to them.
However, it remains important to warn that a repetition
of such behaviour would not be tolerated. This warning
had to be evident from a balanced sentence that does not
prejudice the accused and is not unfair to him …
It is unlikely that the accused will ever be put in the
same situation again and a balanced sentence would be
sufficiently preventive of similar behaviour by others.'

6

Whose side is God on, anyway?

Willie Nortjé was once Eugene de Kock's good friend and confidant. Side by side they faced – and survived – the onslaught of the Border War, and later worked together at Vlakplaas. Nortjé would become one of the key witnesses for the state during Eugene's criminal trial in the 1990s. In my search for a better understanding of Eugene, Koevoet and Vlakplaas, it was inevitable that I would get to know Nortjé better.

By the mid-1970s Nortjé was a young policeman stationed in Springs. He came to know Eugene by chance – he was a friend of Eugene's brother Vos.

'On occasion Eugene visited us at the SAP canteen in Springs. He spoke a great deal about Koevoet and what they were busy doing in South West. For a young guy like me it all sounded very exciting,' said Nortjé.

'I am mechanically inclined and could fix any vehicle. I often repaired police vehicles at the station. Gene can't even handle a spanner. And so in January 1981 I joined Koevoet as part of Eugene's Zulu Delta team. He needed me to fix the vehicles and the two of us got on very well.'

Nortjé was just like the other Koevoet members – young, fit, eager to work in the unit. He, too, became a hardened and

Eugene's long-time Koevoet and Vlakplaas colleague Willie Nortjé
talks to Koevoet members in Oshakati some time in the late 1980s.

respected soldier. He and Eugene share a long history, having spent
several years in Zulu Delta before eventually working together at
Vlakplaas. In time, he became Eugene's confidant. According to
another former Koevoet member, Nortjé often took the radio and
assumed command of Zulu Delta during contact.

During our many discussions about Koevoet and Vlakplaas,
Nortjé spoke candidly and answered every question thoroughly.
He described his service at Koevoet as a wild and reckless time
when they virtually lived on adrenalin. Koevoet only had one goal
and, as in any war, rules meant very little. The fighting was intense
and Koevoet members looked death in the eye on a weekly basis.

'War … blows away the illusion of safety from death,' writes Karl
Marlantes in *What it is Like to Go to War*. 'In a combat situation

you wake up from sleep instantly aware that this could be the last time you awake, simultaneously grateful that you're alive and scared shitless because you're still in the same situation.'[1]

I tried to imagine what it would be like to walk out, almost daily, rifle in hand, possibly to your death. In a TED talk called 'Why Veterans Miss War' and filmed in January 2014, American war correspondent and documentary producer Sebastian Junger discusses warfare's neurological effect on soldiers. He says while soldiers may be afraid before and after operations, they aren't so during the firefight itself. Then something strange happens.

'Time slows down. You get this weird tunnel vision. You notice some details very, very, accurately and other things drop out. It's almost a slightly altered state of mind. What's happening in your brain is you're getting an enormous amount of adrenalin pumped through your system. Young men will go to great lengths to have that experience. It's wired into us.'[2]

The intensity of the fighting made alcohol abuse commonplace. 'After hours in the canteen, fights with army troops often broke out. Sometimes Eugene initiated these fights,' Nortjé said with a twinkle in his eye.

Larry Hanton told me that in one such fight, a member of Eugene's Zulu Delta team, Rodney Bradley, was cut on the chin by a broken bottle wielded by an army troop. Until the day he died Bradley wore a beard to disguise the scar. 'Some of the army troops came from the East Rand, from Brakpan and Benoni, among them ducktails who fought in bars and hotels with motorbike chains. Eugene knew guys like them from his Benoni days and showed them no mercy,' said Larry. 'They were certainly not gentlemanly fights.'

'But you need to look at everything, including the drinking, in context,' Nortjé reasoned. 'When you went into the bush, you didn't know who would come out. If you spent too long in the bush – at Oshakati – you became reckless. I remember Gene going on holiday for two or three weeks once … when he came back he was horrified, shocked by our indifference. He was right – we had started taking chances. There were basic rules, like not driving on certain roads after dark. We had started breaking all those rules. We never took leave. You didn't want to go away, not even for a weekend – you didn't want to miss the action.'

I thought again about something Hennie Heymans told me about alcohol abuse in the police. 'We took refuge in drink. It blunted us, gave us moral courage.'

The bottle was the only debriefing the Koevoet men knew. Interestingly enough, it was standard SADF procedure for any soldier involved in more than three contacts or firefights to be released from service and sent home to rest. This seldom happened in Koevoet, a police unit.

Eugene was involved in more than 300 firefights in Koevoet. 'But even if it were only 30 without an opportunity to recover, one can only imagine what it must have done to his psyche,' writes Maritz Spaarwater in *A Spook's Progress*.[3]

Eugene's former colleagues all agree that before long he perfected Koevoet's classic tactic of tracking down and then attacking the enemy. According to Larry Hanton, it was Eugene who suggested intense mobile infantry deployment exercises for each Koevoet member. 'This was a change from a beat-walking policeman to a light, fast and eminently mobile fighting unit of infantrymen.'[4] Because Eugene's team had, in the early years, been one one of the few groups who had tracked on foot, the terrorists had hunted them. In his report for Professor Anna van der Hoven, Eugene explains how he developed this fighting technique, and describes some of his combat experiences and challenges – including those involving his superiors.

Initially, at the beginning of our counter-terrorism action, we moved on foot. We were very well armed and usually heavily laden. Because we fought the enemy man to man, we often landed up in violent clashes, outnumbered twice or even three times. Sometimes we decided to storm with only our second last or last magazine left.

I would give the signal by standing up and giving the order myself. To the credit of every black member, only the dead or wounded failed to respond. They moved behind or with me as one man. We never surrendered so much as an inch of ground. At the beginning of 1980 we began using Unimog vehicles that were so battered they broke down where they stood.

In February 1980 I began to test the Ovambos' tracking abilities. Three or four trackers, with only their rifles and an extra magazine, would track on the run. We reached a point at which the trackers could track while running practically at full speed. We would catch up with SWAPO – exhausted by then – and force them to fight.

More and more groups started using this technique, which increased the number of terrorists killed and captured dramatically. Koevoet became by far the most effective combat unit in South West Africa. Later, the SADF also started to work on this basis.

Two incidents in Ovamboland, however, contributed to my growing disillusionment with the attitude of those in control towards us in the bush. In the first a Constable Schreuder was shot dead after a terrorist indicated that he surrendered. The terrorist's hands were in the air and he had no rifle with him, but we did not realise there were three SWAPO members hidden behind him. Exploiting

Top: Lukas Kilino (left) was an Angolan who joined Koevoet. For many years he and Eugene (middle) fought side by side. **Bottom:** This gun turret on the Zulu Delta Casspir was built by Koevoet member Willie Nortjé. The weapons at the front are from left to right, an R4, .50 Browning and a Russian 12.7 mm machine gun.

our members' hesitation on the ground and in the vehicles, they opened fire. Constable Schreuder was shot dead; I had another four wounded.

Colonel Dreyer's attitude towards Schreuder's father, who was also a policeman, made me seriously reconsider matters. Dreyer told me to come to Oshakati from the bush to speak to the bereaved father. I arrived there to a devastated man. On reporting to Colonel Dreyer for orders, I was told to take 'the old bugger' off his hands because his 'crying was getting on my nerves'. I also had a great deal of trouble securing the Police Cross for Bravery (Gold) for Schreuder, which he richly deserved for his heroism. It was all I could give to a father and mother in exchange for a fine, promising young man.

In the other incident we went to help one Sergeant Kruger with a follow-up – his relatively new group was still struggling with trackers. When we began picking up loose equipment I realised this small group of four terrorists was very professional. Experience had taught me these small groups were reconnaisance groups and that they usually, but not always, caused fatalities. I could see the helicopters landing at Ondangwa airstrip and could even see vehicles in the distance moving between Oshakati and Ondangwa. I immediately called for air support but was told that there were no officers at the base. They were at a farm just outside Oshakati, busy braaiing and drinking.

I contacted Koevoet's SAP representative at Eenhana base and asked if he could help. He asked if I was sure they were terrorists … he was also having a braai. I needed air support to prevent the terrorists from laying an ambush or planting anti-personnel mines – which they would not be able to do if constantly forced by the helicopters to hide. The woman sergeant at the base, who was in charge of all heavily armed Koevoet groups in the bush, did not have the authority to send helicopters, because the boss was with the others, drinking and partying. Shortly afterwards we triggered a PROM-2 anti-personnel mine. I had three dead and twelve wounded.

An enemy death never hits a soldier as hard as the death or injury of his comrades. We wiped out the entire enemy group but it left a bitter taste in the mouth.

As time passed I started withdrawing from the daily discussions at the base and from any attempts to be drawn into them. I moved out on my own, deciding for myself whether I would go out and where, ensuring that I lost no more men.

Dreyer asked me one day why I had not followed a set of tracks. I responded by saying it was my call. That did not go down too well. I would dictate how I would engage the enemy. Many of the operators thought it was a big deal to round up terrorists and shoot, say, eight of them, losing some of your own soldiers in the process. In the same week on deployment I would also shoot eight terrorists, but lose no men.

Divide and then destroy the enemy. Your success lies not in the number you shoot, but in how many you kill without casualties on your side.

In another incident, at about eight o'clock in the morning we had our first contact in which we lost one SADF troop and two of my men were wounded. That day the entire group of eight or nine terrorists was shot dead, the last one dying with the last light at about seven thirty in the evening.

Two crucial elements in the Koevoet arsenal were, firstly, gunships such as this Alouette, which was used in air-to-ground attacks and, secondly, a proper radio connection with the base. In the image below Koevoet member Daan 'Radio' du Toit sits in the radio control room.

At such times and when possible, I took enemy soldiers captive and sent them to Oshakati. A captain who helped to interpret intelligence information asked me one day why I sent so many prisoners. It transpired that I was the only one, or one of very few, who did this. However, I don't want to create the impression that I was this great humanist. It was a tough time on both sides; mercy was neither given nor expected. You got blunted and had to take great care not to handle your enemy inhumanely.

Certain incidents I took up with Colonel Dreyer: a woman in Angola who was shot dead innocently in front of her children, and when two children died when a phosphorus grenade was thrown into a kraal. It also happened that Unita soldiers were shot dead and claimed as SWAPO terrorists. But nothing ever came of my complaints in this regard.

I reflected, sometimes, on my enemy. Many of them had died courageous and heroic deaths, leaving a permanent impression on me. Had they been on our side, they would have been highly decorated. Yet we just left their bodies in the bush, took their rifles and equipment and continued with the follow-up and the fighting. These people's parents, or wives and children, would never know how their loved ones had fought, how brave or frightened they really were or what had become of them.

However, the empathy I felt would disappear like mist before the sun with each attack SWAPO launched. Then they had to deal – again – with our mercilessness, about which they complained.

Yes, our unit committed offences. But, without justifying it and bar a few exceptions, I had no knowledge of

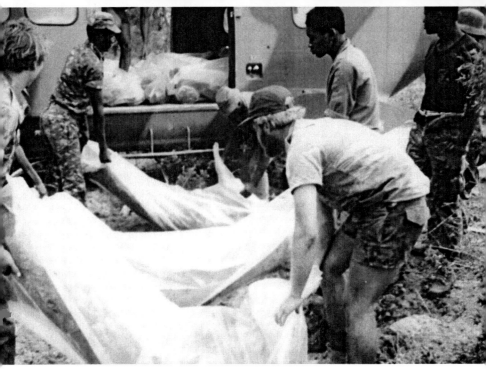

The killing fields … The bodies of SWAPO soldiers killed in action are loaded on to a helicopter and taken back to base.

these offences. One case does, however, stand out. A certain captain – someone I got on well with and who was regarded as well educated – told me about a so-called contact they had had one day. He and a lieutenant had apparently shot seven terrorists. When I congratulated him on his success, he said he would tell me the story later.

Late that afternoon in the base canteen he told me there was in fact no contact: seven people had had to 'go'. In other words, seven SWAPO members in captivity (Koevoet had its own cells) had been murdered. The captain and lieutenant had decided to 'test' the weapons SWAPO and our units used on these seven prisoners. They tied them up and observed the effect, for example, of shooting through the leg with an AK-47. Various rifles and calibres were tested and all seven prisoners died this way.

I don't know why they had to test these weapons. To me it was sadism – all weapons were tested scientifically during their development. It put the personalities of the so-called security policemen in a new light. In hindsight I have come to believe that you had to be as fanatic as a PAC member to qualify as a 'security policeman'. Yet I have also met many who were not like this.

In later years at Vlakplaas, one colleague told me openly on more than one occasion that I should rather have joined the army, that I had military aptitude. After starting at C1 (Vlakplaas), I met many individuals in the business world who offered me good positions. They felt I did not 'belong in the police', but in the business sector, that I was 'wasting my time in the police' or that the force was 'messing with me'.

At no stage did I doubt my loyalty to the government, the SAP or my religion, but I did sometimes wonder who

Enemy weapons and ammunition confiscated by
Koevoet members after an operation.

was right or wrong, whether there was another perspective from which to see things. Whether on the base or in the bush, we had a short service every day with scripture and prayer, a few guards surrounding us. Mine was one of the few groups, if not the only group, that did this.

At the same time, we also shot SWAPO members who carried well-used Bibles. One Sunday morning a chaplain on the Ogandjera base read scripture and prayed, among other things, for the enemy to be delivered into our hands that day. We captured two SWAPO terrorists that afternoon, killing one. When we emptied the dead man's rucksack we found a Bible. It occurred to me that he may have said the same prayer that very morning. He was a believer, not a communist.

Who was right and who was wrong? Whose side was God on, anyway? These questions surfaced regularly, but not their answers.

There were gruesome scenes during and after combat. The devastation of war, low-intensity or not, never left you. Over the radio, the harried and anxious voice of a driver carrying dead or wounded; the hopelessness and impotence of collecting dead comrades; watching a man die as you fight to keep him alive. A wounded soldier's faith in you, despite your limited medical knowledge … his entrails on the ground and you washing them with water from a drip bag before pushing them back inside him. The hate that wells up when you ask for a helicopter to fetch your wounded, only to be told officers' wives and children were being flown around a game reserve.

Then there were my heated exchanges with Colonel Dreyer about the better and heavier weapons I needed to resist the enemy more effectively, and the lame arguments offered in response. In my mind, these and many other issues raised questions about whether the people at the top – the generals and the politicians – cared, or even thought about, the people on the ground. Would we even have had a war if the politicians and their families and grandchildren were on the frontline? I doubt it ...

Among other things that grated me was how the captain and sergeant would steal some of our provisions and trade them for other tasty foods. Operational members' fresh produce was also stolen and sold in Cuca shops, and bush rations were dished out to people who were not entitled to them at the expense of the operational members. This sort of thing made you cynical about the real goals of our struggle against socialism and communism.

I also picked up problems with small but important things, such as the difference between the rations for white and black operational members. The black members received inferior rations despite working just as hard – if not harder – than the white members in the bush. The solution was simple: to give the white members the black members' rations. The light went on very quickly ...

I spent a lot of time on the ground, moving, sometimes for long periods, with the black guys to show them I would never ask them to do something I could not do – both physically and as far as being in dangerous situations was concerned. I used every tactic and plan imaginable, some highly unconventional, to avoid suffering losses. They were my men and I was responsible for them. They were more than just trackers who were being used to reap glory for the unit.[5]

One of Eugene's distinguishing characteristics stands out clearly: since his days as commanding officer at Koevoet he always acknowledged unit members who had performed well. The medal for bravery awarded posthumously to Constable Schreuder on Eugene's recommendation is evidence of this.

Eugene expands on this in his manuscript: 'Always, without exception, I gave recognition to my people, black or white, man or woman, for service or good work. Medals or certificates of commendation or for promotion in rank or even financial compensation were duly recommended. I never asked for anything for myself. As the leader of a group the recognition was theirs because they followed me, which must have required much more courage of them than of me. I never even prayed for myself, but for those who served under me ...'[6]

In a letter Eugene once wrote to writer and publisher Peter Stiff, two Koevoet-related matters about which he feels very strongly come to the fore. Firstly, that the Ovambo Koevoet members had never received the respect and recognition they deserved for their contribution to the war; secondly, that an abscess of corruption festered in the unit, which would later burst open. Of the Ovambo members he said, among other things, that he hadn't known any 'trackers' only 'battle-fit veterans who fought with heart and soul' and who 'could shoot fearlessly and accurately'. He went on to write that calling them trackers 'detracts from the honour these soldiers richly deserved as true fighters'.

Eugene's right-hand man and faithful Koevoet comrade-in-arms was Lukas Kilino, a former FNLA soldier who later also served in 32 Battalion. At fifteen, Kilino was trained in China in the use of heavy weapons and as a paratrooper. It was Kilino and other black Koevoet members Eugene had in mind when he wrote this letter.

The corruption in Koevoet, Eugene said, sticks in his craw. It was all about 'head money (*kopgeld*) and tracking money, and money claimed from the SAP's secret fund and from the SADF'. According to him, at that time there were all sorts of similar money-making schemes on the go.[7]

In Eugene's report for Professor van der Hoven he mentions how – on three occasions, and on Dreyer's orders – he went to bury landmines for a certain captain. Thereafter, large sums of reward money was claimed from the SADF for finding them. Half of the money went to the 'source', a black man who was known to Eugene, and the rest to the captain. The captain told Eugene that he and Dreyer were going to use the money to buy a farm in South Africa where Koevoet members could go to relax when they were back in the country.

'I also saw the register of amounts to be paid out to the Ovambos for contacts in which terrorists were killed or captured and weapons reclaimed. The sums that were received – for example, R20 000 – were written in pencil and the amounts paid out were written in ink. The amounts paid out would only be R8 000 or R10 000, for example. This register was not the official claims register, but the one the group leaders had to sign to claim their group's money.'

According to Eugene, this money was also meant for the farm in South Africa, but he doesn't know whether the farm was ever bought.[8]

Another sensitive matter was Eugene's growing disillusionment with Dreyer. He seems to have lost faith in his commanding officer's leadership, partly because he did not agree with Dreyer's methods and felt he was not getting the support he needed. Dreyer's alleged involvement in certain activities did not sit well with him either.

Eugene thought the Koevoet units got too big, at the expense of professionalism. He believed all Dreyer wanted was 'heads' – and heads started, increasingly, to roll, with fatalities rising on both sides.

By this time Eugene and Dreyer's work methods differed so much that Eugene no longer wanted to go to Ovamboland – not even several years later during the SWAPO infiltration just before the 1989 election. 'I just didn't want to serve under him again. And, at that stage I was not prepared to fight SWAPO and have people killed and maimed for the politicians to give the country away a few days later. That is exactly what happened. I was only prepared to go up and fight if we retained South West.'[9]

Dreyer in turn criticised Eugene's lack of discipline, regarding him, later, as out of control. In May 1983 he sent the following telex to police headquarters in Pretoria: 'The officer has been involved in many contacts with SWAPO terrorists. It is in his own interest to return to normal service and I therefore request his urgent transfer.'[10]

Eugene realised himself that it was time for a change: 'I wanted to go, too. I had lost myself and would become a danger to my men.'[11]

During the Border War, the Onhangwena border post between South West Africa (today Namibia) and Angola was one in name only. Below, Koevoet members cross the border unperturbed in their Casspirs.

7

Brothers in arms

As I see it, there are two ways of looking at Koevoet: as an outsider or as part of the inner circle. These perspectives are hard to reconcile.

I watched the former Koevoet members closely when they got together – square-shouldered men who fondly recalled the 'old days'. They would joke a lot and get nostalgic when they listened to 'Green Boots', the Koevoet song.

One of the countless interviews I conducted the past four years was with Eric Winter, one the first Koevoet members. Winter told me that Koevoet's cult status made many policemen want to go to the Border to be glory boys. Those who did not fit in were spat out.

Inside Koevoet there were also subcultures. The Alpha and Bravo groupings came about when Dreyer realised the men were not getting enough rest. He divided the teams into two groups, deployed in alternate weeks. Eugene was the automatic and undisputed leader of Alpha. The Alpha guys, I gathered, were the rough guys – the drinkers and troublemakers, the dedicated supporters who worshipped the ground Eugene walked on.

Bravo, of which Winter was part, was the more moderate group of older men. Yet some Bravo men embraced the Alpha culture. There was intense rivalry between the groups – it was all about the successes – the number of kills – also for Eugene. According to Winter, Eugene saw everyone as competition. He only socialised with the group of guys close to him.

Time and again after being around the former Koevoet men I felt a sense of discomfort. My intuition told me that much had been left unsaid. The brotherhood of silence was alive and well: 'What happened in Oshakati stays in Oshakati.'

Will we ever know the truth?

And how do you differentiate between justifiable actions and misconduct in war? To what extent are some actions ever justifiable in war? In his application for presidential pardon in 2002, Eugene wrote as follows: 'I was part of a war without rules, conventions or decrees. Everything was admissable in the struggle against the enemy and the effort to defeat it … I testified in court that the terrorists who were captured and interrogated and refused to co-operate were executed and buried. They were the enemy, they showed no mercy and we showed no mercy. They cut people's throats with bayonets. We used this to justify killing them but we knew that what we were doing was wrong.'[1]

In her evaluation report Professor Anna van der Hoven wrote that Eugene learnt on the Border to fight the enemy in an 'unconventional manner' using 'guerrilla tactics'. In this way he 'learnt to disregard the rules to survive in a situation where no rules or laws applied'.[2] According to her, this mindset might well have influenced his later deeds.

Van der Hoven also mentions the Church Street bombing that took place during one of Eugene's visits to Pretoria and the significant impact it had on him. It was his first encounter with the methods of the ANC. In his words, the liberation movement had shown 'total disregard for the lives of innocent people, whoever they may be'. According to Van der Hoven, it was after this incident that he vowed to fight the ANC in every possible way.[3]

I still struggle to imagine what it must feel like to be in a life-or-death combat situation. What would I do? Would I be able to pull the trigger? Could I get fired up for the contact? Would ideology and an unshakeable conviction have driven me to kill someone in the name of a greater struggle? Would I also have seen the enemy as 'the other'?

In Koevoet, Eugene became involved in covert operations for the first time.[4] In 1982 he and Captain John Adam, another Koevoet member, were approached by former spy Craig Williamson[5] to bomb the ANC's head office in London. During a visit Eugene told me more about this operation:

> Craig knew John Adam, so he came to Oshakati to recruit people for the destruction of the ANC head office in London. Jerry Raven [of SAP intelligence], among others, was also there that evening at Oshakati. Williamson stayed in the background. They were looking for someone who could kill with his bare hands if there was trouble, as it wouldn't be possible to get weapons through customs.
>
> I could use my hands very well. I could kill a man with the point of a pen, with a shard from my glasses, with a chain around my neck, a piece of wire, anything. I also had my blue belt in karate and was accomplished in free fighting, a sport where blows and kicks are not retracted before you make contact with your opponent.
>
> We went to England with a great deal of money. Each of us had about £12 000 in cash and more in traveller's cheques. The name on my passport was Alexander Knox. The cash was in case we had to split up quickly to get away. Additional passports were ready for us at the South African embassy.
>
> The rest of the group – we were eight in all – got through customs easily and quickly, but I got caught up in a group

of Chinese or Taiwanese tourists. So, there I stood in the middle of the European winter, over six foot tall in the middle of this group, tanned and with wide shoulders – I stuck out like a sore thumb. Whereas everyone else went through easily, I was held for four hours and interrogated. To make things worse, without me noticing John Adam had slipped his £12 000 into my bag.

The money was discovered but I denied all knowledge of it and said it must have happened by mistake: 'How must I know? The luggage must have got mixed up,' I said to the customs official.

'Oh, so you're flippant,' he said to me.

I had no clue what 'flippant' meant so I just said 'no', hoping it was the right answer. After that I tried to keep a low profile in the interrogation. Eventually they let me go, but allowed me to stay for only two weeks while the others were allowed to stay for six months. In London we were followed almost everywhere: you know, guys on bikes, on street corners, in strange places. Adam told me I was neurotic – I responded that my survival in the bush depended on my observation skills, so I trusted my intuition.

We met Craig Williamson in a London pub called Dirty Dicks that overlooked the backyard of the ANC's head office. It was the kind of place that dated back to the 13th or 14th century, complete with a dusty rat in the corner. We watched the ANC office for two weeks from the pub. On the night of the operation, bangers and mash was on the menu. To get there Jerry Raven, Vic McPherson [with Williamson at police intelligence], John Adam and I had to switch trains to shake two people off our trail. That night the gates of the ANC office were locked for the first time since we had started our watch.

Raven was the first over the gate, then me. McPherson sat across the road from the pub on the pavement, and Adam was further down the road. When we were both over the gate Raven realised the rucksack with the explosives was still lying on the pavement. I called McPherson to give it to us. Meanwhile, I searched the grounds for tramps – if I found one I would have had to take him out. I had a screwdriver and a Parker pen with me for the purpose. We placed the explosives behind an old bench and got out of there. Adam was only just visible in the misty distance – he was not wasting any time getting away. Williamson came to collect us in a vehicle.

On the morning of 14 March, the explosion rocked the suburb of Islington. Windows in buildings up to 360 metres away were shattered and an ANC volunteer who lived in a flat above the office was lightly injured.[6] Johan Coetzee, the former head of the security police and later police commissioner, Williamson, Eugene and another six were granted amnesty for the incident by the Truth and Reconciliation Commission (TRC).

In his criminal trial Eugene implicated Williamson in another international incident. He claimed the apartheid spy 'played a role' in the much-publicised assassination of the Swedish prime minister Olof Palme in 1986.[7] Eugene testified that Operation Long Reach, a military intelligence project headed by Williamson, played a role in Palme's death.

Palme's murderer has never been brought to book.

'Can you tell me more about Craig Williamson's alleged involvement in the assassination of Palme?' I asked one day.

I realised I was taking a chance by broaching this sensitive subject, and watched Eugene closely.

'I have nothing to add to what I said in my trial,' he said, withdrawing.

According to many former Koevoet members, Eugene shared virtually everything with his friend and colleague Willie Nortjé. 'If Gene was involved in any way, he would have told me about it,' Willie told me.

I left it at that.

After the successful mission to London, the Security Branch at the police headquarters in Pretoria sat up and noticed Eugene. He

Zulu Delta's Casspirs were often parked opposite Eugene's house in Klein Angola in Oshakati.

received the South African Police Star for Outstanding Service for his part in completing the operation, then returned to Koevoet.

In 2013, with Larry Hanton and Paul Fouché of the Koevoetbond, I visited General Dreyer and his wife Marietjie at their home in a Rooihuiskraal housing complex. Dreyer had photos of Eugene and allowed me to work through all of his albums and to make copies of his Koevoet video tapes.

Before long we were talking about the past. Dreyer told me how he and his first wife regularly had Eugene and some of the other unmarried men from Klein Angola,[8] a suburb of Oshakati, over for Sunday lunch.

Eugene's manners were impeccable: he would never arrive without a bunch of flowers or a little gift. In Dreyer's voice I heard his pride in his men, the men who brought in the kills for him.

I asked him about his request to have Eugene removed from the theatre of operations. 'I wanted to protect him. I wanted to get him out of the bush and out of Ovamboland. The man was completely battle-weary. He should not have been exposed to further combat situations,' said Dreyer.

He did say, however, that he blocked two requests for Eugene to transfer to South Africa when he realised what the Security Branch wanted to use him for.

In January 1983 Eugene told Dreyer that he was seriously considering returning to South Africa at the end of the infiltration period, usually around July and August. He wanted a transfer to the counter-terrorist department of police headquarters, because he 'knew the work'. Dreyer did not think this was a good idea. He offered to get Eugene out of the bush and keep him busy with other assignments.

'He thought I was battle-weary,' said Eugene, 'but I didn't think so at the time. I had just had enough of everything at Oshakati and was disillusioned by what Koevoet had turned into. I could see how more and more people were starting to run it as a business for personal gain. This was one of the main reasons for the big fallout between me and Colonel Dreyer. I stood firm on my point that the misuse of funds was wrong and in the process Dreyer's attitude towards me started to cool.'[9]

The final showdown took place in Dreyer's office in Oshakati. The tension, under the surface for a long time, flared after an incident the previous weekend. Willie Nortjé was party to the build-up and was present on the day of the altercation.

'The previous week, Eugene and I had been to Etosha, to Namutoni, with a few others. When we returned from the pans on the Sunday, there was drinking at the new Ongediva base. It got rowdy and the guys ended up tearing the place up. Eugene only stayed for a short while. He had nothing to do with the fighting. Back at the base the guys made more trouble, and started shooting in the base,' remembered Nortjé.

According to Nortjé, Dreyer had listened to all the versions of the incident beforehand. 'The impression was created that Eugene had instigated the whole thing. At that time Eugene already believed that the welfare of the guys in the field was no longer a matter of much concern – that there were other priorities. He was very angry about this. Dreyer, however, was angry with Eugene about what had happened at Ongediva.

'Eugene eventually walked into Dreyer's office with an R5 over his shoulder,' said Nortjé. 'We had come straight out of the bush from the Ogandjera side and drove straight into the base in the one Casspir. The other Zulu Delta Casspir was parked outside in the street. Gene was agitated; he told us to shoot at the slightest sign of resistance. I didn't hear everything they said, but there was shouting and swearing.'

When I discussed the fallout with Eugene he admitted that he was also partly to blame. 'In my last days at Oshakati people may have got the impression that I hated Colonel Dreyer. I didn't – it was more a question of being disappointed in him. I didn't make things easy for him, either. Some of my own actions were wrong … uncalled for, such as the arguments and physical reaction to any criticism that was directed at the unit or its members. I also started to butt heads with others, especially other Koevoet members. I put that down to a lack of proper social infrastructure in Oshakati.[10]

Eugene told me at that time he had already submitted a request to be transferred to the Western Cape rather than the Pretoria Security Branch. 'I knew I was fucked. I was tired of war. Too much war. I wanted to get away from the bush, from the East Rand, from Pretoria.'

However, his request was turned down; he was transferred to Pretoria. He left Ovamboland in May 1983. The business with Dreyer meant that he arrived in Pretoria under something of a cloud; his new commanding officer did not exactly welcome him with open arms.

Today Eugene thinks differently about a number of aspects of his time in Koevoet. His blind loyalty to certain individuals and a specific cause has made way for a desire to speak with greater honesty about his time in the bush and what it did to his spirit.

'The myths about Koevoet must be put into perspective and tempered by the truth. I expect much criticism, because I have kicked the sacred Koevoet bull in the testicles. I intend to keep kicking the bull so that all this worship of heroes with feet of clay comes to an end. I want to stop young people from making this mistake, from finding themselves in my position one day having chased false glory.

Eugene (second from left) with Captain George Steyn (on the ground)
and Brigadier Hans Dreyer, commanding officer of Koevoet.

'History must not be repeated.'[11]

On Sunday, 15 July 2012, at 09h00, Eugene and his former commanding officer General Hans Dreyer met once again – this time, at Pretoria Central. Earlier, Eugene had indicated that he wanted to make peace with the general, but was uncertain which course such a meeting would take. It was an emotional moment for both men.

'Our paths separated 29 years ago. It was a very bad time. I would like you to be there,' Eugene had said in a phone call the day before the meeting.

The traffic flowed free on the motorway to Pretoria. My thoughts turned to the oath every policeman takes – the same oath Hans Dreyer and Eugene de Kock once swore: I dedicate myself to the enforcement of law and order, the prevention of crime and the maintenance of the internal security of the Republic ... So help me God.

I found a parking place in the shade. My friend Carina

had come with me. We filled in the visitors' form and walked through the first turnstile. You could smell the many hands that had touched the metal. Eugene had arranged for his friend Daan du Toit, who had been a radio operator at Oshakati, to bring Dreyer. We got into the small bus that took us to Medium B. It dropped us off at a group of warders. They watched us, closely. I got out, looked past them at the prison's sports fields to the right, then left at the high brick wall behind which Eugene spent his days. The monstrous building stared back at me, as if blindfolded.

We bundled forward to hand our visitors' forms to the warder. Black women with head scarves, young women with bags, brothers and fathers. To one side, people hung around in the sun. I looked closer and saw Dreyer and Du Toit, waiting on a wooden bench. The general's face was stern, his cap pulled low over his eyes. Du Toit's beard was snow white. He was wearing a tracksuit.

You wait for anything from ten minutes to half an hour before being called. I spoke to a young man from Benoni who was visiting his uncle. He came once a month, he said. Then he tried to be positive: his uncle only had two years left to serve. Who was I coming to see?

'De Kock,' I said.

'De Kock? Is he a changed man now?' he asked.

'Yes, I think so,' I said. Nearly twenty years is a long time.

Brown uniforms filled the stairs. Hopeful, everyone looked up.

'Jansen! Dreyer!'

We walked through the heavy wooden front door. That day, the female warders searched us thoroughly. I showed my ID book and they peered at the see-through bag in my hand – my car keys and lip balm. Through the final gate and out into the square. A few rays of sunlight managed to squeeze through the gaps in the corrugated-iron roof. I looked left to the door that separated us from the prisoners and saw Eugene through the steel railings.

'Where is he?' General Dreyer looked uncomfortable, tense. I pointed to the gated room beyond the warders who shepherded the prisoners through. When he saw Eugene coming forward, Dreyer's face transformed into a broad smile.

Eugene signed in, set the stopwatch on his wrist, then strode over quickly to Dreyer, hand outstretched. Their eyes met. Dreyer swung his right arm in a wide gesture; the two hands clamped tight. They clapped one another on the upper arm, pulled together, embraced. The general took Eugene's hand again.

'You are going to break my hand,' laughed Eugene.

'You look good!'

Was I imagining it, or was the general suddenly standing taller? They went to sit opposite each other, knees almost touching. The rest of the group comprised me, Carina, Du Toit and another prisoner whom Eugene had arranged to join us because each prisoner was only allowed two visitors at a time.

The general sat very quietly. His left side leant forward, his gnarled right hand holding his right knee. His khaki cap was pulled down low over his eyes and his bifocals. His eyes did not leave Eugene's face for a second. For an hour and fifteen minutes he sat beside him, looked at him, listened to everything he said.

Eugene had much to tell in very little time. How things were in jail; how the discipline he had learnt in the police and Koevoet was standing him in good stead. How, for two years and ten months in C-Max, they had not been able to break him; how he had emerged even stronger. How it helped to live a clean life inside. How he was never involved with drugs, sodomy or any other dubious activities.

Then Eugene leant forward. The general changed hands. The eyes behind the glasses narrowed. Eugene spoke more slowly, softly. Their private conversation. Saying thank you, saying sorry. Making right.

'What you taught me helped me to survive,' said Eugene. 'The things you cannot learn in books, but from the person who was there himself.'

He looked down for a moment. 'I'm sorry. Sorry about all the things that happened.'

General Dreyer patted him on the leg, his eyes calm. 'It's over, son,' he said, patting his leg again. 'It's in the past now, that.'

I sat very quietly, then handed Carina a R100 note. The tuck-shop queue was short. She rose to take our orders.

'Who is that man?' the general asked Eugene, nodding towards the other prisoner who was part of our group. 'Is he a policeman?'

Eugene explained. The conversation turned to Koevoet and Operation Vlakvark.

'How many kills, again?' asked the general.

'That was Piet Stassen,' said Eugene. 'He was the most successful that day. Thirty-eight kills.'

The general's body rocked back, his head nodding in recollection, the ice broken. They looked like father and son.

Carina came back with the Melville Koppies murderer, who was carrying the tray for her. He placed the tray on my lap and greeted me. The general took a Coke, but forgot to drink it. The guy carrying the tray only has one eye, whispered Carina. There's a story to that, I whispered back. Her eyes widened. She turned to the other prisoner at the end of our bench, gave the blue mark on his wrist one look and leaned forward.

'Show me your tattoo,' she said.

He squirmed, embarrassed, then unbuttoned the top of his orange overall to show us. A big bicep, and a big tattoo.

Carina sighed. 'A thing of beauty will always be beautiful.'

I egged her on: 'Show him yours.'

'This is all I can show,' said Carina. She lifted up the hem of her shirt, a fig leaf with two tendrils just visible on her stomach.

The prisoner could not believe his eyes. Then he threw his cropped head back and laughed a belly laugh. 'Now this one's a real woman!'

The general shifted the brown, calloused hand on his knee. 'Who is this man?' he asked Eugene again. 'Is he a policeman?'

Eugene explained again, then his words became automatic rifle fire. He told of the workshop in the prison, the books he read, everyday life in jail. The general listened without moving a muscle.

I looked at Eugene, at his neat profile. Who is Eugene de Kock? To his Koevoet and police colleagues he was a dispassionate soldier, a comsummate hunter of men. A member and, later, commander of Vlakplaas. In the Pretoria Central hierarchy he was classified as an 'assassin', which set him apart from the others.

A prison guard came past and asked Eugene for his ticket. The piece of paper, dirty from overuse, fell. He bent down to pick it up. Number 50.

I remembered an earlier visit when the paper square had also fluttered to the ground and landed under the bench. 'Fuck off,' he had said under his breath when a greasy-looking guy sidled too close to our bench. Paedophile, he told me. He had no respect for them.

'It's time,' said the warder. 'Sorry.'

'That's fine,' said Eugene. 'We had fifteen minutes extra today.'

It is in the focus of his eyes that Eugene shows his emotion, I realised. It is when he really looks at you that you see the soul of a tempered man.

'How should I approach Eugene?' I had asked Piet Croucamp after my second visit in July 2011.

'Quietly,' Piet had answered. 'He is a bit like an abused child – unsure how to handle compassion.'

A year later, everything was different.

We moved towards the exit. Around us, people came and went through the security gates. The general pushed his hand into his trouser pocket and fished out a wallet. He counted off a roll of notes. Thrust a thousand rand into my hand.

'For Gene,' he said. 'For whatever he needs. Contact me any time, *meisie.* I'll gladly help.'

He shook my hand and walked out with Daan du Toit and Carina.

I stayed for a moment with the man whose eyes were shining. His hair, still dark and neatly cut. Each hair smoothed flat. The orange overall immaculate and neatly ironed. Hi-Tec boots polished bright for the visit. His skin looking like it belonged to someone far younger than the 63-year-old who stood before me. It was the skin of someone who gets no sun.

'How was it?' I asked.

"Good, very good. Please tell the general I am sorry for everything I got up to.'

He talked fast, looking back at the door to the gated room.

'You know it's not necessary,' I said. 'Those things are over.' He put his left arm around me, hugged me firmly – looked back, again.

'Tell him anyway. I'm just sorry things came between us as they did. It felt as if my heart was too big for my chest. He was a mentor, just like my father; he taught me how to be and how not to be.'

His eyes were empty, as if the wind blew through them.

'The court then summarised the aggravating circumstances taken into account in respect of the seriousness of the offences. The offences had been planned and executed with meticulous precision. There had been time to recant.

Nevertheless, the offences had been committed and attempts were made to conceal the offences and prevent their being traced back to the police. Some of the offences were cold-blooded and cruel, with no compassion for the victims or respect for their bodies after their deaths. Innocent people, who had not constituted a threat to the accused or other members of the police, were killed. In certain cases, the victims' only offence had been their intention to reveal crimes committed by the police. Even members of the SAP or askaris who had worked with the police were victims of violence and killings.'

– QUOTED FROM JUDGE WILLEM VAN DER MERWE'S
SENTENCING PROCEEDINGS IN EUGENE DE KOCK'S
CRIMINAL TRIAL, 30 OCTOBER 1996.

8

A place called Vlakplaas

'It's here, somewhere,' said Larry Hanton, bolt upright like a meerkat while scanning the surrounding area. 'I remember the Hennops River.'

We had taken the Erasmia off-ramp on the outskirts of Pretoria and were driving up and down a dirt road looking for the farm entrance. There was no sign trumpeting 'Vlakplaas'. After a while we stopped at a building site.

'Do you know where Vlakplaas is?'

The workers immediately knew what I was talking about. 'Dikoko's place?' One of them remembered Eugene de Kock. 'It's that way. Where the cattle are.'

We followed two herders who were rounding up some cattle and calves, and stopped right in front of the main entrance. The farmhouse was small, half hidden behind tall trees and overgrown shrubs. We got out, peered through the wire fence. The homestead looked deserted; the metallic taste of blood settled in my throat. I felt nauseous and dizzy.

'Let's just get out of here,' I said to Larry.

'Wait, let me take a photo of you at the gate.'

Two scraggy dogs ran up, barking hesitantly; a 4x4 and a bakkie were parked under a large lean-to. The Hennops River murmured in the background. The wind played softly through the long grass and the trees.

Top: The author at the main entrance to Vlakplaas.
Bottom: Former Vlakplaas operative Nick Vermeulen at Vlakplaas with the bullet-proof vest custom made for Vlakplaas members to look like civilian wear. In the background are what used to be the living quarters of the askaris.

Photos taken, I got behind the steering wheel with unsteady legs. It was 2012, my first visit to Vlakplaas, the headquarters of Section C1 – the SAP's death squad, as it became known in the media.

Vlakplaas fell under the jurisdiction of the security police. This unit, known as Section C, was earmarked for the founding of a South African equivalent of the Rhodesian security forces unit. The unit had three divisions: Section C1, the operational wing at Vlakplaas; Section C2, tasked mainly with identifying and interrogating activists and deciding which terrorists to recruit as askaris and which to prosecute; and Section C3, involved in compiling statistics about acts of terror.[1]

Having read everything about Vlakplaas I could lay my hands on, my awareness now teeters on the brink of understanding. I may know the facts about the history of Vlakplaas, but a true understanding of the violence of apartheid and the abuses by the security forces still evades me. My fingers may have meshed with the fence around that farm, but I cannot comprehend the physical pain, torture and fear of death that Section C victims must have experienced. I have to force myself over the edge of innocence into the abyss of this inhumanity.

'There's another entrance behind the house. The chopper pad is there too,' said Larry. 'Maybe we can enter there.'

We found the small two-track through hip-high grass to the second entrance. The helipad was a few hundred metres from the fence. A large wooden cross had been erected beside the helipad; I photographed Larry next to it. A man unlocked the gate and allowed us to look around and take photos. He behaved like the owner of the farm; I wondered who would want to live in a place like Vlakplaas. Suddenly it looked like just an ordinary, neglected farmstead.

'The living quarters of the askaris were here, on the left,' Larry explained as we walked in – a brick building with a long row of rooms. We also went to the rondavel that was Eugene's office, the farmhouse and the undercover entertainment area. It looked like a braai area you'd find on any South African farm.

The building that was once the canteen was locked. I peered through the window – no sign of pool tables, bearded men or bottles of *leeutande*: 'lions' teeth', a mixture of liquor dregs and garlic that newcomers to Vlakplaas had to drink.

The voices of the past no longer even whispered here.

Vlakplaas is about 20 kilometres outside Pretoria. It was purchased in 1980 and registered as state property. Section C1 was established to convince members of Umkhonto we Sizwe (MK), the ANC's military wing, and other struggle organisations to work for the Security Branch. These men would be used to identify and capture their former comrades who had infiltrated the country. The captives would then have to choose between co-operation with the Security Branch, which included a salary and benefits, or imprisonment. Those who decided to work for the Security Branch were called askaris, a Swahili word meaning 'fighter'.

In his application for presidential pardon in 2002, Eugene refers to a memorandum called 'Die stigting van Vlakplaas en die Teen-Terroriste Eenheid' (The establishment of Vlakplaas and the Counter-Terrorism Unit)[2] compiled by General Johan Coetzee, a former police commissioner.[3] According to the memorandum, the police rented Vlakplaas from as early as June 1979, primarily to provide central accommodation for 'contaminated witnesses', also called '*makgemaakte terroriste*' (literally, terrorists who had been tamed).[4]

According to Coetzee, the Vlakplaas project was not initially a permanent one. Little money was put into the initiative. '[The] project was somewhat disorganised both as far as location and purpose were concerned and there were no clearly formulated guiding principles, especially considering that the project was initially not intended as a permanent undertaking, and was operated on rented property.'[5]

Later, due to the escalation of 'the terrorist onslaught against the Republic of South Africa', it was decided to buy the property. 'General Coetzee's opinion, as can be deduced from the memorandum, was that Vlakplaas's primary goal was the fight against terrorism. The services of the askaris were used to identify terrorists, after which they were arrested and taken to court, or were persuaded to join the unit,' wrote Eugene.[6]

In the last months of 1981 the Vlakplaas project became better organised after a directive, issued on 11 September 1981 to all departments and commanding officers of the various security branches, announced and outlined the objectives of Special Section C1. According to Eugene, the intention of this directive was to make the services of C1 available to other security branches of the police; it was clear that they were available for a wide variety of actions.

However, he later wrote that the amnesty hearings of the Truth and Reconciliation Commission had shown that Vlakplaas was never meant exclusively for the purpose Coetzee and others had in mind. He went on to say:

> In my time as a commanding officer of a Koevoet unit in the erstwhile South West Africa, I earned the reputation of being a merciless hunter of terrorists. I never received any formal training as a security policeman, nor did I have any practical experience in investigative work related to security

matters. I was not even trained as an ordinary detective. For practical purposes, I was a trained 'soldier' in the armed conflict against SWAPO ...

The other police members of Vlakplaas, both before and after I took over command of the unit, were in a similar position in that they had no specific skills in this regard either. Most of the members, including myself, were used to conduct operations of a military nature.

Many of the men at Vlakplaas had been involved in Koevoet, the SAP's task force or counter-insurgency unit. They were all trained in the use of explosives and had attended intelligence courses. During these courses, a great deal of emphasis was placed on the dangers that communism, the ANC, trade unions, and so on posed to the government.

These officers, including myself, were already used to the idea of violence, human pain and suffering as a result of the gruesome acts in which we participated and to which we were exposed during our service in the aforementioned units. I am therefore convinced that we were appointed as a result of our ability to deal with the threat of violence and because killing would be nothing new to us.

There is no doubt in my mind that the hierarchy in the South African Police was well aware of the requirements for police officers wanting to transfer to Vlakplaas.[7]

During one of my visits Eugene told me about a strange experience he'd had, which had touched him deeply. It was just after he had left South West under the cloud of his fallout with Dreyer. He was driving alone on the road between Vryheid and Babanango when something suddenly shifted in his consciousness. At that moment everything he looked at appeared completely surreal:

the flat landscape, the sun, the feel of the wind against his skin. 'I thought: how the fuck have things reached this point? Why the fuck did I end up doing what I do? How can this be possible?'

But a few weeks later he was part of a cross-border operation in Swaziland and everything was back to how it had been. Without hesitation he had lifted his rifle and shot Zwelibanzi Nyanda dead. Nyanda was a commander of MK in Swaziland and the brother of Siphiwe Nyanda, later a general and head of the South African National Defence Force (SANDF). He told me about Zwelibanzi Nyanda ... an exceptionally big man. The incident took place in November 1983 at a house in Swaziland. Eugene could not get Nyanda to go down. And he was an excellent shot.

The postmortem showed that Eugene shot Nyanda nine times, from his left shoulder to his stomach. Nyanda still tried to get away. The fatal shots were the three Eugene fired into his back, causing Nyanda to crash through the garden gate. A colleague then appeared from behind the fence and fired two more shots at Nyanda's head. But he was already dead.

From June 1983 until early 1993 – when Eugene was attached to Vlakplaas – several people died in one way or another at the hands of Vlakplaas operators. Eugene was not directly involved in all these incidents, but after his appointment as commanding officer of C1 in 1985, he saw to it that most assignments handed down to him from the SAP's top structure were executed.

Many of the attacks on members of the liberation movements took place in South Africa's neighbouring states. The attacks were often in collaboration with other branches of the security forces or, in some instances, with members of the defence force's Civil Cooperation Bureau (CCB).

After the Swaziland operation in which Zwelibanzi Nyanda

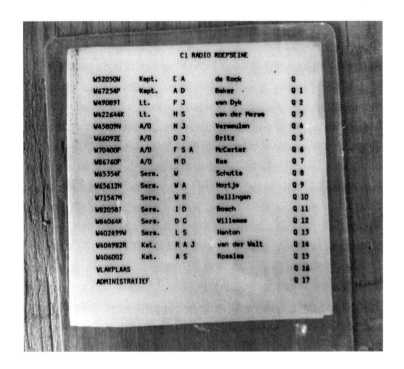

The radio call signals for the covert police unit Special Section
C1, stationed at Vlakplaas.

was shot dead and for which Eugene received the SOE (the South
African Police Star for Outstanding Service)[8] other murders by
members of the Security Branch followed – such as those of the
Cradock Four: Matthew Goniwe, Fort Calata, Sparrow Mkhonto
and Sicelo Mhlauli.[9] On 8 May 1985 the three community leaders
known as the Pebco Three – Sipho Hashe, Qaqawuli Godolozi and
Champion Galela – were abducted at the Port Elizabeth airport
and murdered at Post Chalmers near Cradock. Their bodies were
burnt and thrown into the Fish River.[10] Eugene pointed out in
one of our conversations that the Port Elizabeth Security Branch

in particular was responsible for the deaths of the Cradock Four and the Pebco Three.

Oliver Tambo's bodyguard, Sidney Msibi, was also captured by Vlakplaas operatives and assaulted. Paul Dikeledi, Cassius Make and an MK member named Viva were murdered in Swaziland on grounds of information provided by the askari Glory Sedibe.[11]

The activists Pansu Smith, Sipho Dlamini and Busi Majola died in Swaziland at the hands of Vlakplaas operatives. After this operation, Eugene and the others went to General Johan Coetzee's house in the early hours of the morning to report on what had happened. Eugene later wrote: 'I remember the general was in his dressing gown. Coetzee shook everybody's hands. When he got to me, he said that he did not know whether he should touch my hands because they were drenched in blood.'[12]

Four alleged MK operatives died in 1986 in an ambush near Amsterdam on the Swaziland border.[13] In the same year, four members of the Chesterville Youth Organisation were murdered,[14] and a body was blown up in Pretoria by Vlakplaas members and another in Jozini. The Durban activist Sheila Nyanda, wife of Siphiwe Nyanda, was abducted in Mbabane, Swaziland, and tortured.[15] According to Eugene, the Middelburg Security Branch was involved in this incident.

Eugene also applied for amnesty for the attacks on Cosatu House in March 1987; on Khotso House, the headquarters of the South African Council of Churches, in September 1988 in Johannesburg; and on Khanya House in Pretoria, the offices of the Southern African Catholic Bishops' Conference, in October 1988.

Massive quantities of weapons were moved regularly via Koevoet from South West Africa to South Africa, and weapons were also supplied to Renamo in Mozambique.[16]

Mbuso Tshabalala and Charles Zakhele Ndaba died in July 1990

Top: An aerial photo of Vlakplaas. **Middle:** The main building at Vlakplaas can be seen on the right, with Eugene's office on the left. **Bottom:** Former policeman Larry Hanton in front of Eugene's office.

after being held captive for about seven days and tortured cruelly. They were murdered on 14 July 1990 at the mouth of the Tugela River (now Thukela), their bodies thrown into the river.[17] The Durban C1 branch operating under the command of Colonel Andy Taylor was responsible for Tshabalala and Ndaba's deaths, Eugene told me.

In the words of the commissioners serving on the TRC: 'The killers of Vlakplaas have horrified the nation. The stories of a chain of shallow graves across the country, containing the remains of abducted activists who were brutalised, tortured and ultimately killed, have left many South Africans deeply shocked. The media has understandably focused on these events – labelling Eugene de Kock, the Vlakplaas commander, "Prime Evil".'[18]

The things I read and heard were extremely disturbing. My ongoing exposure to stories of cruel murders and brutal violence plunged me into a spiral of depression. Then there was the hard reality of my visits: the knowledge that the man with the soft voice who sat opposite me had committed some of those murders with his own hands – those neatly groomed hands, resting in his lap.

It took me three, four years of regular contact with Eugene to start understanding the appalling extent of human viciousness on both sides – security forces and freedom fighters. To realise that I, too, carry the seed of evil, as we all do. To understand that there is no such thing as normal behaviour in war. The security forces' underworld of crime and terrorism became a breeding ground for unthinkable acts.

One day I plucked up all my courage: 'Eugene, what does it feel like to kill someone?'

He grimaced. 'The person, the victim, gives off a smell,' he said. 'To this day I recall that smell. It nauseates me to the depths of my soul. It is the smell of fear bursting from the person's pores and through their body's fluids.'

That day, a door to greater understanding opened in my mind. At the same time, I felt something die in my soul. I experienced terrible anger and powerlessness at the thought that apartheid had been maintained for so long, so cruelly, by the death squads at Vlakplaas, the Security Branch and the defence force though their covert activities.

Torture had been the order of the day for the security forces and murder and robbery squad detectives, I gathered.

Eugene explained it like this: 'You must understand, from the time of Koevoet onwards, we used torture to gain information. [The security guard] Japie Maponya, for example, was interrogated by others before he was brought to Vlakplaas. There he was tortured with tear gas and tubing [a form of torture in which the victim's head is placed in a plastic bag or tied up with a piece of inner tubing so he cannot breathe].'

Eugene told me with shocking honesty how the Durban Security Branch, for example, smeared Vaseline on gas masks (to keep every last bit of oxygen out) before spraying tear gas inside them and placing them over victims' faces. 'The prisoner then lost control over all his bodily functions and began to talk ... In Koevoet I preferred to tie a piece of cloth around a SWAPO prisoner's hands and to pull him up until his toes were just touching the ground. You use his own muscles against him, everything cramps and later the muscles become stiff. Then he starts talking.'

In *A Long Night's Damage* Eugene admits it became part of their modus operandi to kill activists to protect the information obtained during interrogation. The identities of informants also had to be protected. 'Part of my job was to gather information about ANC members or collaborators. If necessary, the people I questioned had to be eliminated to prevent them from exposing security force members or the location of Vlakplaas. Sometimes we had to conceal the crimes of the security police.'[19]

Legislation that the National Party government put in place in the 1960s created a fertile breeding ground for the police's abuse of power. In 1963, John Vorster – minister of justice, police and prisons at the time, and later prime minister – pushed the General Laws Amendment Act through Parliament. This made provision for 90 days' detention without trial, extended to 180 days about 20 years later. It marked the decline of the constitutional state and made some police members believe they were above the law. Countless detainees died in detention. It was a mindset that led some policemen to mercilessly track down enemies of the state and to take it upon themselves to murder them.[20]

The Sharpeville Massacre on 21 March 1960 – which saw panicked policemen open fire on unarmed demonstrators, killing 69 – preceded Vorster's legislation. Sharpeville was a watershed in SAP history, claims former brigadier Hennie Heymans. In the aftermath of the shooting, the ANC and PAC were banned and went underground. The era of police death squads had begun.[21]

Vlakplaas operators worked not only in death squads, but also to cover up the transgressions of the security police.

In 2002 Eugene wrote in his application for presidential pardon how in June 1984 Brigadier Jack Cronjé had ordered him to supply activists with hand grenades and limpet mines from which the fuses had been removed. The activists – Congress of South African Students (Cosas) members from KwaThema – were suspected of attacking the homes of police members in the Springs district.

'The intention of removing the hand grenades' timing

mechanisms was to injure or kill their users. To ensure that the leader of the group of activists would not be able to identify Joe Mamasela – the askari who would hand over the hand grenades – a limpet mine from which the fuse had been removed was given to him, which would explode and kill him. These activities show once again that Vlakplaas was unquestionably the operational wing of the security police in the struggle against the terrorists.'[22]

Vlakplaas was also roped in as a 'clean-up' unit: 'Vlakplaas was used to assist in the concealment of crimes committed by members of other branches of the security police and to avoid the serious embarrassment that would result if [police] involvement in such crimes was revealed. When security branches found themselves in a dilemma, an appeal would be made to Vlakplaas to assist them,' Eugene writes. 'Usually C1's commanding officers would be approached, but in some cases I was approached for help directly. Examples include the [Johannes] Mabotha, [Japie] Maponya and Goodwill Sikhakhane incidents.'[23]

Eugene also told of how he had been approached by Lieutenant Schoon of the Jozini Security Branch to help with the kidnapping of an unidentified activist from Swaziland. Gert Schoon was the brother of Brigadier Willem Schoon, Vlakplaas commander and later the head of Section C. 'With Brigadier Schoon's blessing, we had a situation, once again, in which other security police used Vlakplaas to do their dirty work. The activist was handed over [by C1 officers] to the Security Branch at Black Rock or Island Rock. I understood the man was badly hurt during interrogation. He was then killed and Gert Schoon blew up his body on the missile range near the sea.'[24]

Vlakplaas's obligation to other security branches did not sit well with Eugene. A former Koevoet member and Vlakplaas operative with whom I spoke told of how Eugene once said to a police officer, 'We are not a butchery. We can't just do your dirty work for you.'

Eugene's dissatisfaction with this type of work did not prevent him and his colleagues from performing another part of their job: being a death squad. This may be because they were militarised policemen, trained not in normal policing but in wiping out the enemy.

As a former Koevoet member and Vlakplaas operator Johnny (pseudonym) put it: 'We left Ovamboland [Koevoet] with a certain mentality – we were losing the war there, but it had shifted, as we saw it, to South Africa. This, among other reasons, was why we acted so aggressively. We were soldiers, it was ingrained in us. Ordinary policemen did not have that mindset – they had families and stable jobs, they were in comfort zones. So, we were used to do the dirty work that these ordinary policemen were not prepared to do.'

'That being said, at Vlakplaas we were all volunteers,' Eugene remarked when I mentioned Johnny's comment to him.

Committing ongoing acts of violence and heinous crimes leaves scars, Karl Marlantes writes in his book *What it is Like to Go to War*: 'The violence of combat assaults psyches, confuses ethics, and tests souls. This is not only the result of the violence suffered. It is also the result of the violence inflicted. Warriors suffer from wounds to their bodies, to be sure, but because they are involved in killing people they also suffer from their compromises with, or outright violations of, the moral norms of society and religion.'[25]

A close bond between Koevoet and Vlakplaas was inevitable. It was important for C1's activities to remain covert so, in the late 1980s, Eugene received orders from Brigadier Schoon to fetch weapons from Ovamboland and to store them at Vlakplaas.[26] The weapons included machine guns, mortars, automatic rifles, small arms, landmines, hand grenades, ammunition and large quantities of military explosives.[27]

TRC hearings revealed that much of the weaponry supplied to the Inkatha Freedom Party (IFP) prior to the 1994 election came from Koevoet. Several Vlakplaas operatives applied for amnesty for the transport of weapons from Namibia (previously South West Africa) to Vlakplaas. It would appear that this occurred on Brigadier Schoon's orders. The weapons came from Koevoet stores and from the SADF's Oshivelo base. It included AK-47s and ammunition, M26 and Russian hand grenades and explosives, SADF explosives, Russian and SADF limpet mines, light machine guns, SAM7s, mortars, RPG pipes and ammunition, and various other items.

'The weapons were not recorded in the weapons register. No official registers were held in respect of the nature and extent of weapons stored. Initially, I attempted to keep records, but later stopped doing so, largely because no officers appeared to be interested in these details or ever requested to inspect such records.'[28]

As commanding officer at Vlakplaas, Eugene had total control over these weapons. The purpose of having them, he said, was to carry out Vlakplaas operations. Over and above the Ovamboland weapons that had been sent to Vlakplaas, any weapons and ammunition of Eastern Bloc/Soviet origin that the security brances had seized were ordered to be sent there. According to Eugene, 'we used these kinds of weapons when we deemed it necessary to create the impression that terrorists were involved in violence and killings. Vlakplaas was also free to request commercial explosives from the SAP's task force, and did so on occasion.'[29]

According to Eugene, Brigadier Schoon sometimes accompanied him when they went to fetch weapons that had been seized but could not be fed back into service in the SAP. 'Among other things, some of these weapons were used on request of the SAP and SADF to build arms caches which, when discovered, would justify attacks on ANC bases in neighbouring states.[30]

'[H]and in hand with total onslaught went total denial. Under no circumstances should the state be seen to be involved in, or responsible for, violent unrest. The government attributed violence in black townships to radical elements in the townships and not to state-affiliated operatives. Denial was so important that we received orders from high-ranking officers to kill some of our own comrades when they threatened to spill the beans,' writes Eugene.[31]

I thought again of David Klatzow's words in *Steeped in Blood: The Life and Times of a Forensic Scientist*: 'The truth was a complete misnomer in the turbulent 1980s. The state propaganda machine trumpeted out "official" versions of events, portraying the "successes" of the government in fighting the total onslaught in an attempt to brainwash the public at large. Unbeknown to most average South Africans, a common denominator in many of the political stories at the time was a place called Vlakplaas. It was truly a place from hell … No law applied here other than the eleventh commandment: Do not get caught. The men from Vlakplaas lied, raped, murdered and thieved their way around the country …'[32]

When I go through the TRC reports, read book after book, and study Eugene's documents, a movie plays out in my mind – one that illuminates the dark corners of the human psyche. One of Eugene's favourite sayings when plans were being laid was 'Just between us sparrows on the roof …'

Eugene and the Vlakplaas operators did everything they could to keep the existence of Vlakplaas, the presence of the askaris and the nature of their activities hidden. To maintain this guise of anonymity no official police vehicles were used on the grounds and the officers were not uniformed. Two armed men guarded the grounds by night, and an officer with a concealed weapon by day. Anyone without official authority or business was refused entry.

> Great care was taken to ensure that Vlakplaas operations could not be traced to us or to the SAP. False alibis were created; we used vehicles that could not be traced to the police, false registration numbers and weapons of Eastern origin.
>
> [The askari] Brian Ngqulunga was shot dead in Bophuthatswana with AK-47 rifles to create the impression of a revenge killing by ANC members. We also believed Bophuthatswana lacked the resources and skills to investigate his death. The officers involved in this incident and I booked rooms in a Braamfontein hotel to create an alibi.
>
> [The askari] Goodwill Sikhakhane[33] was also shot with an AK-47. [Krugersdorp security guard] Japie Maponya[34] was killed in Swaziland. False travel and accommodation claims were submitted to create the impression that at the time of his kidnapping and murder, Vlakplaas members were in Jozini.[35]

I was stunned by the Vlakplaas operatives' cloak-and-dagger lives. According to Vlakplaas operator Riaan Bellingan, their work was intelligence-driven. It was not the art of killing – 'it was the art of staying out of shit'.

I gathered that police units also hid things from one another. For example, Eugene mentioned how the heads and commanders of the various security police units met daily in Pretoria to discuss security matters. These meetings were referred to as the

Sanhedrin.[36] According to him, the heads of C2 and C3 attended these meetings regularly, but he was never invited.

'I believe there were two reasons for this. Firstly, with Vlakplaas being the operational arm of the security police, I could make no valuable contribution to security matters. Secondly, as commanding officer of Vlakplaas I might report on matters not meant for the other security branches' ears.'[37]

I wondered anew about the levels on which life-and-death decisions were made. In his application for presidential pardon it was important for Eugene to show that most Vlakplaas operations were ordered by higher authorities – or, at least, that his commanders were aware of them.

He wrote: 'During December 1985 Vlakplaas was involved in another attack upon so-called activists in Lesotho. I received the order from Brigadier Schoon and he led me to understand that he had received it from "the top" – that is, from the state president, Mr PW Botha. As far as I can recall, approximately seven people were killed in this attack.'

Eugene also indicated that General Johan van der Merwe, former commissioner of police, had admitted in his testimony before the TRC that he had known about C1 operations in neighbouring countries. General Van der Merwe testified: 'I had used the C1 unit and knew personally that we were involved in cross-border actions in some cases. The members of C1 were very experienced and competent, had undergone counter-insurgency training and were capable of working under difficult circumstances with clear minds. They were essentially the only operational unit in the security forces.'[38]

Eugene mentioned the high praise he and his team members received for their actions, although he refers to the medals as 'trinkets'. How proud he must have been, though, when – at last – he received the recognition he had craved as a child on the highest level. As he pointed out, it is inconceivable that these awards would have been made without the police hierarchy's full knowledge of the reasons for them.

'The SOE [Police Star for Excellent Service] was awarded to me for the London bombing [1982] and the Nyanda/McFadden incident, and I received the Silver Cross for Bravery for the Lesotho incident [1985]. We were were also congratulated on a number of occasions for other incidents. General Johan van der Merwe testified before the TRC that I was one of the most highly decorated policemen in the force. In addition to cross-border operations, Vlakplaas was involved in a number of domestic incidents in which people were killed, injured or assaulted or had their property damaged.'[39]

As far as former brigadier Hennie Heymans can establish, Eugene is the country's most highly decorated post-war policeman for bravery and military expertise. There were also several covert operations for which Eugene received no recognition, for obvious reasons.

The large sums of money channelled into Vlakplaas also gave Eugene the impression that the apartheid government approved of the unit's activities.[40]

Some police generals knew what was going on at Vlakplaas, or must have had a very good idea. The nature of C1 had to be kept secret right up to the top – but at the same time it became apparent from my discussions with Eugene and former Vlakplaas members that all the senior members of the Security Branch in Pretoria, and of the security branches countrywide, knew about Vlakplaas and had even visited the facility. Likewise, the police generals' political heads must have had some kind of idea of what happened at Vlakplaas – but the politicians, in particular, accepted no responsibility in their TRC submissions.

In an open letter written in 2014, Eugene alleged that decisions about life and death were made on three government levels. He said the decision-making began in the Counter-revolutionary Information Committee (Trewits), which consisted of members of the security police, military intelligence service and national intelligence service. 'This group was the first of three levels at which it was decided who would be shot dead or abducted and who would live. The recommendations of this committee were seldom, if ever, turned down.

'The next two levels were the Co-ordinating Information Committee and the State Security Council. When an action or operation was approved, the group or unit to which the task would be assigned for execution was decided.'[41]

According to Hennie Heymans, however, this allegation is incorrect: 'I can swear to this under oath because as a policeman I was seconded to the secretariat of the State Security Council. The Counter-revolutionary Information Committee (Trewits) never decided who should die! Their task was, among other things, collecting information about where bases and things were located, how things were looking there and the best attack methods – tactical information, mostly. [For example] should the SADF decide to take out a house in Matola in a reprisal operation, this inter-departmental task team knew how things looked there.

'The Co-ordinating Information Committee (CIC) met under the chairmanship of the director-general of the national intelligence service. Its aim was to co-ordinate the collection of information – who does what, training, sources, that kind of thing.

'Then there was the working committee of the State Security Council. The heads of the security forces and information services met here and only two weeks after this meeting would the State Security Council meeting be held under the state president's chairmanship. The working committee would go through everything thoroughly before putting it before the state president and the State Security Council.

'It was never decided at Trewits, the CIC, the working committee or the State Security Council who would be killed. It just wasn't done this way. Yes, some highly secret ad hoc meetings were held at which it was decided to neutralise some individuals politically or to eliminate them, but these meetings were extremely, extremely secret and operated on a need-to-know basis.'

General Johan van der Merwe published two reactions online in July 2014 to the objection raised by a Democratic Alliance (DA) spokesperson that Eugene was still sitting in prison while those who had issued the orders were free.[42] In an open letter to DA leader Helen Zille, Van der Merwe writes that there was 'not a single case for which Eugene de Kock was sentenced in which there was any evidence at all that he had acted on instructions from a superior.'

In an article – ironically enough – that issued a plea for De Kock to be pardoned, Van der Merwe wrote that the impression that Eugene de Kock was left with the mess while the generals walk free stems from 'ignorance of the facts ... There is no evidence whatsoever that any of the generals were implicated in any of the murders for which Colonel De Kock was found guilty.'[43]

Eugene's response in his open letter was that all statements for the various commissions of inquiry – particularly the Harms Commission, which examined Vlakplaas operations among other things – were drawn up by General (then brigadier) Krappies Engelbrecht. 'We just had to sign it. We compiled none of our own statements. Claims registers, travel and accommodation registers, documents such as security reports and every vestige of evidence was traced and then removed or destroyed. In effect we had to wipe out all the records and documentary evidence that [later] may have indemnified us …

'General Van der Merwe claims that no general ever committed perjury or defeated the ends of justice, or committed murder and/or a series of other offences. To think that I – who knew so little because I was held in the lowest esteem before the change of government, and then had, so prominently, to become the scapegoat for the old dispensation – knew so much. How much more, then, do you and the others know, General Van der Merwe?'[44]

'The offences were committed over a long period and covered a wide range of crimes. Many were committed in a way that falsely implicated innocent people. In some cases, officers who had acted as executioners on the orders of the accused or other senior officers were rewarded financially for their transgressions. In addition to the concealment of offences, courts and commissions were misled by false testimony. Witnesses were discredited freely.

Some of the victims must have experienced mortal fear for considerable periods before their murders. No mercy was shown to victims. The violent crimes must have caused the victims' families deep suffering and pain. The weapons used in the commission of certain offences were efficient and destructive and may have been in the accused's possession illegally. The accused's actions surrounding the fraud charges were cunning and deceitful and led to the accused and others acquiring money to which they were not entitled.'

– Quoted from Judge Willem van der Merwe's imposition sentencing proceedings in Eugene de Kock's criminal trial, 30 October 1996.

9

Askari

In his book *Askari,* Jacob Dlamini writes that double agents – *izimpimpi* (an Nguni word for 'spies') or *amaMbuka* (Zulu for 'traitors') – are nothing new in our society, and points to the treason that took place among Afrikaners in the Anglo-Boer War. The terms describing traitors or askaris are always loaded, writes Dlamini, 'and their meanings are always context-specific, politically constructed, contested and subject to change. Collaboration is marked by ambiguity ...'[1]

The askaris were unique to Vlakplaas, members of freedom movements like the ANC and PAC whom the Security Branch had arrested and persuaded to work for their former enemy. In exchange for their co-operation, they were remunerated and escaped prosecution. The askaris were indispensable to the Security Branch, helping them to identify their former comrades.[2]

'The purpose of Vlakplaas at this stage was ostensibly as a place to rehabilitate "turned terrorists" or, as they were called, askaris. The askaris were eventually divided into units and supervised by white Security Branch members, and it was this change that transformed Vlakplaas into a counter-insurgency unit,' concluded the TRC in its final report.[3]

The askari system was an effective and ruthless weapon in the Vlakplaas arsenal.

According to former Vlakplaas askari Gregory Sibusiso Radebe, the average askari blended into society with ease: 'Ordinary South Africans like you see every day were there. There were also guys of notable intelligence ... and that probably is what made that unit the spearhead in the Security Branch's fight against the ANC. I think it was probably the only unit that could blend in anywhere in the country and bring information in the shortest time possible.'[4]

Most of the askaris were not prepared to work with the Security Branch of their own accord – they were 'persuaded' to do so. According to former brigadier Hennie Heymans, their motivation for becoming askaris varied. Some were disillusioned with the freedom movements they belonged to, others were just plain homesick, while some let themselves be bribed by the salaries and perks. Some clearly knew the consequences of refusing to work with the Security Branch.

Eugene denied, again, to me the allegation that under his command an askari was burnt to death at Vlakplaas while operatives were having a braai. According to him, when the askaris arrived at Vlakplaas they had already been recruited, and were consequently not tortured there. 'What would actually happen was that on a new askari's arrival, he would get new clothes, a salary and a pistol for personal protection. Of course, some askaris deny this now because they feel guilty. When the askaris got a hiding, it was because they asked for it. Almost all of them were extremely difficult people.'[5]

Under Eugene's command, a few askaris who 'went astray' and threatened to leak information about the unit were murdered by Vlakplaas operatives. When I spoke to former Security Branch members, I learnt that in the intelligence world it is common practice to get rid of a source or a colleague whose loyalty is in question. One such askari, Moses Ntehelang, was murdered at Vlakplaas itself.[6] (In late December 2014, the Missing Persons Task

Top: Two askaris during training. **Right:** A certificate that was issued to askaris who completed their parachute training successfullly.

CLOUD BUSTERS SKYDIVING CLUB

FIRST JUMP CERTIFICATE

This is to certify that

Tsotetsi

has successfully completed a recognised 1st jump course and 1st parachute descent on the 30th day of July 1989

CERTIFIED:

INSTRUCTOR

CLUB SECRETARY

Team of the National Prosecuting Authority traced Ntehelang's remains with Eugene's help.)

For Eugene it was important not only to maintain control over the askaris, but also to improve their living conditions. To secure remuneration for them without revealing their involvement in the Security Branch, they were registered as informants. They lived in their own quarters at Vlakplaas; Eugene felt as responsible for them as he did for his black fellow policemen in Koevoet:

> I encouraged the askaris to study and improve their knowledge, with the assurance they would get the fees back for all the subjects they passed.
>
> The retraining of the askaris was upgraded to special forces standard under my command, and they were also trained in the use of all types of weapons of Eastern and Western origin. Helicopter drills followed, as well as lectures on the Police Act, standing orders, regulations and law subjects.
>
> There was a large framed copy of the ANC Freedom Charter in the lecture hall. I put it up myself in 1986 and said, 'Let's see what I can provide for you on this list.'
>
> A programme resulted that encouraged further studies with financial rewards and saw askaris appointed as permanent SAP members to secure housing subsidies and medical and pension benefits. In this way I provided stability and security for them and their families, and their children had a future and could go to school.'[7]

Dlamini also refers to the training of the askaris in his book: 'According to the former askari Gregory Sibusiso Radebe, "we did intense physical training at places like Penge mine and Maleoskop ... There was not so much theory, though De Kock

Askaris at shooting practice and performing other training exercises at the Penge mine.

liked to have us watch war movies – he seemed to like the movies of the Vietnam war".[8]

With colleagues Nick Vermeulen and Lionel Snyman, Eugene also began training the askaris in parachute jumping. Some of the askaris in the first and second group received their wings from Adriaan Vlok, Minister of Law and Order. 'I received no support whatsoever from my senior officers in this regard. While they were not opposed to the training, I had to devise plans myself to acquire money and parachutes – which we did,' wrote Eugene.[9]

Former Vlakplaas operatives whom I talked to all agreed that the first black parachute unit was founded more as a team-building initiative than a fully-fledged parachute unit. Johnny (pseudonym), a former Vlakplaas operative and instructor, explained: 'The askaris were difficult people. When people compete in dangerous sports or activities, group solidarity develops. That was primarily what we wanted to achieve.'

As Vermeulen – a former task-force member and Vlakplaas operative – said: 'If you can jump with me, you can fight with me too.'

The main question for Eugene and the Security Branch was the extent to which they could trust the askaris. They were always a source of concern and uncertainty: 'Consequently, they were reminded in subtle ways that they could not afford to betray the Security Branch,' Eugene wrote in his application for presidential pardon. 'I established an internal counter-intelligence unit within Vlakplaas. All the telephones the askaris used were tapped. I used some of the senior black members to listen in on their conversations and report back to me. In this way I tried to find out timeously when an askari's loyalty to Vlakplaas came under suspicion.'[10]

At the same time Eugene sympathised with the askaris and

their families, knowing that their former organisations labelled them informants.

ANC supporters were directly and indirectly requested to act against these informants. There was no greater treachery, for the freedom movements, than that of the askaris. People suspected of working with the Security Branch were brutally murdered: '[I]ndividuals accused of collaboration would have tyres doused with petrol placed around their necks or on their bodies and then set alight … the necklace was a weapon … of the masses themselves to cleanse the townships [of] … collaborators.'[11]

According to Eugene, firearms could not be officially issued to askaris because they were not members of the SAP. Many did not qualify for weapons licences either since some had criminal records, but they were issued firearms in any event.

'Some askaris were attacked and had their firearms stolen; others lost – or simply sold – theirs. During the period of unrest and riots I devised a system in which members would guard the homes of those who were on duty. The children of askaris would also be protected at their schools, if necessary … [but] no such situations arose.'[12]

There was always a chance the askaris' weapons could by used by freedom fighters in terror attacks. For this reason, Eugene viewed askari weapon losses with deep suspicion. 'Many of them, according to information we received, considered approaching– or threatened to approach – the political organisations they had betrayed. The murders of Brian Ngqulunga and Goodwill Sikhakhane fall into this category.'[13]

Eugene described many askaris – and some white Vlakplaas operatives – as 'difficult people' who tried his patience endlessly. In addition, he alleged that most of the askaris committed crimes while working at Vlakplaas. He had to use his influence to prevent

Top: A rare photo of a group of askaris with their instructors during training at the Penge mine. **Bottom:** Braaiing was a favourite pastime for many members of the police.

them being prosecuted, because he feared they would disclose their involvement with, and further information about, Vlakplaas. He found it difficult to discipline the askaris because the danger was always that they might reveal their involvement at Vlakplaas in revenge.

In Dlamini's book, former askari Oscar Linda Moni admits to being terrified of Eugene: 'I had the fear of God that was instilled in me … life as an askari and at Vlakplaas was governed by violence.' Moni tells of 'extreme military discipline at Vlakplaas, which was accompanied by occasional beatings, almost on a weekly basis, on the various members who happened to indulge in unauthorised use of alcohol or ill treated their wives'.[14]

According to Moni, Eugene doled out punishment regardless of race. '[A]nybody was a candidate if they should transgress the disciplinary lines that were set.'[15]

Involuntarily, I thought again of Eugene's nickname from his Koevoet days: Fok-fok de Kock. He swung between being 'furious, hopeless, or both' about the behaviour of his white and black colleagues at Vlakplaas. 'I controlled the use of dagga and alcohol when I took command at Vlakplaas. Dagga smoking was not tolerated and the use or abuse of alcohol was restricted to times when the men were off duty. I even had to keep an eye on the men's use of cough medicine because of its addictiveness. One morning I punched Tok Bezuidenhout, a so-called white askari, from under his bottle of cough medicine.'[16]

I asked Eugene about Moni's allegation that they got beatings almost weekly. He denied it happened that frequently and explained that corporal punishment was only meted out after a council of black members had decided on it. This council comprised a black SAP captain, two former ANC members, two former PAC members and two black SAP members.

'A few of them were properly thrashed, but they asked for trouble and got it. One askari challenged me in front of the entire unit: Jimmy Mbane said he was the ANC light-heavyweight boxing champion and would fuck me up. I hit him only once – broke his false teeth, top and bottom, clean through the middle. He had to have another set made when his mouth had healed. He lost his title.'

When Vlakplaas disbanded, all the askaris who were still SAP members were given retrenchment packages. 'We did this because they were clearly not in a position to do ordinary police work. However, a number of askaris became loyal policemen and kept silent when they were discharged,' wrote Eugene.[17]

The extent of the murders, torture and kidnappings by Vlakplaas operatives was revealed in great detail during Eugene's criminal trial, the evidence he and others gave before the TRC, and in books such as *A Long Night's Damage*, which he wrote with Jeremy Gordin, as well as in *A Human Being Died that Night* by psychologist Pumla Gobodo-Madikizela.

One incident that drew considerable media attention was that of askari Glory Sedibe. Sedibe was one of the young protesters who left the country after the Soweto riots in 1976, joined the ANC and became a member of Umkhonto we Sizwe (MK). Code-named MK September, he rose high in MK structures. In 1986 he was arrested by the Swaziland police, then abducted from a Swazi jail by Vlakplaas operatives under Eugene's command. After lengthy torture and interrogation sessions in Piet Retief, he turned. He worked as an askari at Vlakplaas until the early 1990s, when he joined the directorate of covert information. In 1994 he died of a heart attack, although it is alleged that he had been poisoned. In the police file opened on Sedibe while he was still an MK member, a note struck Eugene: 'He cares greatly for his operatives and agents and takes good care of them.'

A man to respect, even as an enemy.

Eugene's description of Sedibe's abduction gives a glimpse not only of operatives' actions during covert activities, but also of the complexity of the issue of betrayal, specifically in the askaris' case. In an unpublished manuscript, Eugene writes about this as follows:

On 12 December 1986 there were discussions in General [Johan] Van der Merwe's office about September Machinery, an Umkhonto we Sizwe unit in Swaziland that was giving the Security Branch a headache. Glory Sedibe was the head of September Machinery.

In terms of an agreement between the South African security police and the Swazi police, Sedibe [after his arrest by the Swaziland police] was held in a small, unremarkable police station with only one policeman on duty at night. This was to give the South African Security Branch the opportunity to kidnap Sedibe and bring him to South Africa. He was well known to the Security Branch as an excellent and successful operative: astute, one who knew the basic rules of security and counter-espionage and was consequently difficult to track down.

On our arrival at the police station, we approached it from a distance to avoid attracting the police official's attention. Only one light was on in the police station; it was locked up and there was no sign of the policeman. Not a good sign. It was raining, freezing cold in fact. I forced my AK-47 bayonet into a small gap in a window in the administration building, then climbed through with my model 92 Beretta pistol and silencer ready in my hand. I had no doubt that either we had received shit information, or that the situation had changed since we had crossed the border into Swaziland.

The other Vlakplaas operatives followed me in dead silence. This was an ambush. In my mind I could already smell the gunpowder and see the blood, shit and snot spatter as I had seen so often in the past, especially with fights at close quarters.

I heard a shuffle in the corridor and saw a young Swazi policeman with a G3 automatic assault rifle creeping up on us. At three metres I aimed my pistol directly at his face and told him, softly, to put his weapon down. He looked at me, flicked his eyes to his rifle barrel, looked back up at me and saw in my eyes that I knew his safety was on. In my eyes he saw what he had seen in the pistol barrel aimed directly between his eyes – his death. He lowered his weapon, slowly.

Our immediate problem was to find out how many more policemen and weapons there were. We then found the person in charge, who had no rifle. If he'd had one, we would have bled to death in that police station in Swaziland that night.

I took the keys from the official in charge. Opening the cells, we came upon one cell that had three people in it. We locked the two police officials in the cell and chased the other two prisoners – two stock thieves – out into the cold. They were highly annoyed, and moaned about the cold and being fucked around by a bunch of strangers.

Meanwhile, the other six Vlakplaas operatives were fighting Sedibe for their lives. Desperation and the litres of adrenalin pumping through his system were making him give six hardened and fit men – three of whom were big and heavy – pure hell. He was eventually throttled unconscious and carried to the vehicle.

In the vehicle, he came to and got violent again. Out of sheer desperation, one of the black operatives hit him so hard in the face with his Makarov pistol that the silencer bent. Then Sedibe went down. He would wear those Makarov scars on his nose as a medal of honour. As he should have – with pride.[18]

The askaris' fates were sealed, from the outset, by their decision to commit treason. Discussing Dlamini's book, journalist Andrew Donaldson suggests that Dlamini tries 'to understand Sedibe's motives, to "explain" Sedibe, and understand why he made the choices he did, to collaborate with a sworn enemy, and to do so without buying, as Dlamini puts it, "into apartheid assumptions about how race determined the moral choices and political loyalties of individuals".'[19]

Eugene claims Sedibe's comrades in Swaziland betrayed him for financial gain. 'I made it clear at the TRC hearings that MK September was not the traitor they [the Security Branch and the ANC] made him out to be. He was abducted from a prison and brought to South Africa. He was neither a defector nor recruited traitor. He was true MK, and did not do a single thing for money. When I countered the allegations by Colonel Visser [head of the Security Branch in Nelspruit] and his allies during the TRC hearing that MK September was a traitor, they knew only too well not to let the discussion go any further: more answers from my side would inevitably have lead to the disclosure of their ANC sources active in Swaziland and Mozambique.

'They [the Security Branch] were protecting their ANC sources by creating the false impression that all the information was generated by MK September ... Even today they have to protect these sources, some of whom are high-ranking, because these same sources protect them now that the times and the government have changed.

'MK September's fate was sealed – in a way, he was already lost when he said goodbye to his wife and young daughter on the morning of his departure to Swaziland. His Judas Iscariot was very well rewarded. In the final instance he was really responsible for MK September's death; it was as if he had pulled the trigger himself and sent a friend and comrade into the abyss.'[20]

Eugene believes Sedibe was betrayed a second time in 1994, that he was murdered by 'the man under whose control he was and who worked for the directorate of secret intelligence ... Sedibe was murdered by those whom he had no option but to trust.' He maintains that Sedibe was killed by the same poison used to murder Knox Dlamini, a Swazi supporter of the ANC.[21]

There are so many untold stories in the ranks of the erstwhile security forces on one hand and the former freedom fighters on the other ... far more than came to light during the hearing of the Truth and Reconciliation Commission. Sedibe's story is only one of them, writes Jacob Dlamini: 'But it complicates how we think about apartheid and its legacies, and reminds us of the stories that still refuse to be told. As a nation, we would do well to examine the taboos, the secrets and the disavowals at the core of our collective memories.'[22]

10

Divide and rule

Eugene remembers the sense of feeling dirty all too well. He calls it 'contamination'. After an operation like the one in Swaziland or the one in which Japie Maponya was murdered, he would strip off his clothes before setting foot in his house. Sometimes, he would cut up and burn his work clothes, destroy everything but his Hi-Tec boots. Work clothes were never washed with his wife and children's clothes – they were always kept separate.

I wanted to know what he thought about in the middle of an operation. He explained that he could shut himself off completely from his surroundings and focus on the task at hand. He would answer a question without it registering, accept a beer he was offered robotically; he was not entirely present. His brain would 'empty'; sometimes, he couldn't even talk to the men around him. This feeling of isolation started before an operation and could last for up to two days after it. Then he would recall the events and replay them, over and over, in his mind's eye, like a film. Frame by frame.

His answer to my asking why he did this: 'The enemy has his script and you have yours. I always tried to do everything perfectly. In South West Africa this must have had a negative influence on my health. You do and give your very best, but during an operation nothing goes exactly as you want it to. This taught me to reevaluate everything, and I mean everything: first your performance, and then every other facet of the operation. From deployment to

Eugene de Kock during a visit to Oshakati and his
former unit Koevoet in 1987.

withdrawal, from medical to cover, even the colour of the vehicles
we used in neighbouring states and which vehicles were most
common in that state. *Nothing* was left to chance. I also watched
my men's behaviour for a few days after the operation for any
negative reactions and other aspects that were atypical of their
normal daily routine.'

According to criminologist Professor Anna van der Hoven, who
gave evidence for mitigation of sentence in Eugene's criminal trial,
he felt mentally exhausted after an operation and had to reevaluate his value system. He experienced guilt and inner conflict
if a life had to be taken, but he also believed that he had to look
after himself.[1]

Eugene told me how one day someone from the Security Branch
asked him how he managed to do what he did and still function
so normally. When he thought about this, he realised that all the

violence and death was like a very thick, transparent door. Once the door had slammed shut behind him, there was no going back. Ever. He left everyone, including his wife and children, on the other side. He could still see everyone on the other side, and they could see him. They thought he was okay – he looked normal, but knew he wasn't. He knew that if he turned around and looked behind him, he'd see nothing but blood, loss and destruction.

This is the price you pay for the loss of innocence.

'Even my wife did not know me completely,' he said.

I asked Eugene about his wife and children. He was always very private about this.

'I married late in life, at 36 only. Audrey and I were married in 1986 in Pretoria. She was only 22 … a beautiful woman, the second great love of my life. She wasn't just all pretty and innocent, you know. She was part of a large group of policewomen who worked at head office and Charmaine Gale, the former high jumper, was one of her friends.'

'You know, I've just remembered something,' he said. I watched him go back in time. 'I have no dress sense. Audrey couldn't handle this and always picked my clothes.'

They lived in Pretoria: 'After my wedding I bought a flat in Pretoria North, in Burger Street, while Audrey and I were on the waiting list for one of the Lynnwood police houses. When I finally got a house, of course it was the dirtiest, worst one of the lot. It didn't even have a fence. I fixed everything up myself. The same happened at Vlakplaas. When I took over in 1985, Vlakplaas was valued at R94 000. There was no electricity, proper water supply, toilets or entertainment area. A team of workers transformed the place into a paradise. It became a microcosm, later, with a workshop and its own motor mechanic. In 1993 the farm was valued at R5,5 million.'

Eugene and Audrey have two sons, Eugene and Michael, both of whom are now in their twenties. He regularly took the boys with him to Vlakplaas. Journalist and writer Jim Hooper, Eugene's good friend, remembers how he always insisted that the boys address the black Vlakplaas operatives as *Oom* (Uncle): 'I was a regular visitor to Vlakplaas. At the weekly braais for Security Branch members from around the country, Eugene would take a quiet delight in introducing me as "an American journalist" – anathema to anyone in the SAP or SADF – and watching them whiten and choke on their beers.'

Eugene sent his wife and sons out of the country before he was charged in 1995. He had already realised how things were likely to turn out for him. He last held his sons in his arms when they were four and seven years old.

He wanted to protect them. 'I did this for two reasons. Firstly, the media would destroy my family. And secondly, the children are not the father. My sons were innocent. They had to go. I knew, for the generals it would be a matter of: talk, and there will be harm. And for the ANC: if you don't talk, there will be harm.'

'Audrey and I divorced just after they left the country. She was still so young … that's why I divorced her. I wanted her to have a second chance, make a new start. She started at the bottom in a foreign country and has worked her way up to management level. She is an excellent mother to our sons, the proverbial iron fist in a velvet glove.'

How does one reconcile being a soldier – an assassin for the state – with everyday family life? Eugene told me it became difficult to listen when people spoke about run-of-the-mill problems, like the milk that had gone sour or the child who was struggling at school – these matters were no longer part of his frame of reference.

In many respects the De Kock family lived an extraordinary

life. Not even going out for a meal was straightforward: 'normal' for Eugene meant carrying a concealed weapon and watching not only the whole restaurant but also the waiter for the slightest hint of trouble. He would even ask for their cold drinks to be brought sealed to the table. One former operative claims that Eugene became paranoid at Vlakplaas, constantly looking over his shoulder, suspicious of everyone.

It's been years since he was last in contact with his family. 'We used to keep in touch through letters and phone calls. Later, they broke contact.'

Does he expect to see them after his release? 'The boys are adults now – it will depend on them whether they want to see me again.'

During one of my visits to Pretoria Central, we sat opposite each other, each of us with a Tex in our hands and a shared bottle of mango juice on the prison bench. We talked about his memories of Vlakplaas, his recollections rising, coming to rest just beneath his skin. He leaned back, his voice growing softer, eyes hidden behind the glasses.

An hour at a time is very little, too little time really for a coherent conversation. But that's how we did it, Sunday after Sunday, month in and month out.

The more time I spent with him, the more he opened up to me. I asked difficult questions that day. Questions about emotions, what motivated him, decisions he had made. Without saying it in so many words, I wanted to understand where things started to go wrong for Eugene de Kock. Had he lost the ability to distinguish between right and wrong on one specific occasion, in one particular moment? Or had it happened progressively?

To grasp this I had to listen – without judgement – to him, as well as to those who worked with him most closely.

'Go and talk to everyone,' he said. 'Don't write only good stories about me. Write everything.'

So began my conversations with the 'voices of the past'. Larry Hanton was once again invaluable, helping me to arrange meetings with former Vlakplaas operatives and other colleagues in the police. Over three years, countless discussions took place over lunches and coffee, beer, Red Heart rum and whisky sessions. Each encounter presented an opportunity for 'storytime' – whether it be at the Kia-Ora Backpackers Lodge in the Pretoria city centre, the International Police Association (IPA) in Arcadia, a suburban veranda, the Blikkantien at the Voortrekker Monument, Quay Four at the V&A Waterfront, Villains Pub in Durban, a Mugg & Bean somewhere, or a pigeon club at Boknes.

No one's recollections were there for the taking: the stories surfaced in fits and starts from the windblown paths of memory. The more comfortable they became with me, the more easily our conversations flowed. Yet I realised there were many stories I would never hear all the details of; I also did not want to.

Because most of the former Vlakplaas operatives were prepared to testify against Eugene in exchange for indemnity from prosecution and imprisonment for offences ranging from kidnapping, malicious damage to property and torture to murder and conspiracy to murder, they lived reasonably good lives after Vlakplaas. They had seemingly found ways to adapt to the new South Africa.

They ranged in age from the early fifties to almost 70. The operatives were outdoor people, men who got things done. They still worked, or had active lifestyles – although they mentioned that a few of the guys had 'fallen off the wagon'.

I spoke mostly with Johnny, Neil and Greg. To protect their families and jobs, they chose to use pseudonyms. As time passed, however, I won the confidence of some operatives who allowed me to use their real names.

'What was it like to work with Eugene at Vlakplaas?' I asked them.

'If you wanted to see Gene angry, you only had to drink on the job,' said Neil. He leaned back, took a swig of beer and laughed into his beard. 'The guys didn't like it, but it was one of his rules. After hours you could do what you wanted.

'We didn't have fixed working hours at Vlakplaas. For the most part we'd be busy for three weeks at a time on an operation somewhere in southern Africa, then we'd spend another week on the farm doing administration. All in a day's work. It must have been hard for the wives. On many nights we came home late and very drunk.'

Those were wild, rough times. Eugene joined in, especially in the early years. Shortly after he began working at Vlakplaas in 1983, he shared a flat on the corner of Schubart and Pretorius streets in central Pretoria with Vlakplaas colleague Riaan 'Balletjies' Bellingan. Bellingan told me their rent was R90 per month and they'd bought a double-door Bosch fridge that he still uses today. Ouboet, as he called Eugene, had a preference for Grolsch beer, he recalled. In those years, Lukas Kilino, the former Angolan soldier who had fought at Eugene's side at Koevoet, often stayed with them.

Bellingan still eats lots of garlic and drinks Red Heart and Coke, as he and Eugene had done all those years ago. 'We were fucking naughty and fucking happy then.' He also remembered that in those days Eugene had outlined, for him, the important things in life: 'There are three things that count – rum, a good steak and a good screw.'

However, in the work environment Eugene did not trust people easily – not even his friends. After his appointment as commanding

Eugene de Kock

Top: The final gathering of Vlakplaas members took place on the Natal coast. To the left of Eugene is his colleague Chappies Klopper and to his right Dawid 'Duiwel' Brits. **Bottom:** The Vlakplaas operative Riaan 'Balletjies' Bellingan during an askari training session.

officer of Vlakplaas, his modus operandi was divide and rule, said Johnny, a neatly groomed man in a trademark cap. 'That's just how he was.'

Bellingan also shed light on this aspect in his submission to the TRC. 'He distrusted everyone. It was normal for him to say, "Riaan, I don't know if those guys are telling the truth, you go and investigate." He would do the same thing when I was doing something. He would send some guys to go along with me and say: "Who says Balletjies is telling the truth?" He always distrusted everyone, it was ops normal for him, to use some military terminology …

'You know what Colonel De Kock would do … perhaps he kept it compartmentalised to prevent leaks, but he would take me to one side and say: "Riaan, go down to Cape Town and do this and that." Then he would also talk to Mbelo and the askaris individually on the side. So you had no idea what he told them, he would just say to you, here are two weapons … You never knew what he had told the other guys and so he kept you off balance … [Sometimes] Eugene could be paranoids [*sic*] … also with white members.'[2]

Bellingan testified further that Eugene constantly had to keep the operatives in check. 'The moment the guys enjoyed working in a certain area, they went back to Pretoria and wrote colourful reports – because there was a girl or a good drinking hole there – and old Eugene was always paranoids [*sic*] about this. He always said, surely the man is not on the road [working], is it because there's a girlfriend?'[3]

Criminologist Professor Anna van der Hoven wrote that Eugene described the intelligence world as a 'paranoid underworld in which as a member you are consumed, used and abused. It is a world in which you have no friends. You have to distrust people to survive and must constantly be cautious of false information.'[4]

Eugene did not have many friends, Johnny told me, his holster lying unobtrusively on the chair next to him. 'His actions were always calculated. He always emphasised that people's first impressions of you as a person were extremely important. He bought people and friends with money or by doing things for them. It was just a question of time until he had them in his pocket. Right up to the generals. Then they were compromised.'

In the Vlakplaas underworld, ego, money and testosterone became a deadly cocktail. As Johnny put it: 'We were untouchable. We literally did exactly what we wanted.'

According to Johnny, Eugene always had to be in control. He told of the time when Eugene broke his leg during an operation in Botswana. Eugene was beside himself and wanted to postpone the operation. It couldn't wait, so his men went in and handled it successfully. He could not handle the fact that they were able to execute an operation without his direct involvement.

When and how did things start going wrong for Eugene? I asked time and again. What was the seed of his moral decline? Was it post-traumatic stress disorder that crept up on him, the disorder he developed during his time at Koevoet but was never treated for?

'No, it wasn't the time at Koevoet,' reckoned Greg, a quiet man with impeccable manners. 'At Vlakplaas Eugene became obsessed with power. It all started with the money, the false claims. That was when things went off the rails.'

Greg's answer made me think twice. Eugene was supposedly the one with the strong morality, the rigid black-and-white outlook on life. His conflict with Colonel Hans Dreyer at Koevoet was precisely because he'd opposed the misuse of money from the SAP's secret funds for private purposes.

From April 1985, the funding of covert operations – including those of Section C1 at Vlakplaas – were regulated by the South African Police Special Account Act 74 of 1985.[5] This clearly made a great deal of money available for false claims about which no questions were ever asked.

I again turn to Hennie Heymans. 'Yes, you need to bear in mind that in covert units, three things are important: the unit and everything it did had to be highly secret, untraceable and easily repudiated [deniable],' he explained.

As commanding officer of Vlakplaas, Eugene thus had unlimited funds at his disposal. This was common knowledge among members of the Security Branch.[6] Submitting false claims to generate funds was not unusual.

In his application for presidential pardon, Eugene wrote: 'All improvements to Vlakplaas were … financed through false claims. We entertained regularly at Vlakplaas – often ministers, generals and other high-ranking officers. We were equipped with ice machines and pool tables. Astronomical amounts were paid out in false claims. Eventually, it led to much foolishness and we started to draw up false claims in my favour and in favour of other Vlakplaas operatives.'[7]

According to Eugene, he and other Vlakplaas operatives, acting on the request of Section C1's finance department head, submitted a large number of false claims for fictitious informants. However, they never received any part of the proceeds of these claims.

It was also common knowledge that claims by Vlakplaas for the payment of informants were always processed rapidly. 'Several other security branches then started submitting their claims for informers through us,' Eugene said.[8]

One of my last encounters with a few former Vlakplaas operatives took place in 2014 at the Mugg & Bean in the Irene Village Mall in Pretoria. Five of us sat talking in the watery winter sun, clasping cappuccinos. I studied the four faces around me. Despite sun damage, crow's feet and a look of vigilance, their faces also exuded something akin to youthfulness, almost a boyishness. There was plenty of laughter. The apartheid era was a lifetime away.

'At one stage we knew what we were doing, and how we were doing it, was wrong,' said one. 'One day towards the end Balletjies and I said to each other, yes, they will still finger us as the white askaris. That one, the one sitting there in the corner, and him also – it was them …'

11

The writing on the wall

Friday 17 November 1989 was the beginning of the drawn-out, messy end for Eugene de Kock and Vlakplaas. By then rumours about police death squads eliminating anti-apartheid activists were already doing the rounds. Dirk Coetzee, the first commanding officer of Vlakplaas, confirmed the existence of these death squads in an interview published on that day in *Vrye Weekblad*, and in more startling articles that followed in the weeks after. Coetzee's revelations followed the allegations made in October by Almond Nofomela, a convicted prisoner on death row, that he had been part of a police death squad at Vlakplaas.

Coetzee maintained that the death squads left a trail of death and destruction wherever they went – that people were shot, stabbed, poisoned or blown up in their beds at night.[1] 'I was the commander of the South African Police's death squad,' he said. 'I was in the heart of the whore. My men and I had to murder political and security opponents of the police and the government. I know the deepest secrets of this unit, which is above the law. I myself am guilty of, or at least an accomplice to, several murders.'[2]

The local and international outcry in the wake of these allegations forced the National Party government to investigate them. Judge Louis Harms was appointed to head up a commission of enquiry into the death squads. He began his proceedings on 5 March 1990. Earlier that year, allegations of another death squad – the Civil

Cooperation Bureau (CCB), funded by the South African Defence Force – had also surfaced. The Harms Commission eventually investigated the activities of both Section C1 and the CCB.[3]

However, it was business as usual at Vlakplaas despite the Harms Commission and the fact that Eugene had to testify before it: 'I believed unequivocally that as long as our actions targeted the political enemy, our commanding officers would approve of them. In practice, this certainly seemed to be the case. It also gave me the impression that we were above the law, that we could not be prosecuted for the crimes we committed as long as we had committed them in the course of the struggle against the political enemy. This perception was, to a large extent, strengthened by the fact that even during the course of the Harms Commission, we received orders from our superiors to commit various crimes, such as the murder of Brian Ngqulunga, the attack on the Chand home and the Motherwell incident.'[4]

On 2 February 1990, President FW de Klerk announced in Parliament the unbanning of the ANC and other freedom movements and Nelson Mandela's release. Eugene was informed beforehand about these imminent political changes. In his evidence before the TRC he said that a meeting of 60 senior officers was held in December 1989 or January 1990, where they were told Mandela was to be freed.[5]

In his official report released in 1990, Judge Louis Harms found that there were no death squads at Vlakplaas. Opposition parties criticised the report as a whitewash, an attempt at exoneration.[6]

After the Harms Commission, there was talk that Vlakplaas should be disbanded – a suggestion Eugene initially supported:

Following the unbanning of the ANC, PAC and the SACP, I recommended to General Engelbrecht that the Vlakplaas unit be disbanded. At that stage, the unit was already divided into three components: one at Vlakplaas,[7] another at Midrand[8] and the third under my command in Waterkloof.[9]

General Engelbrecht replied that the ANC and PAC had not foresworn violence and that the political negotiations could easily fail, which would mean resuming the armed struggle of the past. In that instance, Vlakplaas had to be ready to fight them immediately.[10]

In 1991 C1 was transformed into C10, ostensibly a crime-fighting unit. While a number of former operatives told to me that their focus increasingly moved to crime and solving criminal cases, they remained involved in covert actions and political activities. In the course of his TRC evidence, Eugene was asked how he felt about Vlakplaas's new role: 'It brought no additional tension for me. It was not a case of us being sidelined … there was some tension, at times, between the different parties and we saw that things could go wrong. I did not have a specific negative feeling with regard to my work … We were never told "now you will cease all counter-terrorism" and the askaris were not taken away. As I said, none of our equipment was handed back and we did not disband.'[11]

In one of our meetings Eugene mentioned that political violence escalated after the unbanning of the ANC, instead of abating. He and other Vlakplaas members executed Operation Excalibur, for example, on the grounds of information they received after the ANC's unbanning: 'I can mention that especially on the East Rand, especially in the areas such as Daveyton and Duduza, in that vicinity, we picked up information that the Self Defence Units were being provided with ammunition by the ANC …'[12]

During this time there were also several attacks on SAP members. In his application for presidential pardon, Eugene writes that their information indicated that the ANC and PAC were still responsible for these attacks and were involved, along with the Inkatha Freedom Party (IFP), in the so-called black-on-black violence. Trafficking of unlicensed weapons that were used in such black-on-black violence increased drastically:

> Vlakplaas therefore clearly still had a role to play, a role that was almost the same as it was before the unbanning of the organisations. We continued the struggle against political violence and the trade in terrorist weapons.
>
> The accuracy of the information we received about the involvement of the ANC and PAC was confirmed when General Siphiwe Nyanda gave evidence against me during my criminal trial. Under cross-examination by my legal representative, he admitted that the ANC was involved in weapons trafficking. Indeed, Vlakplaas confiscated and used some vehicles with modified fuel tanks that concealed large quantities of weapons.
>
> Despite the negotiations taking place after the unbanning of the political organisations, the continuation of the struggle was still being discussed, planned and executed. Operation Vula [an ANC operation started in the late 1980s aimed at importing weapons secretly and setting up an underground communication channel between local ANC activists and ANC exiles in Lusaka and London[13]] was a classic example of this ...
>
> A number of subsequent incidents, and information we received from informants, left us with the impression that the political negotiations between the parties were clearly not going to end the confrontation between those parties.
>
> As far as I and other members of Vlakplaas were

concerned, the ANC and PAC were still the enemy. The PAC allowed the armed struggle to continue for some time after the commencement of Codesa [the multiparty negotiations]. It was for this reason, too, that I was prepared to support the IFP by providing them with weapons to protect themselves against attacks by ANC members and their supporters.[14]

The Goldstone Commission was appointed in October 1991 to investigate political violence and the allegation that a so-called third force was responsible for it. Among the findings of the commission was that third-force activities stoked political unrest, that a system of oppression was still in place, and that the architects of this system still controlled the police.[15]

Vlakplaas members were involved, among other things, in supplying weapons to the IFP in their struggle against the ANC. Padraig O'Malley, a conflict expert and academic who has conducted over 2 000 hours of interviews about South Africa's transition to democracy, writes the following in his historical reports on apartheid: 'The March 1994 Goldstone report into criminal acts committed by members of the SAP, the KZP [KwaZulu Police] and the Inkatha Freedom Party (IFP) implicated senior policemen not only in the supply of weapons to the IFP, but in attempts to thwart the Goldstone investigation into the issue. Subsequent evidence in the State vs Eugene de Kock and before this Commission corroborates the fact that the SAP, largely through Vlakplaas operatives, supplied the IFP with a considerable amount of weaponry during the 1990s.'[16]

Testimony before the Goldstone Commission revealed that many of these weapons came not only from Koevoet stores but also from those at the SADF's Oshivelo base in the erstwhile South

West Africa. Various generals, among them General Krappies Engelbrecht and Major-General Nick Janse van Rensburg, also instructed Eugene to supply handmade weapons to the IFP.

With the Durban Security Branch as intermediary, Eugene met former IFP member Philip Powell, to whom he supplied sophisticated weapons for the training of self-defence units in KwaZulu-Natal.[17] Journalist De Wet Potgieter wrote in 2013: 'The weapons were part of a 70 tonne, six-truck consignment De Kock delivered to Powell in 1993, in preparation for possible war during the 1994 general elections. It came from the "managing director" of the Civil Cooperation Bureau (CCB), Joe Verster. The CCB was the notorious front organisation of the apartheid era's military strategy to disrupt the ANC's underground networks and assassinate target people in the struggle.

'Sixty-four tons of weapons are still outstanding, and it is believed the majority of these are in KwaZulu-Natal. Powell, a former member of the Security Branch with strong links to Vlakplaas, oversaw the training of more than 8 000 IFP-aligned self-protection unit militias in preparation for a possible civil war ahead of the 1994 elections.'[18]

Padraig O'Malley writes: 'According to De Kock, he kept a register of the recipients of weapons and ammunition but handed this to General Krappies Engelbrecht before his arrest. De Kock also claimed that he had given General [JA (Bertus)] Steyn of Durban a complete list of all the firearms given to [former IFP leader] Themba Khoza.[19] This is confirmed by Rausch [a former member of the Rhodesian police], who states that "Eugene told me that he was ordered by the generals to destroy all of [the documentation] which we did".[20]

In the early 1990s – when the NP government had already started negotiating power-sharing and a democratic

Top: Eugene in a typical pose when he is concentrating. To his left is his Vlakplaas colleague Willie Nortjé. **Bottom:** Damaged mortars and mines piled up at Koevoet over the years. Eugene destroyed these weapens when he went to Oshakati in 1987 to collect other weapons destined for Vlakplaas.

election – transgressions by Vlakplaas members continued on various levels. Former Vlakplaas operatives told me about large-scale fraud in this period – that the misuse of the Security Branch's secret funds was in fact perfected over the years at Vlakplaas.

They created, among other things, false arms caches, claimed large sums of money for them from the SAP's secret fund, then appropriated the money for personal use. A Vlakplaas-controlled 'source' would supply another Security Branch with information about an arms cache that had ostensibly just been discovered, former operative Johnny told me. A Vlakplaas operative would then put in a 'source' claim at the secret fund. The source would receive a share, with Vlakplaas taking the rest.

The funds would be used for improvements at Vlakplaas, such as upgrading the canteen and entertainment facilities or purchasing pool tables. According to clinical psychologist Dr Annemarie Novello, who gave evidence in Eugene's criminal trial, Eugene (and his fellow operatives) therefore created their own world at Vlakplaas that functioned beyond the boundaries of normal society.[21]

Eugene admitted openly that after the Harms Commission, he had made a conscious decision to enrich himself: 'We knew it was all over. I now had to look after myself and my family. That was my primary motive.'

So, with his superiors' permission, he founded a front company to export and import weapons and for this he travelled to Eastern and Western Europe frequently in 1992 and 1993. In the company's name – Honey Badger Arms and Ammunition – he acknowledged, again, the badger of his childhood days. A security contract for the guarding of an Absa property followed[22] – former Vlakplaas operative Brood van Heerden had already left the SAP and was working for the bank at this stage.

In the early 1990s Eugene was also involved in the cover-up of several murders, including those of an Inkatha member who died while being interrogated by the East Rand Security Branch and of Johannes Sweet Sambo. The askari Goodwill Sikhakhane was murdered by Vlakplaas operatives, and the Nelspruit incident – one of two incidents for which Eugene was not given amnesty by the TRC – also took place in this period.

Sambo was arrested after a police informant alleged that he was illegally in possession of a firearm.[23] He died in detention at the Skwamaans police base near Komatipoort, after torture by the tubing method. An agitated Flip de Beer, commanding officer of the Security Branch at Komatipoort under which Skwamaans fell, contacted Eugene.

'"Help, we've murdered someone" are not words I want to hear at any time, especially late at night …' writes Eugene in his application for presidential pardon. 'We were only good for the dirty work!'[24]

Eugene tried to get permission from General Krappies Engelbrecht to help De Beer, but Engelbrecht was unavailable. He decided to go ahead on his own, sending a group of Vlakplaas operatives to get rid of the body. They took Sambo's body to the Verdracht training camp outside Middelburg and blew it up.[25]

Eugene went on to explain that he informed a police colonel and a general about the incident. 'They summarily flew in the Security Branch helicopter to the Skwamaans police base near Komatipoort … things needed "cleaning up". Colonel Herman du Plessis told me the next day that they had found the inner tube [used in the tubing torture method] covered in spit, mucus and blood – and other evidence – at the murder scene. There were no prosecutions …'[26]

In his criminal trial, Eugene was found guilty of the five

murders that resulted from the so-called Nelspruit incident. In this incident, Sergeant Douglas Holtzhausen, a Vlakplaas operative, approached him in 1992 about a potential operation. 'One of Holtzhausen's sources … had told him that a trained member of the ANC, and the personal driver of Mrs Winnie Mandela, was smuggling weapons and that he and other MK cadres were going to commit an armed robbery in either Pretoria or Nelspruit,' Eugene said in *A Long Night's Damage*.[27]

Although Eugene had no further information, he ordered Holtzhausen to go ahead with his planning. On 26 March 1992 Khona Khabela, Masilo Mama, Mxolisi Ntshaota and Lawrence Nyalende were brutally attacked when their vehicle was led into an ambush outside Nelspruit. A fifth member of the group, Tiisetso (Tiso) Leballo, was not in the vehicle but was killed by Vlakplaas operatives shortly afterwards. In Eugene's court case, Captain Chris Geldenhuys testified about the trauma he had suffered during the incident. One of the victims had been blown out of the vehicle by an explosion but was still alive. He was on fire, groaning with pain. According to Geldenhuys, Eugene walked towards him to shoot him, but then lowered his weapon. The man died shortly afterwards.[28]

According to Eugene, the Nelspruit shooting was 'wrong'. 'Even more wrong was that I was there that evening. I could have stopped it; probably in time. I was only in Nelspruit because General [Krappies] Engelbrecht and I had to meet the head of the SADF for the Kruger Park region the next morning. I had traced two large shipping containers of weapons, dynamite and ammunition on the Mozambique side of the game park's border and wanted to blow it up … Statements were "corrected" that morning by General Engelbrecht who was on the scene after I had told him about the murderous mess. We did infiltrate groups like these that planned robberies … and this group was without doubt going to commit robberies … but it was wrong to kill them before they had done so.'[29]

The dramatic upheaval in the political landscape in South Africa brought with it an equally dramatic upheaval in Eugene's life. Within a year or two he had gone from being virtually untouchable—a god in police circles—to an officer the police needed to get rid of.

The writing was on the wall for the security forces and for Vlakplaas. The Goldstone Commission's investigations were central to this. In November 1992, Goldstone investigators raided a building in Lynnwood Ridge, Pretoria – the operational headquarters of Trewits, a secret military intelligence unit.[30] The cat was out of the bag.

'During the negotiations [for a peaceful settlement between, among others, the NP government and the ANC] it quickly became clear that a new government would take power, in all likelihood the ANC. General Engelbrecht instructed us to destroy sensitive documents that could link C1 to covert and unlawful activities,' wrote Eugene in his application for presidential pardon.[31]

Former SAP members told me that about 40 tons of documents and other evidence were destroyed at Wachthuis, SAP headquarters. 'Many of those documents would have been of great help to me in my application for amnesty before the committee [TRC]. Following the revelations in the Goldstone Commission report about Vlakplaas activities I proceeded to destroy additional documents that I had withheld.'[32]

This marked the end of Eugene's career in the SAP. 'On 30 April 1993 at the age of 44, I went on early retirement. The state granted a sum of R17,5 million to be paid out to Vlakplaas operatives, but

Port Reference: HAH/611
Home Office Reference: K448273   IS 82B

HM IMMIGRATION OFFICE
PARKESTON QUAY
HARWICH
ESSEX
CO12 4SX   Tel: 0255 504371

IMMIGRATION ACT 1971 - NOTICE OF REFUSAL OF LEAVE TO ENTER

DE KOCK EUGENE ALEXANDER

THE SECRETARY OF STATE HAS PERSONALLY GIVEN DIRECTIONS FOR YOU NOT TO
BE GIVEN ENTRY TO THE UNITED KINGDOM ON THE GROUND THAT YOUR
EXCLUSION IS CONDUCIVE TO THE PUBLIC GOOD.

The Secretary of State has given directions for you not to be given entry to the United Kingdom on
the ground that your exclusion is conducive to the public good.

I therefore refuse you leave to enter the United Kingdom.

REMOVAL DIRECTIONS

I have given/propose to give directions for your removal at 11:30 hrs on 28-AUG-93 by STENA
BRITANNICA to
(county/territory) HOLLAND

RIGHT OF APPEAL

You are not entitled to appeal against refusal of leave to enter because this was in obedience to
directions given by the Secretary of State personally on the ground stated above.

This notice has been explained to you in English /

by me /

Date 27-AUG-93   Immigration Officer:

In 1993 Eugene was refused entry to England 'on the
ground that your exclusion [from the United Kingdom] is
conducive to the public good'.

this was later increased to R25 million so others could also be paid
out under the Vlakplaas name, too, including all the askaris in the
two other C1 sections in Durban and East London.'

Jeremy Gordin writes in *A Long Night's Damage* that the state
undertook to pay Eugene's legal expenses if he was prosecuted for
offences while in the force's employ.

He was placed on special leave due to extraordinary circumstances – suspended, effectively. For Eugene, this was indescribably

humiliating. According to Dr Novello, Eugene and Audrey's marriage suffered during this time; she wanted to leave him. She felt she could no longer continue with that kind of life – in the wake of the Harms Commission, for example, she'd had to change jobs. The fact that Eugene refused to leave the country because he wanted to support his men was the last straw.[33]

Remarks made in his application for early retirement in 1993 indicate that he battled to make sense of how he had been treated. He said, among other things: 'I am currently still in command of Section C1, described as a death squad, and am seen, therefore, as the leader of the so-called death squad. Taking into account how the local and international radio, television and news media have assassinated my character and destroyed me both at work and socially, there is no alternative for me but to request an early retirement.

'The government gave in to political pressure and appointed the Harms Commission to inquire into the allegations of death squads. The news media alleged nothing – instead, they made direct accusations and findings, creating perceptions among the public as well as within the department that would never be officially or socially erased. This also led to my suspension from the SAP, under the guise of leave.

'As a proud member of the SAP, with 22 years of uninterrupted service, this suspension (leave) was the greatest humiliation that I have ever experienced and has, I feel, irreparably damaged my image and status within the SAP – as well as in the public sector, where I have a wide circle of friends.'[34]

Why were Vlakplaas activities not halted at some point? Why was there no attempt to intervene? These questions, raised by a former Vlakplaas operative, haunted me.

Johnny, another former operative, answered them: 'For the

The document on the left, dated 17 February 1993, informed Eugene that he was being considered for promotion, but little more than two months later his service in the South African Police was terminated on 30 April 1993 (document on the right).

Right document

67-5 600-006

SAP 55

SUID-AFRIKAANSE POLISIE ● SOUTH AFRICAN POLICE

SERTIFIKAAT VAN ONTSLAG
CERTIFICATE OF DISCHARGE

Verwysing
Reference 52050-1

Hiermee word gesertifiseer dat ..... EUGENE ALEXANDER DE KOCK ..... in die Suid-Afrikaanse Polisie gedien het
It is hereby certified that ..... served in the South African Police for the

Identiteitsnommer 4901295009000
Identity No.

vir die tydperk(e) soos hieronder vermeld:
for the undermentioned period(s):

..... 1968-01-03 - 1993-04-30

Rang beklee met ontslag ..... COLONEL
Rank held on discharge ..... COLONEL

Opmerkings ..... DIENSBEËINDIGING WEENS RASIONALISERING
Remarks ..... TERMINATION OF SERVICE DUE TO RATIONALISATION

Datum van ontslag 1993-04-30
Date of discharge

Plek ..... PRETORIA
Place

Datum 1993-04-30
Date

H/ Kommissaris: Suid-Afrikaanse Polisie
F/ Commissioner: South African Police

Left document

ONDERNEMING

Hiermee verklaar ek,

..... 0052050-1 ..... (magsnommer),

..... lt.-kolonel ..... (rang),

..... E.A. DE KOCK ..... (naam),

die ondergetekende, die volgende:

* Ek is in kennis gestel dat my bevordering onder oorweging is.

* Dit is die prerogatief van die Kommissaris van die Suid-Afrikaanse Polisie of sy gevolmagtigde gedelegeerde, om, indien ek bevorder word, my te verplaas na enige plek binne die grense van die Republiek van Suid-Afrika waar die Kommissaris van die Suid-Afrikaanse Polisie of sy gevolmagtigde verteenwoordiger meen die rôg my die nodigste het.

* Daar is geen onstandighede omtrent myself of my gesin of enige afhanklikes van my, wat verhinder dat ek na enige polisiestasie of polisiekantoor op enige plek binne die grense van die Republiek van Suid-Afrika, verplaas kan word nie.

* Ek sal enige verplasing wat in belang van die taak nodig is, uitvoer en gee die versekering dat my gesin of enige afhanklikes van my, my na my nuwe standplaas sal vergesel.

* Ek neem kennis van die bepaling dat indien ek bevorder en later verplaas word en by so 'n geleentheid besware teen so 'n verplasing sou opper wat op redes gegrond is wat reeds bestaan het voor ek hierdie onderneming gegee het, ek op die voorrangslys in 'n posisie geplaas sal word asof ek nie bevorder was nie.

* Ek onderwerp myself vollo aan voornoemde bepaling en ook die feit dat dit my verdere bevordering kan benadeel.

ALDUS gedoen en geteken deur die ondernemer te ..... Pretoria

op die ..... 17de ..... dag van ..... Februarie 1993

ONDERNEMER
E A DE KOCK

AS GETUIES:

1. .....

2. .....

* Skrap en parafeer waar van toepassing. Motiveer op aparte bylae.

mw/13 V 13.

simple reason that it was too late.' His hands, their fingernails clipped short, lay folded, at rest, on the restaurant table. 'There was no turning back; there had been too many covert operations. It was a unit out of control; we only relied on ourselves. During Eugene's court case he thought the generals would cover for him, as they had always done for all of us – but they didn't. There was already too much blood on the hands of Vlakplaas members.'

The political winds had already changed. Now, it was every man for himself.

'The court considered the nature of the punishment to be imposed. Counsel for both sides had accepted that imprisonment was called for. The court held that, in view of the nature of the crimes of which the accused had been convicted, the only fitting sentence was imprisonment. The defence had contended that the effective sentence on all the charges should not exceed 25 years. The state had requested that effective imprisonment of many years be imposed. The defence had submitted that the accused was no longer a danger to society and that it was therefore not necessary that he be removed from society for the rest of his life.'

– QUOTED FROM JUDGE WILLEM VAN DER MERWE'S
SENTENCING PROCEEDINGS IN EUGENE DE KOCK'S
CRIMINAL TRIAL, 30 OCTOBER 1996.

12

Betrayal in courtroom GD

On 4 May 1994 Eugene de Kock was taken into custody at Johann Rissik House, a guesthouse of the International Police Association (IPA), in Arcadia, Pretoria.[1] When I asked around for more information about his arrest the ranks closed.

A few trusted colleagues were with Eugene that day but they wouldn't talk to me about it. I found it strange – after all, it has been twenty years? And back then Eugene had known it was coming. His brother, Vos, told me how Eugene had been warned not to venture near Pretoria, but was at the IPA that day nonetheless. Like so much else, what took place at the IPA guesthouse remains wrapped in a web of intrigue. 'Ask those who were there who the Judas Iscariot was who phoned to say I was at the IPA house,' was Eugene's terse offering when I asked him about it. With him, nothing is ever straightforward.

Eugene was initially held at the Adriaan Vlok police station (now the Lyttelton police station) before being transferred to the maximum security section of Pretoria Central, where he was confined to a death row cell. In reply to my question about why he did not receive bail, he said, 'I was refused bail … when I walked into the court the judge said he would supply reasons later, but he refused bail.' Eugene said it would have been the highest bail ever granted in South Africa: the state suggested R303 000.

Eugene's trial commenced about ten months later on 20 February

Top: Eugene was arrested in 1994 at the guesthouse of the International Police Association (IPA) in Pretoria. **Bottom:** The bar at the IPA House.

1995 in courtroom GD of the Transvaal High Court in Pretoria. He was charged with 129 counts, ranging from fraud to murder. According to Eugene, the number of charges changed constantly during the trial because of the large number of fraud charges, but he was eventually found guilty of 121 charges. The judge who heard his case was Willem van der Merwe and the prosecutor, the deputy attorney-general at the time, was Anton Ackermann SC – who eventually called upon 87 witnesses to testify for the state. Flip Hattingh SC defended Eugene.[2]

It was a sensational court case in which the extent of the transgressions by C1 and Security Branch members became public for the first time. Not only was Eugene and Vlakplaas's dirty linen hung out in public, so too was that of the National Party government. Eugene de Kock became the face of apartheid – in his words, 'an icon' who was 'almost too good (or rather too repellent)' to be true. 'I became the living symbol of the horrors and offences of apartheid,' he said.[3]

In his application for presidential pardon, Eugene wrote that he had realised the seriousness of the charges against him from the outset.

> I knew that the evidence was so overwhelming that I stood virtually no chance of being acquitted. My legal team advised me that I was, nevertheless, entitled to test the state's case, despite having no defence against the charges. This was consistently done and … throughout the trial … I neither lied nor instructed my defence team to present … false versions to state witnesses.
>
> During the trial it also became apparent that I could have asked for the suspension of the prosecution pending a possible submission to the Truth and Reconciliation

> Commission (TRC). I realised I would still be afforded
> this opportunity after the trial … The case and the charges
> against me had, at that stage, generated such a high degree
> of sensation and interest that I felt I could use the opportu-
> nity to expose some of the commanders and senior officers
> who had issued my orders and who were as guilty as I was
> of the injustices committed in the name of apartheid.[4]

At this point Eugene made a critical decision – he would testify
himself in mitigation of his sentence. He wanted to reveal information about the security environment, name those who had given
him direct orders and identify the politicians who had issued the
orders. 'After the state had closed its case in about April 1996, I
began to testify in mitigation of my sentence. In doing so, I made
several aspects known.'

During the court case his health took a significant knock. 'After
I suffered a pulmonary embolism [a blood clot in the lung] and
had lung capacity of only 20%, Advocate [Anton] Ackermann and
[Torie] Pretorius made the court sit, regardless, for one hour per
day. This was very difficult for me. There was no time for me to
recover, which further compromised my health. The prosecution
apparently hoped that [the stress] would lead to another attack,'
he told me on one of my visits.

Eugene would reveal a great deal – but not everything – in his
testimony:

> I decided on this specific approach to ensure that these
> people [those who gave him his orders and the politicians
> behind them] would be publicly exposed and to ensure
> that they would have no alternative but to approach the
> TRC for amnesty. I decided, purposefully, not to divulge

everything in which I had been involved and not to name all fellow perpetrators.

This may have given the perception that I was not going to make all the names and operations public and lulled them into a false sense of security. It could have led them to believe that they only needed to apply for amnesty for the incidents to which I referred during my testimony in mitigation of sentence.[5]

Eugene's intuition about his former colleagues and commanders' actions proved correct, as later became evident in the Motherwell case: the Security Branch members involved tried to deny their involvement.

Three black police members – Amos Faku, Glen Mgoduka and Desmond Mapipa – and an informant were killed when members of the Security Branch in the eastern Cape bombed their car at Motherwell outside Port Elizabeth in December 1989. The police initially maintained that the ANC was responsible for the explosion. Eugene was involved in planning the operation and sent Vlakplaas members to help with its execution. Gideon Nieuwoudt[6] of the Port Elizabeth Security Branch was eventually sentenced to twenty years for his role in this incident.[7]

Eugene mentioned to me that halfway through his criminal hearing in Pretoria, he heard that the attorney-general of the Eastern Cape had brought criminal charges against several members of the Security Branch in connection with the Motherwell case.

I followed the proceedings closely in the press … Of course, I realised immediately that there was far more to this trial than met the eye. I knew exactly what the orders had been as I was also involved in this operation and knew that all

Moorde in PE: De Kock se vriende getuig

Deur DAWIE VAN HEERDEN:
Port Elizabeth

DIE staat se twee "geheime getuies" in die moordverhoor van vyf voormalige veiligheidspolisiemanne is oudlede van die nou al berugte Vlakplaas-polisie-eenheid en ook vriende van kol. Eugène de Kock, voormalige bevelvoerder van dié eenheid en die beskuldigde in verskeie moordsake.

Mnre. D.L. (Lionel) Snyman en N.J. (Snorre) Vermeulen gaan na verwagting opspraakwekkende getuienis lewer in die verhoor van kol. Gideon Niewoudt, maj. Gerhardus Lotz, brig. Wahl du Toit, kapt. Jacobus Kok en adjt.off. Marthinus Ras, wat daarvan verdink word dat hulle verantwoordelik was vir die dood van drie kollegas en 'n sogenaamde askari in Port Elizabeth sewe jaar gelede.

Die twee voormalige polisiemanne se name het Donderdag in die Port Elizabethse Hooggeregshof opgeduik

toe adv. P.J. (Dup) de Bruyn, vir die verdediging, daarop aangedring het dat die Gautengse prokureur-generaal, dr. Jan d'Oliveira, alle dokumentasie, mediese verslae en ook moontlike videomateriaal van die twee getuies aan die verdediging moet verskaf.

Dr. d'Oliveira, wat gedagvaar is om voor die hof te verskyn, kon weens werksverpligtinge nie die hofverrigtinge bywoon nie. In 'n beëdigde verklaring wat by die hof ingedien is, sê dr. d'Oliveira hy is betrokke by 'n massiewe ondersoek oor Derde Magbedrywighede en dat dit, indien dit bewys kan word, grootskeepse terrorisme, aanhitsing en destabilisering gaan ontbloot.

In die hof het dit dié week geblyk dat sowel mnr. Vermeulen as mnr. Snyman sielkundige behandeling by die Weskoppies-hospitaal in Pretoria ontvang het. Geen rede vir die behandeling is aan die hof verskaf nie, maar mnr. Snyman se vrou het gister aan Rapport gesê die twee het behandeling ontvang nadat "Vlakplaas se goed op die lappe gekom het".

Aan die hof is die week vertel dat mnre. Snyman en Vermeulen in Angola is.

Die saak is tot 19 Februarie uitgestel wanneer dr. d'Oliveira waarskynlik sal bekend maak of hy die inligting oor mnre. Snyman en Vermeulen aan die verdediging beskikbaar gaan stel.

Die beskuldigdes is almal uit op borgtog van R10 000.

De Kock to speak out

Newspaper clippings about the so-called Motherwell court case, in which Eugene testified for the state.

the parties were, without a doubt, guilty of the charges against them.

The defence, however, was highly successful in its cross-examination of the state witnesses and it became clear that they were on the verge of being acquitted ... This particular incident was about the 1989 murder of three black members of the Security Branch and an informer, allegedly because they had committed fraud but in truth because they knew all of Gideon Nieuwoudt's dark secrets and, naturally, the inner workings of the old Security Branch faction based in the eastern Cape.

Almost halfway through my own trial, I made the decision to testify in the Motherwell trial. I testified after the state had closed its case, in fact. It wasn't an easy decision. I had no desire to be a state witness and I had nothing against any of the Security Branch members who were in the dock. But I could see another Harms cover-up looming.

It was clear to me immediately that if the accused were acquitted, virtually nothing would come to light about the atrocities they had committed against freedom fighters and the ANC in general in the eastern Cape. It was common knowledge that the eastern Cape was a hotbed of atrocities by the Security Branch but it had always been practically impossible for the ANC to prove the Security Branch's involvement.

I realised the accused were hoping and praying they would be acquitted and could subsequently close ranks. Then there would be no need for them to apply for amnesty for the Motherwell incident or for related incidents in the eastern Cape.

I knew that the accused in the Motherwell incident

had also been involved in the Cradock Four incident [four activists – Matthew Goniwe, Fort Calata, Sparrow Mkhonto and Sicelo Mhlauli – were abducted and murdered in June 1985 outside Port Elizabeth by members of the Security Branch] as well as the Pebco Three incident [Sipho Hashe, Champion Galela and Qaqawuli Godolozi, members of the Port Elizabeth Black Civic Organisation (Pebco), were abducted in May 1985 and taken to a deserted farm at Post Chalmers where they were interrogated, tortured and strangled. Their bodies were thrown into the Fish River]. I realised, then, how important it would be for the amnesty process, the ANC-led government and the families of the victims to learn what had happened in the eastern Cape.

I decided to testify as frankly as possible. I revealed, for the first time, that these murders were not committed because the (deceased) members of the Security Branch threatened to disclose offences relating to misappropriated funds, but because they threatened to disclose the fact that Gideon Nieuwoudt, [Gerhardus Johannes] Lotz and some of the others[8] were involved in the murders of Matthew Goniwe and the three other members of the famous Cradock Four group ...

I was cross-examined exhaustively, but remained truthful. The court, chiefly on the strength of my testimony, convicted all the accused except two. The attorney-general of the Eastern Cape, Advocate Les Roberts, was so appreciative of my efforts and contribution that he wrote a letter to the Department of Correctional Services setting out my participation, as well as my commitment and assistance.

While I was in Port Elizabeth testifying in the Cradock Four case I was approached by Advocate Chris McAdam

Top: A rare photo of Eugene de Kock at the Hennops River where it runs through Vlakplaas. **Bottom:** The main entrance to the Vlakplaas farm.

Left: 'Invisible, invincible': The badger was again used as the emblem on the Vlakplaas badge.

Bottom: In 1983, shortly after he arrived at Vlakplaas, Eugene (front row, second from left) completed a course in explosives. Jerry Raven, who was part of the group that planted the London bomb, is second from right in the front row.

16-11-1984

****

Die Bevelvoerende Offisier
van die Suid-Afrikaanse Polisie Veiligheidstak,

GENERAAL-MAJOOR S H SCHUTTE,

het die genoeë om

.............MAJOOR HB HEYMANS.................

uit te nooi na 'n geselligheid in die vorm van 'n braai te

Vlakplaas om 12h00 op Vrydag 16 November 1984

ter bevordering van skakeling tussen lede van die Tak Nasionale
Vertolking en ander SA Polisie-lede verbonde aan die SVR en lede
van die Veiligheidstak. Terselfdertyd word ook afskeid geneem
van GENERAAL-MAJOOR GROENEWALD terwyl BRIGADIER R P J VAN VUUREN
verwelkom word as aangewese Hoof van die Tak Nasionale
Vertolking.

****

Major-generals, brigadiers and other senior officials of the South African Police
were wined and dined at Vlakplaas during the 1980s.

Askaris of Section C1 receive abseiling training (top) and are taught how to prepare for a parachute jump (bottom). After qualifying in parachute jumping, the askaris received their wings (insert).

A group of askaris who received training in parachute jumping pose with their instructors from Vlakplaas.

Eugene at home with his firstborn, also called Eugene.

Top: Eugene with his ex-wife, Audrey.
Bottom: From left to right: Vos de Kock and his father, Lourens, along with friends Koos Wilken and Koeks Koekemoer. Eugene is on the far right.

Top: Eugene and his Koevoet comrade Lukas Kilino in Oshakati in 1987.
Bottom: The author in conversation with former Vlakplaas operative Nick
Vermeulen at Boknes in the Eastern Cape.

As late as 1991 Vlakplaas operative Nick Vermeulen received a commendation from the commissioner of police for his role in Operation Excalibur. The operation by former Vlakplaas members was intended to counter weapons smuggling by the liberation movements, by then unbanned.

Vlakplaas-kolonel in arres ná Derde-Mag-bevindinge

Marga Ley

KOL. EUGENE DE KOCK, gewese bevelvoerder van die Polisie se Vlakplaas-eenheid, is in hegtenis geneem.

Daar is onlangs in die Goldstonekommissie se verslag oor die Derde Mag geïmpliseer dat hy inligting daaroor sou hê en betrokke was by georganiseerde trein- en hostelgeweld in die swart woonbuurte.

Die bevindinge van die Goldstonekommissie word ondersoek deur dr. Jan D'Oliveira, Prokureur-generaal van Transvaal.

Kol. De Kock en nog twee mans, na verneem word Snorre Vermeulen en 'n lid van die Polisie se moorden-roofeenheid in Oos-Londen, is deur die Polisie in hegtenis geneem terwyl hulle eergisteraand by die sosiale klub van die Internasionale Polisie-Assosiasie in Pretoria ontspan

het.

Kol. De Kock was ook bevelvoerder van die Polisie se latere Badger-eenheid wat onwettige wapensmokkelary ondersoek het.

Dié eenheid het, soos die Vlakplaas-eenheid, hoofsaaklik bestaan uit oud-ANC-lede wat vir die Polisie werk. Hulle is Askari's genoem.

'n Woord verder van die Polisie het gister gesê hy het opdrag van bo gekry dat die Polisie geen kommentaar oor die inhegtenisnemings moet lewer nie.

Na aanleiding van die Goldstoneverslag is drie Polisie-generaals en tien polisiemanne aanvanklik geskors.

Genl. Basie Smit, senior Adjunkkommissaris van Polisie, en lt.-genl. Johan le Roux, hoof van die afdeling misdaadbestryding en -ondersoek, het vrywillig hulself aan diens onttrek en is intussen terug by die werk.

Genl. Krappies Engelbrecht, hoof van die afdeling teenintligting, en die tien ongenoemde polisiemanne was op verpligte verlof. Genl. Smit het vandeesweek aangedui hy gaan aftree, terwyl genl. Engelbrecht medies ongeskik verklaar is.

Luidens die Goldstone-verslag was kol. De Kock van die polisiemanne wat na bewering betrokke was by georganiseerde trein- en hostelgeweld, sowel as die vervaardiging van eiegemaakte wapens vir die IVP.

Kol. De Kock het onlangs in 'n onderhoud gesê hy weier om vrywaring te vra en hy sal ook nie die land verlaat nie.

"Ek wil nie aan ander doen wat aan my gedoen word nie. Ek sal die laaste mens wees wat hierdie land verlaat," het hy gesê.

Hy beskou dit as verraad dat oud-polisiemanne oor die werk van die Vlakplaas-eenheid praat.

The Star

More hit squad reports
...Pages 2 and 25

No way out for De Kock

Cold-blooded killer given two life sentences and 212 years told he does not qualify for parole or full amnesty

Newspaper clippings from the time Eugene was arrested and tried in a court of law.

As a result of Eugene's testimony at the Truth and Reconciliation Commission several apartheid crimes related to the Security Branch and the Defence Force came to light.

Son Eksklusief

Eugene de Kock resenseer vandeesweek vir Son Peter Stiff se boek The Covert War. De Kock het natuurlik eerstehandse ervaring van dit waarvan Stiff skryf.

PETER Stiff is 'n bekende skrywer oor Afrika se bos-oorloë. So ook is hy die skrywer van boeke oor die Koevoete (geheime eenhede), hul operasies en al die onaangename dinge wat saam met hierdie eenhede en hul operasies gaan.

Hy vertel in *The Covert War* van moed, heldemoed, dapperheid, opoffering, die vloei van die bloed van manne en van die manne se vyande.

Hy kon, wat my betref, meer met die swart vryheidsvegters van Koevoet gepraat het. Hulle het aan die begin van die stigting van die gevegseenhede die absolute meerderheid uitgemaak.

Weet

Die eerste gevegsgroep, die fondasiegevegsgroep was Roepasein Zulu Delta; tagtig swart lede en een wit lid. Ek weet! Ek was die wit lid! Net soos die skrywer Jim Hooper, wat ook oor Koevoet en Unita geskryf het, het Stiff nie met die swart vegters gepraat nie.

Ek kry die idee dat die manne, die wit manne, die operateurs, nie 'n probleem het om alles met hulle swart mede-vegters te deel nie — veral die glorie. Dis is my vinger wat na die RKMFS wys, die Jam Stealers, die Remington Raiders.

Die manne wat in die hoëvertkoeëlie kantore gesit het, en verwerk hoeveel koppeld geskim kon word. Nie vir toerusting nie, nie vir die manne in die veld nie. Vir hulleself. En ek sal dit kan bewys.

So terloops, REMF is die afkorting vir Rear Echelon Mother Fucker. Kom reeds van Vietnam se dae af. My eie gesprekke met Hooper oor lang glase bier, of enigiets anders, het gehamer op die verhaal van die swart lede.

Hoe hulle die oorlog sien, dit is tog 'n burgeroorlog, broer teen broer, pa teen seun.

Hooper skryf niks van die swart lede se oordeel oor hul wit kollegas nie. Peter Stiff het nog 'n groter probleem. Hy kon nie in die veld ry saam met die manne nie. Hy het geen toegang tot die swart manne nie. Hy het slegs genl. Hans (sterk Hans of skelm Hans) Dreyer se woord. Dreyer se lakeie se woord en dan video-opnames waarin die wit manne hulself en ander ophemel en verheerlik. Dieselfde selfverheerlikingbendes vertel die van hul nederigheid in die aangesig van redelike of goeie toestand vanaf Swapo se kant nie. Peter Stiff kry nie die oorspronklike Koevoet telekes nie (daar was nog nie fakse nie), hy sien nie die oorspronklike kontakverslae nie en hy hoor nie hoe die kontakverslag en wat op grondvlak gebeur van mekaar

verskil nie. Ek het so 'n paar afdrukke van my kontakverslae. Lees meer vorentoe in die Son-koerant.

Tog het Peter Stiff goeie navorsing gedoen. Hy pluis soveel moontlik uit. Hy vlieg die feitlik onmoontlike verhaal netjies en helder vir die leser. Ongelukkig vir die menigte swart operateurs kon Peter Stiff nie met my 'n onderhoud voer nie. Ten spyte van herhaalde pogings sedert 1996-2001 en selfs daarna, toe ek en hy skriftelik aansoeke gerig het aan 'n sekere instansie. Wat jou sal keer om nie skriftelike aansoeke te rig aan diegene wat nie wil lees nie.

Daar was geen gebrek aan dapperheid aan die vyand se kant nie. Hulle het vanaf Angola ingekom met net dit wat hulle kon dra, wat dam baie was. Hulle het geen 2-rigting radio's, niediese geriewe of hospitale gehad nie. Hulle het ook nie bystand, ekstra ammunisie of vervoer gehad nie.

Man-tot-man

Tog hou hulle nie op nie, en ten spyte van die bravado van sekere Koevoet-lede skiet Swapo

Top: The author at Vingerkraal farm outside Bela-Bela where a group of former black Koevoet members live. In the wheelchair is the former Koevoet member and author Shorty Kamango. **Middle:** In conversation with General Hans Dreyer, former commanding officer of Koevoet. **Bottom:** The author on her way to do a parachute jump with former members of the police's task force.

'Prime Evil' parole hangs in balance

LOUISE FLANAGAN
and KASHIEFA AJAM

THE PAPERWORK on whether apartheid killer Eugene de Kock gets parole is waiting for Correctional Services Minister Sbu Ndebele's decision.

And a little hiccup around controversial suspended SAPS crime intelligence chief Richard Mdluli may be delaying that decision.

De Kock, nicknamed "Prime Evil", commanded the notorious apartheid police Vlakplaas hit squad. He was jailed for a range of offences from fraud to murder, with sentences totalling 212 years plus two life sentences. He remained in jail because he got only partial amnesty.

De Kock was arrested a week before Nelson Mandela's inauguration as president in May 1994 and has been in jail ever since. He was sentenced in October 1996.

As Ndebele makes the final decision on whether he gets parole, the department is understood to have asked the State Security Agency (SSA) to investigate any possible links between De Kock and Mdluli, who also served in the apartheid-era police.

"This matter – we've heard about it," said Brian Dube, spokesman for the SSA, when asked about the Mdluli-De Kock investigation, but referred queries to Correctional Services.

"If a request was made, we would not make that public... We won't be able to comment."

Mdluli could not be reached for comment.

Ndebele's spokesman Manelisi Wolela would last night not confirm or deny whether De Kock's request for parole had been approved but said the minister was applying his mind to each parole application.

"Over the past few months, (Ndebele) has considered the parole applications of hundreds of inmates sentenced to life imprisonment including that of offender Eugene de Kock, (which) is currently receiving due consideration," said Wolela.

LIFE SENTENCE: De Kock was convicted of six counts of murder, one of attempted murder, one of culpable homicide, one count of being an accessory after the fact to culpable homicide, nine contraventions of weapons laws, 59 counts of fraud, two counts of conspiracy in contravention of the Riotous Assemblies Act, one count of obstructing justice, one count of kidnapping, and one count of assault with intent to do grievous bodily harm. His total sentence was 212 years plus two life sentences; the effective sentence was life.

He added that the department was not aware of any communication with the State Security Agency with regards to the alleged investigation involving Mdluli.

De Kock's lawyer, Pretoria attorney Julian Knight, expressed amazement at the suggestion of any Mdluli-De Kock investigation.

"If that is a consideration of the minister then it is bizarre in the extreme," he said.

Knight said he understood the

National Council for Correctional Services had recommended De Kock's parole to the minister in November.

Yesterday he queried the delay in the decision.

"While I welcome the decision to release De Kock, I feel that there is no point in trying to play politics and delay his release," said Knight.

"He is the only member of the apartheid regime that was punished for the sins of the generals

and politicians, whose orders his sin was to obey. While they enjoyed their pensions and the consort of their wives, lovers and families, De Kock had to languish in prison for the last 19-and-a-half years."

Judge Siraj Desai, the chairman of the National Council on Correctional Services, would not comment on De Kock's application.

This week De Kock brought an application to compel the minister to make a decision within two weeks on his parole application.

De Kock said that last year his parole application was approved by the various levels of the parole system and went to the National Council for Correctional Services, which in November made a recommendation – "the contents of which I am not acquainted with" – to the minister.

Since then, the minister has "failed, neglected and/or refused to consider" that recommendation, he said, and called for a decision.

In an affidavit supporting his application for a decision, De Kock said he had served 17 years of his sentence and was eligible to apply for parole.

As a lifer sentenced in 1996, De Kock is entitled to apply for parole earlier than those sentenced under current law. The minister is not obliged to grant parole.

"I am the only member of the South African Police Service that is serving a sentence for crimes which I had committed as part of the National Party's attempt to uphold apartheid and fight the liberation movements," said De Kock.

"Not one of the previous generals or ministers who were in Cabinet up to 1990 have been prosecuted at all.

"I would never have committed the crimes if it was not for the political context of the time, and the position I was placed in, and in particular the orders I had received from my superiors.

"All actions took place under the auspices of an organised system, where I acted on orders given by superior officers, who have never been prosecuted."

Eugene applied unsuccessfully for parole a number of times before it was finally approved at the end of January 2015.

The academic Piet Croucamp helped Eugene with his applications for parole in recent years and campaigned actively for his release. During his incarceration Eugene started assisting the National Prosecuting Authority's Missing Persons Task Team in their search for the remains of murdered activists. These photos were taken on one such an occasion.

Top: Former task-force member Larry Hanton at the cross erected by family members of apartheid victims on the helicopter landing pad at Vlakplaas.
Bottom: The author with Candice Mama (far left), the daughter of one of the victims of the Nelspruit shooting, and Professor Pumla Gobodo-Madikizela, author of *A Human Being Died that Night.*

and Advocate Jeremy Gauntlett (SC) in connection with the criminal prosecution of the former [state] president of South Africa, PW Botha. They discussed Botha's refusal to co-operate with the TRC and allegations that he had ordered his subordinates to commit atrocities.

I immediately felt duty-bound – almost driven – to accede to their request.[9]

Eugene's comprehensive testimony in Port Elizabeth and his willingness to cooperate with the state ensured that astounding evidence about police transgressions was made public. In his own case in Pretoria, however, he stood alone in the dock.

I studied the TRC amnesty reports and applications by the generals who were Eugene's immediate superiors. They ran to hundreds of pages. In answer after answer during questioning, they remained evasive and denied knowledge of, or implication in, any Vlakplaas activities. It was as if Vlakplaas had never existed.

Yet most Vlakplaas activities were executed under orders from senior officers, claimed Eugene. Today he believes that he and his colleagues were simply the 'executioners' of those in control: 'I took the blame during my trial for the police and military generals as well as members of the former National Party government. I stated in court that the National Party had been party to covert activities – more specifically, former presidents PW Botha and FW de Klerk, the former foreign minister Pik Botha, former ministers of police [later law and order] Louis le Grange and Adriaan Vlok, and the former head of the National Intelligence Service, Niël Barnard … I also referred to the roles that police commissioners Johan Coetzee and Johan van der Merwe had played, as well as a variety of other officers, including the generals Basie Smit, Krappies Engelbrecht and Johan le Roux …'[10]

But not one of the police generals or senior politicians was in reality prepared to take personal responsibility for what they had done in the name of apartheid.[11] Former minister Adriaan Vlok and former general Johan van der Merwe applied for, and received, amnesty from the TRC for isolated incidents. Former minister Leon Wessels – deputy minister of law and order, at one stage – testified before the TRC that he and his colleagues could not justifiably say that they were unaware of the offences. But there was no comprehensive admission of large-scale wrongdoing. How, then, did one person alone become the symbol of apartheid's offences?

'I regard Eugene as an Azazel figure, literally a scapegoat,' says Hennie Heymans, who was a member of the top management of the SAP and served in the secretariat of the State Security Council.

'He became the symbolic bearer of a group's sins [those of the security forces]. Leviticus 16:8–10: Aaron had to draw lots for two he-goats. The one was to be selected "for the Lord" and the other "for Azazel" [a demon, in the Jewish tradition]. Aaron was to offer up the goat selected for the Lord as a sacrifice. The goat "for Azazel" was to live, to stand in the presence of the Lord and become burdened with the guilt as an atonement for the sins of the group – and then be chased out into the desert at the mercy of Azazel.' This, in Heyman's view, is what happened to Eugene.

What a terrible price to pay – to be held solely responsible for collective sins. During Eugene's trial, he said to the criminologist Professor Anna van der Hoven that he felt as if the state president at the time, FW de Klerk, had hung the former security forces out to dry. She writes in her report for mitigation of sentence: 'Today he feels as if the struggle was not worth the effort. He asks: "What did we achieve by it?" He no longer knows what he fought for. He feels that his actions were futile.'[12]

Van der Hoven holds that Eugene's prolonged exposure to armed conflict made him susceptible to exploitation. 'His emotions became blunted and he was able to kill someone in cold blood if it made sense to him why he should do so. He was also accustomed to high-intensity situations.'[13]

Where does individual accountability begin and end? Eventually Eugene had to – and did – take responsibility for all his choices. But was he, alone, responsible for them? Was he the only one who had to carry this burden? To what extent were his seniors and political heads also responsible? Should someone have intervened? If so, who? The generals? The politicians?

Van der Hoven wrote in her report that the SAP's line of command 'tacitly' let him have his own way. 'No inspections were carried out at Vlakplaas; top management let things lie. Orders were given to the accused verbally; a blind eye was then turned. The attitude was that it was Eugene's business how he carried out the orders. There was thus inadequate supervision and control from top structures.'[14]

Former Vlakplaas operative Neil also points a finger at the generals. 'Why did no one get involved and say: Stop it, guys – you're going too far? Instead, there was praise and there were medals – medals that didn't fall from the sky, but were awarded from the top.'

Eugene was one of the most highly decorated police officers in the SAP at the time.

But there was no intervention. The same can be said of earlier years when SAP top management transferred a battle-weary Eugene de Kock from Koevoet to Vlakplaas. In his book *Trou tot die dood toe*, former police commissioner General Johan van der Merwe reiterates that General Hans Dreyer, then still a colonel and Koevoet's commanding officer, advised strongly against Eugene

Eugene de Kock

Two of the medals Eugene received during his career in the
SAP: above is the Police Star for Outstanding Service (SOE),
awarded twice, and below is the Silver Cross for Bravery,
awarded once.

being placed back in the Security Branch when he returned to South Africa. This happened, nonetheless.[15]

Why, I wondered, was Eugene sent back there against the express recommendation of his former commander? Why was Dreyer's warning ignored?[16]

The means presumably justified the end. The fighter known for his ruthless killing ability was the SAP's candidate of choice for placement at C1. Brigadier Willem Schoon's testimony before the TRC confirmed police management's reckless attitude in this regard, and the way in which it had put its own interests above all else. When Eugene – still a captain – was appointed to Vlakplaas in 1983, Schoon was the head of Section C1. They knew each other from Schoon's days as commander of the Oshakati Security Branch. In November 1996, when Schoon appeared before the TRC, Advocates Glen Goosen and Dumisa Ntsebeza asked him about Eugene's appointment at Vlakplaas:

> ADV. GOOSEN: Is it correct that you were responsible for his transfer to the Vlakplaas unit at the end of 1984?
>
> BRIG. SCHOON: No, I was not responsible. I was approached and asked whether I could place him and I said yes.
>
> ADV. GOOSEN: And you decided to appoint him and the position you chose to place him was the Vlakplaas unit. Is that correct?
>
> BRIG. SCHOON: Yes, that is correct ...
>
> ADV. GOOSEN: You fully understood what – what kind of work he had been doing prior to being transferred to Vlakplaas. Is that correct?
>
> BRIG. SCHOON: Yes.
>
> ADV. GOOSEN: Yes, that he was in truth more of a soldier than an ordinary policeman in the work he was doing as a

member – or commanding officer – of a unit of Koevoet. Is that correct?

BRIG. SCHOON: Well, I knew that in Ovamboland he performed the work of a soldier and my task was to rehabilitate him so he could be integrated back into society. They could not appoint him in any other position and that is why I was asked to – to take him under my wing.

ADV. GOOSEN: Did you rehabilitate him?

BRIG. SCHOON: I don't know – I don't think so.

ADV. GOOSEN: How did you go about trying to rehabilitate him?

BRIG. SCHOON: Well, for example I allowed him to remain [at home] over weekends so that he could lead a normal life, he was for example almost 40 years of age, still unmarried, and I wanted to give him the chance to begin a family life and felt that this would surely put him back on the straight and narrow.

ADV. GOOSEN: Was this your motivation when you appointed him as head of the Vlakplaas unit?

BRIG. SCHOON: There was nobody else.[17]

Later in the session, Schoon explained how Eugene had 'gone backwards mentally' in Ovamboland.[18] 'They used the expression – I don't know the proper translation – *bosbefoeterd* [messed up by prolonged exposure to bush conflict] … there is a more explicit word that describes it. For example, if he was sitting in the canteen and someone looked at him sideways, he would get up and attack him physically and say what are you looking at?

'You know, he was mentally … one could almost say disturbed. As a result of the stress and trauma that he had experienced in the time he fought there. Because almost every day they shot and killed people and under those circumstances you can't expect a man to last very long emotionally.'

Goosen then indicated that Eugene would surely have been expected to use violence against the state's targets at Section C1 – that there would be little difference between what he was expected to do at Koevoet and at Section C1.

> ADV. GOOSEN: I put it to you, Brigadier, that the real reason why Eugene de Kock was appointed at Vlakplaas was because of the experience that he had gained in his work at Koevoet, that here was a person who could make sure that Vlakplaas undertakings were effective.
> BRIG. SCHOON: I believe that this was indeed one of the reasons.
> ADV. GOOSEN: Yes, it had nothing whatsoever to do with his rehabilitation; you wanted to appoint an effective person in command of a unit whose primary task was the elimination of enemies of the state. Is that correct? [. . .]
> BRIG. SCHOON: I was not unhappy with his appointment – but I did not place him there specifically.

In stark contrast, Johnny – a former Vlakplaas member – said that Eugene blamed those around him 'for everything – instead of looking inwards and taking the blame himself. The things that happened were his own fault, his own choices. He just doesn't want to accept that.'

As I see it, Eugene was just one cog in the workings of a larger, more complicated mess for which one individual could not reasonably be expected to take sole responsibility. The security structures in the police were under huge pressure from all sides – the government, the commanders and the public. The directive to the police was to suppress the freedom movements and ensure that 'white South Africa' slept safely at night.

General Johan van der Merwe helped to compile a police memorandum submitted as part of a parliamentary inquiry into the stipulations of the law that would deal with amnesty. The memorandum required its contributors to capture the spirit of the 1980s – to recreate, in other words, the decade as experienced by a member of the security forces. Van der Merwe writes in his book *Trou tot die dood toe* that policemen had to deal with wholesale violence almost daily in the 1980s, including 'necklace murders, people who were burnt alive, stabbed or chopped up, car bombs that spread body parts, which needed picking up and putting into plastic bags, over a wide area, limpet mines at restaurants and landmines on farm roads ...

'Between September 1984 and April 1992 there were 80 507 incidents of unrest; 9 280 people died and 19 061 were injured. A total of 406 people were burnt alive by the necklace method and 395 burnt alive by other means. The ANC-SACP alliance openly stated that members of the SAP were hard targets; a concerted effort would be made to murder and maim policemen and their families.'[19]

Van der Merwe emphasises that the political leaders were categorical – the security forces had to halt the revolutionary onslaught at any cost. The state president, ministers, churches, academics, cultural organisations and the media all demanded the extermination of the 'terrorists'. As an example, Van der Merwe says PW Botha himself gave the order to blow up Khotso House.[20]

Van der Merwe's book and the accounts of former policemen make it clear to me that the ideology of a total onslaught that had to be averted consumed them totally; it became their reality, as it was for Eugene.

Former policeman Koos Kotze, author of *Mean Streets: Life in the Apartheid Police*, lays the blame for police offences squarely at the NP politicians' door.[21] 'How is it possible that an honourable and proud organisation with respectable and well-educated members became an organisation that instilled fear in the hearts of the majority of the population? What changed?' he asked in an e-mail discussion.

When I went to see him, we spoke at length about this. According to him, the problem was that Security Branch members suddenly started acting as intelligence officers. 'As such, other rules applied and, under a veil of secrecy, the policemen decided to take matters into their own hands instead of leaving them to the courts, which was how things worked traditionally. It is also likely that we started believing our own propaganda, and that fear was an unconscious factor – the war was very real, and had already gone on for decades.'

The politicians relied upon the SAP's strong discipline and believed that it would enforce the laws of the land 'as a police force is legally obliged to do', said Kotze.

He makes the argument often put forward in such cases: Eugene was just following orders. 'Whereas an army in the bush can question unreasonable orders, a policeman cannot … a police force cannot decide which laws to enforce.

'For all practical purposes, the Nationalists forced the SAP to destroy itself – either by refusing to enforce the laws of its political masters (legally impossible), or by enforcing those laws and losing the respect of the people they were supposed to protect. An honourable institution, thrown into disrepute by unprincipled politicians.'

Although apartheid legislation criminalised the liberation movements, it was important for the state to try Eugene as an ordinary criminal and not as a political prisoner. Yet everything about the trial was political – and the Security Branch could just as well have been called the 'political police', said former brigadier Hennie Heymans. Today, Eugene feels that this should have been a stronger focus in his trial. He still feels that the prosecution deliberately downplayed the political dimension of his offences, which could have had implications for his amnesty hearing.

Things may have turned out differently for him if a general amnesty had been granted for members of the armed forces of all parties. It appears, though, that Kobie Coetsee, Minister of Justice at the time, delayed on this issue and missed the opportunity.[22] Jan Heunis, then an advisor on constitutional law and the son of former minister Chris Heunis, writes in *Die Binnekring*: 'The question of indemnity for crimes committed during the apartheid era was high on the political agenda during 1993. Surprisingly enough the ANC made a suggestion in this regard that would have suited the government's representatives perfectly. However (Kobie) Coetsee in his capacity as minister of justice turned the suggestion down and said he was working on his own proposal.'[23]

Initially, Eugene believed the police generals would support and protect him during his court case as they had always done before. In the end, he answered for Vlakplaas's transgressions alone. For the first five months of his trial, his former colleagues visited him in jail; almost everyone then turned against him.[24] When his former Koevoet colleague and close friend Willie Nortjé began testimony against him at the end of August 1995, Eugene was shattered.

In *A Long Night's Damage*, Eugene is quoted on the trial: 'Some people see my trial as the first opportunity for the true extent of covert security force actions to become known; others see it as vindication of the Goldstone Commission's findings and a triumph of justice. I see it as two years of betrayal – first by the state that had given me my orders, and then by my friends, who lined up to testify against me.'[25]

The bond of brotherhood had broken.

But what exactly does this type of brotherhood entail? In a wartime situation, what is the role of the individual, and of the brotherhood? I came across a perceptive talk by journalist Sebastian Junger, who spent some time with the American defence force's 173rd Airborne unit in Afghanistan. He describes the brotherhood as he observed it in the unit as a bond that develops between men who, under normal circumstances, would not necessarily be friends. In a wartime situation, however, they give everything for one another and put the group's interests and safety above their own.[26]

Eugene shared a similar bond with his colleagues at Koevoet and Vlakplaas.

I had already spent a fair amount of time with Eugene's former colleagues when I met neurologist and paediatrician Dr Greg Lamb, an expert in the field of post-traumatic stress disorder (PTSD), specifically in a military context. He cites consistent reliance on brotherhood, the habit of blaming others, the abuse of alcohol and extreme religiosity as ways in which PTSD sufferers try to divert attention from their inherent shortcomings and avoid taking responsibility for their decisions.

In her evaluation report, Professor Van der Hoven also refers to the high incidence of alcohol abuse among Security Branch members. She writes that the policemen were not allowed to talk to their families, or speak out, about work. 'The Security Branch of the police carried out covert operations that could not, in the interests of the state and the police, be made public. The Security Branch developed specific techniques, therefore, to ensure that covert dealings did not come to light. Because of the type of work the accused did, he often had to assume a false identity. He also had to murder people to prevent certain crucial information from reaching the media. It was an underworld world in which the definition of right and wrong became increasingly vague.

'They learnt, therefore, to keep their experiences to themselves. The only recreation they had was to go to the canteen and seek comfort in alcohol. Here, with their colleagues, they could lower their masks. Excessive drinking and partying was part of their subculture.'[27]

In Elaine Bing's book, *Unmaking of the Torturer*, I read that the 'militarised policeman cannot display emotions such as fear and heartache. Nor must he give way to empathy, a soft heart or tolerance. He may indeed show controlled aggression.'[28]

To try to understand, I went too far, once, when I asked a former operative about the effects of violence on those who commit it. Memory can be a horror movie … his rage exploded, taken back to times and places to which he no longer wanted to return.

The former operatives repress not only their own memories but their colleagues' secrets, taking them to their graves as the unspoken rule dictates.

Why this silence? 'Of course avoiding [personal] pain is one of the main reasons for the mystery and silence,' writes Marlantes in *What it is Like to Go to War*.[29] These memories, this 'personal pain', never goes away: it is a can of worms that must diligently be kept sealed.

Why, then, would Eugene's former confidants – his 'brothers' – testify against him? The answer is quite obvious: to save themselves. They were threatened with prosecution if they did not.

It seems, from my discussions with former Vlakplaas operatives, that there had been dissension in the ranks since the early

1990s. The brotherhood was already under pressure; the discord from all sides saw C1 splitting into three sections, at Vlakplaas, Waterkloof and Midrand.

Some former operatives still feel guilty, I noted, that Eugene is the only one of the band of brothers to have served time and that they testified against him; many expressed a need to contact him.

The prisoners in orange who sit around timidly in Pretoria Central's visiting area seem harmless at first glance. A visit seldom goes by, though, that doesn't send a shiver down my spine: the semblance of normality is misleading. The world inside those walls is a desperate, terrible place where inmates give over to gangsterism, drugs and moral decline.

One day, the one-eyed Melville Koppies murderer who liked to carry the tuck-shop trays was gone. He died, silently, in jail. Most of the prisoners around me are guilty of serious crimes.

'If you could choose to do it all again, would you approach your trial differently?' I wanted to know during one of my visits.

The left corner of Eugene's mouth pulled down. 'Well, as I sit here today, I can tell you I could have done what Willie Nortjé did [his good friend from his Koevoet and Vlakplaas days who testified against him]. I should have, from day one. But in my heart, even now, I know I wouldn't have done it at the time. I think I was stupid not to, but I'm still me. I fulfilled my biggest obligation – to make sure that my family was, and is, safe. After all these years, nothing really matters but the present, the now.'

A clear ray of sunshine broke through the corrugated-iron roof. The sleeves of Eugene's overall were rolled up; the bright ray fell on his bare arm. Within minutes, his skin was flecked with sickly red. 'Life happens, we happen, and you have to leave the past behind for ever,' he murmured.

'Why did you stay in the country?'

'I stayed because I felt responsible for my men, that's all. Little did I know they would betray me.'

'The defence had pointed out that a large number of accomplices had been called to testify against the accused. They had also been offered indemnity in terms of section 204 of the Criminal Procedure Act. It was submitted that it had been unnecessary to call all these accomplices to prove the case against the accused and to have done so could create an impression that they had been called merely to make it possible to offer them indemnity. The defence had also pointed out that charges had been withdrawn against many other former members of the police who were accomplices or offenders. Yet others had never even been arrested or charged. This, it was submitted, meant that probably only the accused would be prosecuted, leading to inequality of treatment, contrary to section 8 of the Constitution, Act No. 200 of 1993. The court held that it was true that courts were required to strive for consistency in sentencing. In addition, people who had committed crimes should, as far as possible, be treated equally. However, this only applied after the institution of prosecutions. It was not known who would still be prosecuted. It was true that accomplices who had testified and had committed serious crimes, such as having acted as executioners, would get away scot-free. While this was a factor to be kept in mind, this single factor did not mean that an otherwise appropriate sentence should not be imposed.'

– Quoted from Judge Willem van der Merwe's sentencing proceedings in Eugene de Kock's criminal trial, 30 October 1996.

13

Guilty

After a trial of almost 21 months Eugene was found guilty and sentenced by Judge Willem van der Merwe on 30 October 1996. He was found guilty of 121 charges, including six of murder, one of kidnapping, one of culpable homicide and many charges of fraud. For these, the following sentences were handed down:

> Charge 1 (murder), 20 years' imprisonment.
> Charge 2 (murder), 20 years' imprisonment.
> Charge 3 (murder), 20 years' imprisonment.
> Charge 4 (murder), 20 years' imprisonment.
> Charge 5 (murder), life imprisonment.
> Charges 6 to 8 (infringement of section 32(1)(a) and (e) read with sections 1, 39 and 40 of Act 75 of 1969, taken together for purposes of sentence), five years' imprisonment.
> Charge 9 (fraud), two years' imprisonment.
> Charge 10 (fraud), four years' imprisonment.
> Charge 12 (conspiracy to infringement of section 18(2) (a) of the Riotous Assemblies Act 17 of 1956), 20 years' imprisonment.
> Charge 13 (obstruction or defeating the ends of justice), six years' imprisonment.
> Charge 14 (murder), 20 years' imprisonment.

- Charge 15 (attempted murder), five years' imprisonment.
- Charge 16 (culpable homicide), ten years' imprisonment.
- Charge 17 (fraud), four years' imprisonment.
- Charges 18, 19 and 21 (fraud, taken together for purposes of sentence), six years' imprisonment.
- Charge 20 (fraud), two years' imprisonment.
- Charge 22 (fraud), two years' imprisonment.
- Charges 23 to 42 (fraud, taken together for purposes of sentence), four years' imprisonment.
- Charges 43 to 57 (fraud, taken together for purposes of sentence), three years' imprisonment.
- Charges 88 to 93 (fraud, taken together for purposes of sentence), two years' imprisonment.
- Charges 94 to 97 (fraud, taken together for purposes of sentence), two years' imprisonment.
- Charge 98 (fraud), two years' imprisonment.
- Charge 99 (fraud), three years' imprisonment.
- Charges 100, 101 and 102 (infringement of section 32(1)(b), section 32(1)(c) and section 32(1)(e) read with sections 1, 39 and 40 of Act 75 of 1969, taken together for purposes of sentence), five years' imprisonment.
- Charges 103, 104, 105 and 106 (infringement of section 32(1)(b), section 32(1)(c) and section 32(1)(e) read with sections 1, 39 and 40 of Act 75 of 1969, as well as an infringement of section 6(1) read with sections 1, 6(2), 6(3) and 29 of Act 26 of 1956, and further read with Government Notice R1603 dated 8 September 1972, taken together for purposes of sentence), five years' imprisonment.
- Charges 107 to 117 (fraud, taken together for purposes of sentence), two years' imprisonment.
- Charge 118 (kidnapping), two years' imprisonment.

> Charge 119 (assault with the intention of inflicting serious injury), four years' imprisonment.
> Charge 120 (conspiracy to infringement of section 18(2)(a) of the Riotous Assemblies Act 17 of 1956), life imprisonment.
> Charge 121 (accessory to culpable homicide), 12 years' imprisonment.[1]

I struggle, sometimes, to reconcile the soldier and assassin for the state with the man who sits so calmly before me during my visits to him in jail. However, when I read the judge's summary of Eugene's crimes, I shudder at their brutality. The 44-page summary of the imposition of sentence and some of the remarks made by the judge drive home the reality of who Eugene once was. Among others:

Charges 17 to 22, 98 and 99: All these charges of fraud, as with charges 9 and 10, were planned, calculated and executed with cunning. In most cases stories about events were fabricated with an imagination that testifies to sharp-witted originality ... Whether the proceeds of this fraud were used for an individual's personal gain or for other police activities makes very little difference. The fact remains that money that was placed in the hands of the state by citizens was illegally acquired and wasted. The calculated way in which the fraud was planned and executed fills one with revulsion.

Charges 118 to 120: Japie Maponya's sin was having a brother who the police were after. To interrogate him about his brother, he was kidnapped, badly assaulted and killed.

The kidnapping, charge 118, was not of short duration. Maponya was so heavily outnumbered that he stood no chance of evading abduction. The assault he suffered was cruel and cold. It was perpetrated, once again, by a multitude of people while he was powerless. The accused was charged with, and found guilty of, conspiracy to kill Maponya. As was the case with [Brian] Ngqulunga, the events prior to, during and after the killing could not be excluded when establishing the seriousness of the crime.

After it had been decided to end Maponya's life, regardless of whether permission to do so was given from 'above', the Vlakplaas members acted in a cold and calculated way and every precaution was taken to ensure the murder could not be traced back to the police. Clearly, he was killed in Swaziland for this reason. The journey to Swaziland with Maponya in the vehicle, with him knowing and hearing what his fate was to be, speaks of callousness …

The way in which Maponya's life was ended and his body left in a plantation fills one with repugnance. The lack of compassion for him as a person is also evident in the reaction after the murder. After allegations of the involvement of the accused and other members of Vlakplaas in Maponya's death became known and were investigated inter alia by the Harms Commission, it was covered up with lies and deception.

This incident, in which the deceased launched no attack on any member of the force, deserves serious censure. A dedicated worker who could have provided for his future wife and child was unceremoniously kidnapped, assaulted and killed, merely because he could reveal that the offences of kidnapping and assault had been committed against him.[2]

In her evaluation report for mitigation of sentence, criminologist Professor Van der Hoven wrote that the police was more than simply a career for Eugene – it was a 'calling to defend his country and his people and also to protect them from communism'.

'The reason he joined the police was to help fight terrorists. The ANC and Swapo were seen as communists and worse than wild animals (they were criminalised). The accused made up his mind that he would not allow white people in South Africa to be wiped out as had happened, for example, in the Congo, Angola and Mozambique. Therefore, he focused his efforts on combating terrorism. The SAP was seen as the personification of what was right and just; it had to protect the community at any cost.'[3]

Eugene told her how he had realised that becoming a master of counter-insurgency makes one 'become an even greater master of terrorism'. Whereas a counter-insurgent is bound by the country's laws and codes of behaviour, a terrorist has 'no inhibitions and sees himself as not bound by any laws or norms'. This in fact gives a terrorist a higher success rate than a counter-insurgent, he said.

'In the process you become a terrorist yourself,' he stated.[4]

Van der Hoven also maintained that Eugene's childhood experiences taught him to repress and hide his emotions. As a result, he came across as emotionally cold. 'This also contributed to the relentlessness and determination he displayed when tracking down and killing the enemy. Working for such a long time in a war situation caused progressive emotional blunting.

'Due to the changes in personality that take place, the individual becomes a very efficient murderer. Such a person learns to repress feelings of guilt and views people in terms of diametric opposites – his subordinates are good and worth saving; the enemy is bad and must be killed. During combat, the person emotionally represses events and feels empty, detached and alienated. Later he is only capable of a limited range of feelings.'[5]

According to Van der Hoven, Eugene stressed that killing his enemy gave him no satisfaction. 'He could not simply kill people; he had to know why he had to do it … his objective was to halt the enemy. The risks he ran in these operations were getting tortured, murdered or maimed himself'.[6]

Dr Annemarie Novello is a clinical psychologist who was also approached to evaluate Eugene in light of the signs of post-traumatic stress disorder (PTSD) he displayed. She reported that there were, indeed, 'significant symptoms of post-traumatic stress disorder' in Eugene's behaviour. According to Novello, he had a strong belief system. In the context of this he attached a certain significance to 'especially the traumatic events to which he had been exposed in his work situation'.[7]

Van der Hoven also believed that Eugene had PTSD and should receive psychological treatment for it in prison.[8]

In the sentencing proceedings Judge Van der Merwe mentioned that Dr JA Plomp, the psychiatrist for the state, doubted whether Eugene suffered from PTSD. However, according to Van der Merwe, Plomp could not consult with the accused and had to rely on what he had heard while Eugene and the other experts gave their testimonies. According to Van der Merwe, Plomp did, in fact, say that even if Eugene did not suffer from PTSD, he accepted 'the accused experienced blunting [of the emotions]'.[9]

14

'I cannot tell you how dirty I feel'

After his criminal trial Eugene applied for amnesty at the Truth and Reconciliation Commission (TRC). The TRC investigated apartheid-era human rights abuses by all parties with a view to bringing about reconciliation. Members of the security forces were requested to come forward with information about apartheid offences and were given the opportunity to seek amnesty from the TRC for political crimes.

Eugene's numerous TRC amnesty sittings took place between October 1997 and April 2000 in Pretoria, Durban, Port Elizabeth, East London, Pietermaritzburg, Cape Town, George and Johannesburg. 'I testified constantly,' he told me.

When he thinks back to his trial and his testimony before the TRC, one thing is evident: he was completely alone. But this was not the first time he had been on his own.

Eugene's speech impediment had taught him from an early age what it felt like to be an outsider. I only became aware of his stutter myself after reading about it in *A Long Night's Damage*, which was quite some time after my first visit to the prison. In the four years I have known him, he hasn't stumbled over his words once.

We spoke about this during one of my visits. The previous night a group of prisoners had tried to escape, and the warders were vigilant. We had been searched thoroughly; the brusque warders circled like brown hawks in the visitors' area. The tension seemed to sweat from the walls.

'I've known how it feels to be ostracised since childhood,' Eugene said.

'How so?' I asked.

'You know, I really wanted to see the movie *The King's Speech*, but when I eventually got the chance to I had to keep switching it off. It was so "me" that I almost couldn't watch. The king's experience – his helplessness in communicating because of his stutter – was mine too. School was hell. The hell just got worse later.

'The humiliation, the teasing, the powerlessness, the inability just to be normal. The fear of having to ask for something over the café counter. Just greeting people was torture. But giving up was not an option.'

He also firmly believes that the police generals were hoping that his stutter would inhibit him during his court case and his testimony before the TRC. 'But then I lost it and decided bugger them! For the first time in my life I fucked them over. I shoved their authority and superiority down their own throats. They waited for the stuttering, the swallowing, the sideward glances that make people bow their heads in pity. When it didn't happen I saw only one thing on their faces – doom. For days this expression remained on their faces.'

'But how did you manage to stop stuttering all of a sudden?' I wanted to know.

'A stutter can never be cured, of course, but as a child I went to the University of Pretoria to learn a few techniques to control mine. When my court case started, I decided not to be dismissive of the proceedings; it was important to me to add value and dignity to it. People tend to doubt the credibility of those who stutter. So,

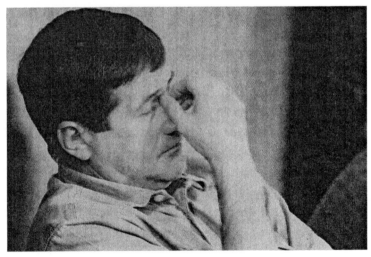

Top: For his testimony at the Truth and Reconciliation Commission, Eugene mostly attended the hearings at the Idasa Building (Institute for Democracy in South Africa) in Visagie Street in the Pretoria CBD. **Bottom:** One of the many photos taken of Eugene during his testimony at the TRC.

I harnassed all the resistance, focus and intensity I had to apply those techniques and to do my best.'

In his book *No One to Blame?*, Advocate George Bizos writes that Eugene's announcement that he was going to reveal all to the TRC forced many individuals to seek amnesty who would otherwise not have done so. 'He did not want to be in this alone, he wanted all to come forward, and, in particular, he wanted to implicate the politicians and the generals who had abandoned him … They suspected that they might have been implicated and could not afford to take the chance and the applications flooded in.'[1]

Each day, Eugene was driven – under heavy guard – from C-Max to the Idasa building in Pretoria where most of the TRC sittings were held. In his application for presidential pardon, he wrote of his experiences at the sittings:

> My legal representative and I worked day and night to complete my amnesty application, which ran to a thousand pages. What interested me was that my legal representative was approached almost daily by those representing some of the other perpetrators, asking if they could see a copy of my amnesty application before submission. It forced others to think very carefully about their applications …
>
> I have no doubt that my approach assisted the TRC and the government enormously in uncovering the truth. It essentially obliged perpetrators to lodge applications for all of their operations and atrocities. At that stage I felt I would do everything in my power to support the TRC process as much as possible. I definitely took the correct approach; it definitely had the desired effect.
>
> The TRC acknowledges the effect of my decision [to keep my application secret] in its interim report – more

specifically, in volume 5A, page 202, paragraph 32 – which reads:

'In reviewing its efforts to uncover the deep truth behind the violation of the apartheid era, the TRC frankly acknowledges that much of its success is due to the fact that large numbers of security police members grasped at the possibility of amnesty in exchange for full disclosure. The commission is not, however, so naive as to believe that it was this alone that had persuaded them to blow the whistle on their past actions. The fact is that they would have preferred the cloak of silence.

'The ironic truth is that what brought them to the TRC was the fullness of the disclosures made by an individual often painted as the arch villain of the apartheid era, Mr Eugene de Kock. Whatever his motives, the TRC acknowledges that it was … he who broke the code of silence.'[2]

In his book *Unfinished Business: South Africa, Apartheid and Truth*, TRC commissioner Advocate Dumisa Ntsebeza writes that many of the initial tip-offs for TRC investigations into apartheid offences came from Eugene: 'De Kock, probably correctly, saw himself as being set up as a scapegoat, the sacrificial lamb for all the ills and brutality of apartheid. He is still widely regarded as probably the only perpetrator to have come clean.'[3]

Eugene is outspoken on the issue: 'I always felt the way in which the ANC leadership accepted responsibility for the actions of their foot soldiers stood in stark contrast to the cowardly conduct of senior officers in the police and army, and the ministers in the former cabinet – our former superiors.'[4]

In his application for presidential pardon, Eugene quotes from Dr Alex Boraine's *A Country Unmasked*, in which Eugene's testimony in the court case against former state president PW Botha is described. According to Boraine, Eugene entered the small courtroom with a stern expression on his face. Botha glanced quickly at De Kock, then turned away to sit with his back to him.

> If Botha imagined that De Kock would in any way be intimidated by being only a few feet away from him when the former colonel read his statement, he was in for a shock. De Kock came out with all guns blazing. I watched him as he passionately described the politicians of the National Party as cowards who sold out the police and the army: 'They wanted to eat lamb but they did not want to see the blood and guts.'
>
> De Kock went on to say that he and his colleagues had been told by politicians on the highest level that they, the security forces, were fighting for the protection of their fatherland. But, he said, they were only fighting for the 'incestuous little world of Afrikanerdom'. De Kock went on to say: 'We did well. We did the fighting. Politicians do not have the moral guts to accept responsibility for the killings.'
>
> He described himself as a lowly colonel, but affirmed: 'I am also an Afrikaner.' However it was as cowards that God would deal with the politicians. I watched Botha carefully as this vitriol was spewed out by De Kock. He was unmoved; he stared ahead and never looked at De Kock again.[5]

Another challenge for the TRC was that the old South African Defence Force (SADF) had no desire to participate in the proceedings and instructed its members not to submit amnesty applications. However, Eugene had been involved in a number of joint operations with the SADF and decided to make information about these public too.

He went on to write: 'In this regard I referred to the co-operation between Vlakplaas and the directorate of covert intelligence, with which we launched an attack in Botswana in which the Chand family died. I revealed all the information I had about the operation against the former Transkei government of Mr Bantu Holomisa and the operation against the former Ciskei government of Mr Oupa Gqozo. These operations were executed in co-operation with the intelligence forces of the army.'[6]

Eugene received amnesty for almost all of his submissions, but not for the murder of Japie Maponya and the Nelspruit murders.

He told the TRC amnesty committee: 'There are times when I wish I had never been born. I can't tell you how dirty I feel. I should never have joined the South African Police. We achieved nothing. We left only hatred behind us. There are children who will never know their parents and I will have to carry this cross forever. I am a very private person and don't like to show emotions, but I sympathise with my victims as if they were my own children. That is all I can say.

'I have since met ... the family members of the Motherwell Four and they have accepted my sympathy and apology. I have also expressed my regret to Mr Joe Slovo's children, which they accepted. One of the children said to me: "At least you have faced your demons and come clean, which is far more than can be said for the other perpetrators."

'The proceeds of my book *A Long Night's Damage* [his story as told to the journalist Jeremy Gordin] have been donated through the Presidential Reparations Fund to the victims of apartheid and their families.'[7]

During Eugene's TRC amnesty hearings, two very different women featured in his life: clinical psychologist Pumla Gobodo-Madikizela and Finnish journalist Katia Airola.

At the time, Gobodo-Madikizela worked for the TRC and was present at Eugene's first testimony before the commission on the Motherwell incident. In his testimony he asked to meet the widows of the murdered policemen so he could ask for their forgiveness. Gobodo-Madikizela then decided to conduct a series of interviews with Eugene in prison to find out more about the inner workings of the man she had come to know as 'Prime Evil'.

The result was her book *A Human Being Died that Night*, based on her meetings with Eugene: 'From one point of view De Kock was simply … a criminal found guilty in a court of law of gross acts of inhumanity. But he represented much, much more. He was the embodiment of hundreds of years of conquest, the hitherto sacrosanct aggressor acting in the name of a higher power, even the Higher Power. And now he was disgraced. He stood for every white man with a whip or torch or gun … and now he was defeated … abandoned.'[8]

Gobodo-Madikizela is an attractive woman whose singularly beautiful features radiate compassion. It is easy to feel comfortable in her presence.

On a spring day in 2014, I had an illuminating discussion about forgiveness and reconciliation with her and Candice Mama, daughter of Glenack Masilo Mama, one of the victims of the Nelspruit killings. The youthful Candice is a striking example of the healing power of forgiveness and reconciliation. The Mama family met Eugene in October 2014 and forgave him for the death of their husband and father.

Gobodo-Madikizela told me that after her book was published she advocated reconciliation in various ways, especially in media articles in which she explained why it was time for Eugene de Kock – the face of apartheid-era transgressions – to be paroled. When an offender like him shows sincere remorse, she believes it paves the way for forgiveness and the possibility for reconciliation. 'Showing remorse is the recognition of deep human brokenness and it is also the possibility – the place where it becomes possible – for the perpetrators to reclaim their rights to belonging in the realm of moral humanity,' she writes in one of her articles.[9]

For Gobodo-Madikizela, moral responsibility is critical. An article by author Karina Szczurek pinpoints the importance of Gobodo-Madikizela's work: '[she] identifies what is missing in our democracy: a spirit of human solidarity that transcends the commitment to membership of one's racial group or political party. Her plea is for a shared humanity, for the understanding and acceptance of our diverse grievances, traumas and complicities, and crucially, for the triumph of moral responsibility.'[10]

During one of my visits Eugene suggested that I contact Katia Airola, whom he had met during his TRC hearings. 'We are still friends today and she visits me without fail twice a year,' he explained.

Eugene's friendship with Airola is an improbable one. Born in Finland, she is a leftist journalist who, from 1984 to 1998, worked at the Angolan government's Press Centre. Today she divides her time between Cape Town, Portugal and Angola.

I met Katia at the Kia-Ora Backpackers Lodge where for the past fifteen years she has stayed whenever she is in Pretoria. The guesthouse is opposite the leafy Burgers Park in the city centre, a stone's throw from the old Idasa building where many of the TRC sittings were held. Our initial meeting was slightly confusing: we first had to explain how and where we fitted into Eugene's circle of friends. The next day I picked her up for a visit to Eugene. I kept a low profile. She wanted all of Eugene's attention and drank in the conversation with every fibre of her being. I laughed when the two of them got hot under the collar during a heated discussion about politics and China's influence in Africa. I got to observe Katia closely. She is an attractive woman with generous features, a mop of light hair and smooth skin. I could see why men would like her. The visit was over too quickly.

'Come and have a beer with me,' she said as we stopped at Kia-Ora. It was a Saturday morning. Jacob Mare Street was filled with pedestrians.

I asked her to tell me about meeting Eugene, their friendship, and her impressions of the TRC. No matter how much I read about it or how many broadcasts I watched, it was not the same as talking to someone who had been there.

After resigning as a journalist at the Angolan Press Centre, Katia found herself in Cape Town with nothing much to do and the sickening feeling that she wanted to crawl into a hole and die. That is until she discovered the bookshops. After the war in which Angola gained its independence no bookshops survived and consequently she was starved for books and also very interested in South African history.

'How did your and Eugene's paths cross?' I asked.

'The first time I became aware of Eugene de Kock's existence I was chatting to a friend with one eye on the TV news. Then I suddenly sat bolt upright: a man with absolutely fascinating hands and long, elegant fingers was arranging papers on the desk in front of him. Not only the hands, but the way he moved them, caught my attention. Who was he?

'It was a TRC broadcast, but I was new in South Africa, uninformed about local news. The next day I went to Exclusive Books and bought everything I could lay my hands on about the TRC and De Kock. In under a week I had read it all and realised that, as usual after all wars and revolutions, a scapegoat had been chosen on whose shoulders everyone could heap blame. My reading material described a man who was made the scapegoat for apartheid crimes. This shocked my sense for justice. I had discovered a new field of interest.'

Chin cupped in hand, I listened to Katia. Two mechanics had arrived in the meantime and decided to occupy the bench beside us.

'But the man, Eugene, fascinated me,' Katia continued. 'At that stage I really felt physically drawn to him. He sat there with an emotionless face. He has a strong appeal that speaks to most women with whom he comes into contact. I don't think he is aware of it.

'My next step was to attend the TRC sittings in Cape Town to find out how things worked. Then I just got on the train to Pretoria, arranged accommodation at Kia-Ora and attended the sittings at the Idasa building. Until the end of the TRC my life comprised travelling to Pretoria whenever Eugene testified, but also to Durban, Port Elizabeth and East London. Not only to listen to him, but also to others who had applied for amnesty and to see how Eugene weighed up against them.'

'Was he different from the others?'

'Yes, he was different. His brutal honesty made a deep impression – also his long, sensitive fingers and almost painful politeness. Back in Cape Town I began to walk, ten to fifteen kilometres a day. I lost weight; my life started revolving around Eugene and his situation. I was alive again. "I am going to meet the person behind the mask of a murderer," I said to my family. They thought I had lost my marbles.'

I asked her how she managed to do it.

'After about a year I asked his advocate if I could give him a book. He said it was fine since Eugene was a book lover, but that I couldn't give it to him myself. He would give it to Eugene. The next day I took a copy of *King Leopold's Ghost* to him. The following day his advocate asked me my name and said Eugene wanted to thank me.'

I wondered about Katia's choice of book. Back at home that afternoon, I learnt that the book is about the politically and morally corrupt king Leopold II of Belgium who colonised the Congo in the late 19th century. During his rule over the Belgian Congo, there were countless atrocities; about half the population – an estimated ten million people – died.

Author Adam Hochschild devotes an entire chapter of *King Leopold's Ghost* to Joseph Conrad's *Heart of Darkness*. Conrad was a steamship captain on the Congo River during the early years of Belgian colonisation; *Heart of Darkness* appears to be based on his experiences there. Hochschild's research led him to four men who could have been prototypes for the evil Mr Kurtz in Conrad's book: all men who boasted that they could kill.[11]

Then I understood. Katia had a very specific message for Eugene. She wanted him to understand that she had empathy for him – that he had been a cog in the machine of an evil government.

'I received a little yellow card, which I still cherish,' Katia continued. 'In the brief, polite message the word "support" was used four times and it led me to understand that he knew I had been there for his testimony. I don't know how he knew this – we sat on opposite sides of quite a large hall; neither of us has good vision and could not see where the other was looking. I was possibly quite conspicuous because I wore African kaftans at that time.

'Through his advocate and the prison warders I started sending him letters and sweets. He told me he could no longer receive books because the warders at C-Max took them away from him. But when I asked him what he wanted, he answered almost boyishly: any kind of chocolate. I started buying chocolates until we found out what his favourite was – Côte d'Or. He liked dark chocolate.'

The mechanics ordered rum and Coke. 'I've seen you here before,' the one with the dark hair said to Katia.

'Mind your own business,' she grumbled, turning her back on him.

'The next step was to arrange a meeting. I had to be careful; people around me tried to find out who I was. I didn't want to embarrass him either; ludicrous women who become fascinated by prisoners is an old cliché.

'Then I had a good look at the guards, the men who had passed the correspondence between me and Eugene. I decided to flirt with the fattest and most unattractive one until he asked me: "Do you want to meet him? I could take you in during the break."'

By this time Katia had scrutinised Eugene so many times during sittings that her impressions of him had already been formed. She found him to be shy, polite and somewhat inquisitive. 'Meeting him for the first time, I noticed he had a strong handshake and a lovely smile.'

Later, she decided to take food for him to the prison. 'Home cooking as a variation on jail food. Yet he said of the prison food: "The food is not bad, I had worse in the defence force." For the Pretoria sittings I sometimes made him lunch. He developed a taste for *bacalhau*, dried and salted Portuguese fish.'

At the end of the TRC process, Katia asked Eugene if she could continue to correspond with him. 'I was learning Afrikaans and told him that he could write to me in his own language. In English he wrote about two pages, but his first letter in Afrikaans was fourteen pages long. But the pen got too heavy for him; I would write, and on occasion he would phone me.'

I thought about Eugene's wife and children having left the country in the nineties, a few years before Katia's appearance, and the divorce soon afterwards.

I had e-mailed Katia previously to ask whether she would put something in writing about her friendship with Eugene but I had not received anything. I asked her why.

She replied without hesitation: 'I must admit, I wrote you pages and pages about Eugene and then deleted them all, because they revealed more about me than about him. It's just like Pumla Gobodo-Madikizela's book: it's about Pumla's reaction to Eugene.'

The sun, and the two mechanics, had moved on; there were empty glasses and beer bottles on the table. We said our goodbyes.

Weeks after our visit to the prison, I received an e-mail from Katia who was then in Portugal: 'Somewhere I read that during his trial Eugene was asked to outline his work. His cold – defiant – answer was: "Assassin for the state". The media latched on to this statement as an admission that he was indeed an assassin. But they ignored the most important part of the statement: "for the state".

'I got the idea that he got bored during the tedious court proceedings and that he then gave confrontational answers to stupid questions. He has a sharp sense of humour and irony,' Katia wrote.

I read into his remark a hidden message from Eugene the outsider, the branded scapegoat. Buried in it is confession on the one side, but a kind of redemption on the other. While not the sort of recognition he had craved since his childhood, his court case and the amnesty hearings that followed gave Eugene an undeniable stature. He had become well known in South Africa – in his own words, a kind of 'icon … too repellent … to be true'. People around the world took note of him during his amnesty hearings.

As a BBC news programme said of Eugene in 1998, 'in the post-apartheid era of truth and reconciliation he has also become something of a hero, a man of integrity in a community of denial.'[12]

During one of his amnesty hearings Eugene remarked that he

felt defiled, dirty, that he sometimes wished he had never been born. He realised the consequences of his deeds, mostly devastating, on the lives of a number of people, that he had caused them unforgivable pain.[13] For Eugene, redemption was only possible if he confessed his offences openly and honestly, faced his demons.

Eugene's public confessions meant that as a persona he took on different meanings for different people. Some empathised: in their opinion, he was the only one being punished for the crimes of many others. Others, who could not make peace with the new dispensation, regarded Eugene as a hero for all the wrong reasons, even though he does not, by his own admission, sympathise with the rightwing. To a number of family members of Vlakplaas and Security Branch victims, he brought closure with the information he provided about how and why their loved ones had died.

His brutal honesty about his offences, his acknowledgement that it was gravely wrong, and his genuine remorse sets him apart from many other apartheid offenders. It is proof of his humanity. His confessions brought deliverance not only for the families concerned, but also for himself. I concluded, after talking to many former policemen, that only those who had embraced the opportunity to speak out honestly and openly about their offences could experience any measure of redemption.

The families of Eugene's victims generally reacted positively to his admission of guilt and attempts to reach out to them. Felicia Mathe is the widow of Theophilus Sidima, also known as MK Viva Dlodlo, a senior MK commander who was murdered in May 1987 by the Security Branch. After Eugene's testimony before the TRC she sent the following message to the commission: 'Mr De Kock, during this meeting, divulged all the information pertaining to this incident to me and I left the meeting with the distinct feeling that he had been most honest and sincere in his dealings with me ... I did not think I would ever be able to say this, but I am extremely grateful to Mr De Kock for his help and assistance and I wish to convey my gratitude to him for having helped me and some of the other victims of this particular very sad incident.'[14]

'The families want closure,' said Eugene when I asked him about this. 'They want to know how their loved ones died, what they were wearing, what their last words were. I alone – as the murderer, the one who was there with them in that most intimate moment of death – can give these answers to those who are left behind. It is very important to do so.'

15

C-Max

Eugene staked his claim wherever he found himself – his bar was his ward, the field of operations his hunting ground. But here in Pretoria Central, the lion was caged.

I kept one eye on the tuck-shop queue. When it shortened, I would join. The prisoners sitting around us talking, animated, to their visitors, looked so harmless, so ordinary – except for the orange overalls.

But this semblance of normality was misleading. Most of them had been convicted of serious crimes. One shouldn't delude oneself about what goes on behind prison walls. Eugene described it as a merciless place where countless inmates give over to gangsterism, drugs and fraud.

Sitting in the sun in the prison courtyard, I had to keep reminding myself that I was in the bowels of a place of punishment and penance.

When he was sent to C-Max – Pretoria Central's maximum security section – in September 1997, practically all of Eugene's police friends and brothers in arms deserted him. Sealed up behind steel and concrete, he was forgotten. He and his wife Audrey had already divorced and she had emigrated with their two small boys. He felt abandoned, by God and humankind alike.

C-Max is designed for violent 'problem prisoners' who are

classified as highly dangerous.[1] Inmates are kept in solitary confinement for 23 hours a day. I wondered how a person could function normally after being in solitary confinement for over two and a half years.

What goes through a man's thoughts when he is locked up with his regret, rage and anguish? It became, for Eugene, a struggle for a different kind of survival – one for which he had to develop a new set of instincts. In a report by his former psychiatrist, Dr JP Verster, Eugene alleges that he was tortured emotionally in C-Max.

Verster, who treated Eugene for post-traumatic stress disorder (PTSD), writes in his report that it took him almost six months to win Eugene's trust – and that Eugene had no 'sociopathic' (psychopathic) tendencies, that he was a person with a conscience.[2]

Eugene and his legal representative decided not to lodge a complaint about his detention in C-Max. 'I had clearly committed very serious crimes and had to take my punishment. I endured the terrible conditions in C-Max for 31 months.'[3] Furthermore, Eugene told Dr Verster:

> When I asked why I had been placed in C-Max, I was told it was because the psychologists wanted to experiment on me. Mrs Helena du Toit, a social worker at the prison at the time, confirmed this statement.
>
> I was repeatedly tortured emotionally. For instance, they left lights on throughout the night or shone them directly into my face. They hammered on the cell door constantly. From the observation platform above my cell there was always hammering and loud noise. I could only move around for an hour a day – I could exercise in a cage of 1×5 metres. They tampered with my food. I was allowed no visitors. I was completely isolated.

Later, when I was in Phase 2 and again in a death row cell, I had human contact for the first time in a few years. After some time I was transferred to the general part of the prison where I was kept reasonably isolated and eventually, from August 2005 – after a period of almost eleven years – I was treated as an ordinary prisoner and held in Medium B. There I had more time to myself as well as the privacy of a single cell.

I was so depressed in C-Max. Mrs Lourentia de Kock [no relation], a psychologist, was the only person who helped me during this deep depression during which I had suicidal tendencies ...

Other than her support, I received no additional therapy. I had no help at all from the prison psychologists. Occasionally a visiting psychiatrist would prescribe medication, which neither treated my post-traumatic stress disorder (PTSD) nor brought any relief.

During one visiting hour a visitor mistakenly dropped a heavy object. On hearing this I experienced a serious panic attack. When I came around I realised that the sound had taken me straight back to the bush in Angola, to a contact. My PTSD was, at this stage, out of control. I also experienced problems with a detached retina and nearly lost an eye before I could persuade the district physician to allow me to receive treatment at the Pretoria Eye Institute.

I feel I was psychologically and physically abused, and emotionally broken, during my 31 months in C-Max. I underwent months of sleep deprivation and long periods of sensory deprivation. For years I saw no daylight. These actions were all of extended duration. I feel I was excessively punished during this time and started to recover from solitary confinement in C-Max only much later.

I realise now, too, that I never really stood a chance and could not defend myself. The worst was the knowledge that the people who were with me, and who had committed much worse crimes than I had, had got off scot-free. I was picked to be punished! I feel no bitterness towards the judge, but am, in every way possible, bitter towards those who issued my orders, and those who were aggressors with me but who now walk free, enjoying their lives.

And I never see the sun.[4]

The struggle between doing the right thing and facing the consequences – thus taking responsibility for your actions – on one side and the knowledge that you are the only one being punished on the other, must eat away at you like a cancer. I tried to broach this with Eugene a few times, but he remained evasive.

So, I started looking around for more information about this dark time of his life. Among Eugene's documents is an insightful article by journalist Jann Turner that appeared in the *Mail & Guardian* on 28 May 1999. Turner's father, Rick, was an anti-apartheid activist and political scientist affiliated to the University of Natal [now the University of KwaZulu-Natal]. In 1978, Turner was shot through the window of his Durban house and died in 13-year-old Jann's arms. While the perpetrators were never found, it was widely believed that he was shot by the security police.

Turner visited Eugene several times in jail after he made it known that he wanted to talk to her: he had information about the members of the Security Branch whose names had come up in the investigation into her father's murder. She did not expect to like him, she writes. 'His glasses are so thick you can't see the colour of his eyes. I found I watched his mouth more than his eyes. His politeness and intelligence disarmed me. His shyness took me by surprise ...'[5]

Turner experienced Eugene as 'starved for company and good conversation'. They talked, among other things, about guilt and forgiveness. 'He talked about the horror that comes back to him at night. How he smells it, tastes it, sees it and can't sleep.'[6]

Although Turner writes of Eugene with hints of compassion, she notes: 'I remember at the time I found that reassuring, such a man shouldn't be able to sleep at night ... he described himself as a "veteran of lost ideologies".'

Three days after their first meeting, De Kock was moved to C-Max; when Turner saw him again, he was thin, depressive and disoriented. He spoke a great deal about death and felt that he deserved to die. In her view he was overwhelmed by remorse.[7]

A handful of interventions were, indeed, part of Eugene's detention in C-Max. Two women, psychologist Lourentia de Kock and social worker Helena du Toit, were involved in his emotional recovery process. Lourentia de Kock began treating him as early as 1996 and saw him until October 2001. In 2002 she wrote as follows in a clinical report:

'We met weekly initially, and then monthly. Mr De Kock is a highly functioning, intellectual person, with excellent insight into himself. His condition is strongly connected with his present prison situation and he is being treated for major depression. He is apsychotic. He is fully conscious and orientated in terms of place, time and person. No personality disorders have been detected.

'Mr De Kock provided excellent co-operation during his individual psychotherapeutic sessions ... He shows intense remorse in respect of the actions that led to his conviction and is highly motivated not to repeat them. His present circumstances have had a destructive influence on him, which have impacted his functioning negatively.'[8]

Helena du Toit, head social worker at Pretoria Central at the time, reported that she had counselled Eugene since 1996 and that topics such as post-traumatic stress disorder, his suicidal tendencies during his incarceration in C-Max as well as his feelings of despair had come up.[9]

According to Du Toit, Eugene's only moral support at that stage was his aunt. 'Both his parents have passed away. His brother does not have regular contact with him. The prisoner was divorced in 1997. Currently his ex-wife and two sons keep in contact by messages. The prisoner was, and still is, of the opinion that his ex-wife and children are in danger. He fears that his former colleagues or members of the Security Police who were in power during the apartheid era may use his family to prevent him from testifying truthfully during the hearings [of the TRC] … He feels abandoned and that his family is suffering because of his actions.

'The prisoner is a person with integrity and an overdeveloped sense of loyalty. He also has high morals. He is talented, ambitious and not inherently criminal. No negative behaviour has occurred in prison. The prisoner is not involved in gangsterism or drugs … He has been able to build relationships with fellow prisoners. He is respected and accepted by the wider prison community.'[10]

Lourentia de Kock's report recommended that Eugene be released to invest his knowledge and abilities into the country as a citizen. Her report was part of Eugene's first application for presidential pardon, submitted in May 2002.

This request for pardon to erstwhile President Thabo Mbeki included representations from generals Mike Geldenhuys, Johann

Coetzee and Johan van der Merwe. Eugene was no longer being held in C-Max by this time.

As part of their submission, the three generals described the circumstances of political unrest, conflict and violence that had prevailed when Eugene had served in the police force. They claimed that covert actions such as those executed by Vlakplaas operatives were necessary, because South Africa had practically been a war zone.

'Seen in its proper perspective … there can be no doubt that this sort of scenario led to the foundation upon which sound and normal policing, namely the will and desire to protect and serve … being seriously undermined and even destroyed … Subsequent to his redeployment in the Republic of South Africa, Colonel De Kock was posted to the ranks of the Security Branch's fighting unit … [I]n this role he was intimately involved with violence and death, often on a daily basis … Very few people would have survived and been able to face the world at large if subjected to the same work exigencies and experiences that Colonel De Kock was.'[11]

The three generals requested Eugene's deeds to be seen in the light of the political climate of the apartheid era and that he should be reprieved as a result.

His application was rejected.

16

Nothing will ever be the same again

One sunny day in 2013, I attended a family day at Pretoria Central, rechristened Kgosi Mampuru II Correctional Centre. Long queues of visitors clustered at reception, beach umbrellas under their arms, camping chairs and cool boxes in their hands, looking as if they were on their way to a beach picnic. The pleasure of an informal contact visit of a few hours is a privilege prisoners are granted only once or twice a year.

Minibusses transported the prisoners to a sports field with a high fence. A dirty-white marquee had been pitched; with the other visitors, I made a beeline to its shade. I spread a rug out on the grass and peered into the cool box. Everything Eugene had asked for was there.

It felt like a public holiday. Kwaito music blared over the loud-speakers; a queue formed at the tuck-shop tent. There were cold drinks, sandwiches, pap and meat, and whole iced cakes for sale.

To one side, in long orange rows under a smaller tent, sat the prisoners, waiting expectantly for their visitors. With every new announcement they stared at the warders at the entrance gate.

'What food should I bring?' I'd wanted to know from Eugene the previous week.

'Steak,' he'd said immediately. 'A big chunk of good meat, cooked medium. And chocolate, pudding and salad, please.'

The ideal would obviously have been to bring a steak still sizzling from the coals. Alas, the Spur steak was cold after a night in the fridge – I had to be in the queue at the prison by eight o'clock that morning. Eventually it took Eugene more than an hour to eat the 300-gram steak. His body was just not accustomed to that much meat any more. He was so full, then, that he ate only a small piece of chocolate and didn't touch the salad. He shared the leftover food with his fellow inmates.

Things got lively. To loud cheering, a woman in a tight-fitting denim outfit started swaying her hips suggestively in front of the food stall.

Eugene turned away from the noise. We talked about music and he told me how he used to listen to Johnny Cash, among others. He also likes classical music. 'When I write I always put my earphones on and listen to Vivaldi ... I'm mad about his "Spring". It makes me peaceful, but also makes the blood surge and bubble in the veins. I don't know why it affects me that way. While I can't play a musical instrument or read music, I can pick up a false note immediately – it's like a blow to the chin.'

I leaned forward.

'Can I ask a serious question? Something I've been wondering about for a long time.'

He nodded.

'Could it be that certain commanding officers – how shall I put it? – function on a certain level, a level determined by their emotional make-up? Could one say that every commander has an emotional Achilles heel?'

I explained that the question arose from a conversation I had with a former commanding officer in the police. The man expressed very little emotion; I wondered whether his limited register of emotions was why he was such a successful commander.

'I see his inability to engage emotionally as a defence mechanism, nothing more,' said Eugene. 'But at night, while he sleeps or lies awake, when he is alone, he knows everything: what is just, unjust, wrong. Some commanders stayed for only a month at Vlakplaas, others two weeks, some nine years – or three and a half years under continuous combat pressure in Ovamboland.

'But then one morning, in the middle of Pretoria, it feels like you're having a heart attack ... after running all the tests, the hospital says you're fine. Then the dreams and the nightmares start. You're too scared to go to sleep and when you wake up, you have sweated right through the mattress. And then you are really alone, with no one to talk to, and the load just never gets any lighter. You learn to live with it, but the uninvited guests stay in your dreams and thoughts, day and night.'

We were no longer talking about the other commanding officer. Eugene's gaze was intense; words fired ever quicker from his mouth.

'Then one day you decide fuck them all, and fuck yourself, and you just keep going. But the load still doesn't get any lighter. The men in the grey suits and black shoes say, "More! More! You're good at this." It brings them prestige, honour, but for me and commanders like me the load gets heavier.'

Eugene reached for a cool drink and snapped it open.

He struggled to sit comfortably – tried sitting cross-legged, but it didn't work: a remnant of the injuries he sustained during the Border War.

Suddenly the family day was over. It was three times longer than the usual hour-long visit, but even this was too short; there were still questions I had wanted to ask.

'See you on Sunday,' I said, while Eugene rolled up the rug and closed the beach umbrella. He slid it carefully back into its plastic sleeve. Passionate farewell rituals were taking place all around us. The cool box was light. He joined the inmates already in line for the minibusses back to the cells.

That Friday morning he called from a payphone. He had queued for a long time: each floor is supposed to have a phone but only one phone on the three floors near his cell was working. I heard shouting and jostling around him. He swore under his breath.

'Let's cancel Sunday's visit. There is no water. Even the fire department's reservoir is empty now. The conditions are dreadful and will be even worse in the visitors' area. I still have enough water to drink and can flush the toilet once more. I've eaten no uncooked food since yesterday because the kitchen doesn't have water either.'

I asked him why the water supply had not been repaired.

'They probably will at some point, but I must admit this morning I feel like a tired old bear,' he said.

I thought about the prisoners getting their supper at three o'clock in the afternoon then being locked into their cells for the night. Eugene is alone, then, in his cell until the next morning. He usually makes himself a small supper with the two pieces of cooked chicken he receives. 'I make a mixed salad of tomato, green pepper, cucumber and a bit of onion, with a splash of vinegar and a quarter of a teaspoon of Aromat or a pinch of salt. It's enough. With a cooked potato chopped into it.'

An extract from a letter I had received earlier from Eugene also streaked through my thoughts. It had worried me because it told of how his experience of the world had shrunk: 'I've always liked cooking with herbs and spices, to experiment with tastes. But food – you know, people really buy cat and dog food to eat. I have already thought about how I would cook mouthwatering dishes with it if I get out. Onions, garlic with tomato, *putupap* [maize porridge] with spices, and other vegetables. I have no problem with that.'

An inconceivable world, on the other end of the phone line.

In his book *Fado*, André P Brink explains that the Portuguese fado is a song 'in which a timeless melancholy is expressed, a nostalgic searching back to a past that is long gone, a deep yearning for a future sensed far in the distance … a call in which yesterday, today and tomorrow will be united … it is always an admission of insignificance against a fate that conquers all.'[1]

I imagine this is the kind of *saudade*, or melancholy, that Eugene experiences regularly in prison. As expected, his is a sombre existence. It is the same thing, over and over, day in and day out. 'It's a grey hell of continuous noise, stench and boredom – everything is coated in dust and rubbish. I move around, but not enough. I don't have a problem with moving among the other prisoners, but they are loud and use drugs. Dagga, *nyaope* … anything you can think of – it's all a big problem here.'

He is a stickler for neatness and has tried to maintain certain standards. 'I get furious and hopeless when some of the inmates throw pieces of food for the rivers of rats that stream past in the corridors every night. But I scrub my cell, keep it as sterile and hygienic as possible. I make a plan, with the cockroaches too and the other pests and plagues.

'Many of the prisoners let themselves go. Personal hygiene and care is the first thing that slips. This is where discipline comes in. I shower every single day of my life. In the morning only the first two or three inmates get hot water – after that, it's cold. But I shower winter and summer, whether the water's cold or not.'

He also told me that he purposely kept his cell in a slight degree of disorder and for a reason. I gathered it had to do with the regular searches to which the inmates are subjected at any time of the day

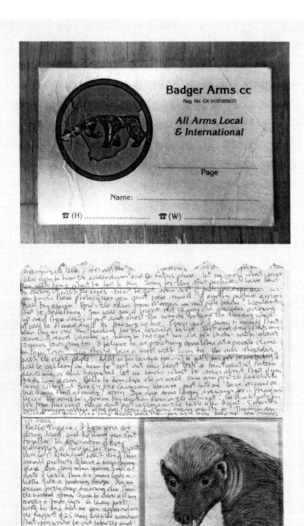

Top: The business card of Badger Arms, a company Eugene was involved in and which imported and exported weapons in the early 1990s. **Bottom:** A letter the spy Kevin Woods wrote to Eugene when incarcerated in a Zimbabwean jail.

or night. 'I get by with very few possessions. The day I am out of here, I'll be able to carry everything I will ever need on my back.'

Gangs control life in the prison. According to a former C-Max prisoner, they even have their own language, called 'Stariaan'.[2] Loners who have no gang affiliations are called 'franse'. Eugene was a frans.

'I can count the friendships I have made with prisoners in the last twenty years on one hand,' he said. 'They will tell you, also: De Kock is a *frans*, he does his own thing. In the prison hierarchy I am classified as an assassin. It's a status others aspire to. Paedophiles are the lowest on the prison ranking. I have never been a member of any gang. I have needed to defend myself before. I will take anyone on – with my bare hands, any time, in any way.'

'But you're in your sixties!' I said in disbelief.

His smile was sardonic. 'I am strong and fit and fear no one. I understand the system and play the game. And I don't look for trouble.'

I was shocked that Eugene has to defend himself physically against other inmates. In the book 6 *Ster: Binne die ingewande van Pretoria-Sentraal* by former prisoner T Rex, I read: 'In prison only one rule counts between the gangsters: Do it to others before they can do it to you.'

This is the law of the jungle and of warfare – the very law that applied during the Bush War and at Vlakplaas.

In Rex's book I learnt that survival methods drive ordinary prisoners' day-to-day existence: 'There are a few things you can choose: get dagga-drunk and forget; learn to satisfy the other gangsters with sex; steal something from another gangster; or survive by scoring off other gangsters.'[3]

Eugene had to develop his own survival strategy too. He was one of the lucky ones who received financial support from outside for practically the entire time he was imprisoned.

When I started visiting Eugene regularly, people approached me, increasingly, to arrange visits for them. I became the unwitting intermediary for former comrades who wanted to make contact. So it happened that Pine Pienaar, chairperson of the Koevoet Bond vir Veterane (the society of Koevoet veterans) phoned me in 2012 to find out if they could assist, possibly by buying Eugene a new pair of boots. Eugene was surprised and very grateful – his boots dated back to 1994 and had just the previous week started coming apart. He had repaired them over the years with glue, but now they were beyond fixing.

He knew exactly what he wanted when I told him about the offer: 'I wear only Hi-Tec boots that come to just above the ankle. Leather is easier to clean and I have Dubbin.'

He told me that while he was moved by the sudden assistance after eighteen years, he was also sceptical: 'The bitterness is just beneath the skin sometimes, which is not others' fault but my own,' he said. 'But I don't know what's going on outside. I must be careful not to alienate people who don't deserve it and who just mean well – not to become my own worst enemy.'

In due time, the Koevoet Bond collected R12 000 to replace Eugene's computer when his old one gave up the ghost. General Hans Dreyer, his former Koevoet commander, contributed R2 000.

Eugene's perspective, however, was that in C-Max, and initially in Medium B, he'd had very little moral support. He still wrestled with the feeling that the SAP and his former comrades left him in the lurch. But studying the massive collection of notes, letters and documents on the hard drive that he gave me for safekeeping, I did find a few faithful supporters.

Wildlife artist Helena Mulder, whom Eugene met during the TRC sittings when she testified about the death of her husband, kept in touch through correspondence, sketches and wildlife paintings she made for him. Katia Airola visited him twice a year and offered moral support through letters, books and journals. A few loyal fellow ex-policemen also stayed in contact.

Another person with whom he corresponded regularly was Kevin Woods, a former senior member of Robert Mugabe's feared Central Intelligence Organisation (CIO) in Zimbabwe. Woods was a double agent for the National Party government, sentenced to death in Zimbabwe in November 1988 for politically motivated crimes for the apartheid government. He was held in the Chikurubi maximum security prison 15 kilometres east of Harare. Eugene persuaded Ferdi Barnard and others to correspond with him, building up a support network.

From 2005 Eugene was eventually treated as an 'ordinary' prisoner, held in a single cell in Medium B. His diary entries from that year show the daily challenges and realities of prison life, and that that survival and parole became all-consuming. I quote parts of this diary directly.[4]

---

12 AUGUST

1. Phoned dentist. Ordered two gum guards. He says I will have to come in to fit them, but don't know when that will happen, nobody and nothing works in this place.

2. Saw Dr Verster. He wants me to undergo narco-analysis to get everything on tape. He says he injects Ritalin, a stimulant, and Valium. As far as I know

Ritalin is a sedative for hyperactive children. I get the idea there is more to the analysis than my best interests and my post-traumatic stress disorder diagnosis. Now he and others will say that I am paranoid and see the world as an enemy. Why am I so 'careful'? …

Why does it take nearly five years to get my medical files and documents? Why the delay? Why – too many whys.

3. Had a problem at the gate to go through to the psychologist. The student/new [staff] member has absolutely no manners and this led to a discussion between me and a member (senior) who resolved the situation. There is virtually, as in 98% of the time, no control in the prison.

13 August

1. Verster cancelled his visit.

14 August

1. Visit from Ina and her husband … M van Biljon cannot come. Blackie Swart was sick and he could not come either.

2. A Coloured man, presumably [from a] gang, don't know which 'number', wants my weights. Don't know why he sought me out. Anticipate problems because

Top: Notes written by Eugene about his experiences in C-Max.
Bottom: Some of Eugene's diaries, as well as a telephone book that dates from the Vlakplaas era.

in the whole prison he sought me out to borrow my weights.

15 AUGUST

1. Visit from Advocate James Clark [one of Eugene's previous legal advisors]. Going to make statements.

2. Bad flu and feel very sick.

3. The same Coloured man and another man came to my cell; he said he wants my weights. Says that I can have my weights back when I need them. He says he stays in Medium A – has a scar on his cheek. He is insistent. I don't think it is about the weights as such – it's about having to pay him to use my own weights, a question of domination by the gang. He, the leader, must seek out the big man and dominate him.

I mix or interact with very few people and ask nothing from anyone – I fear the future as far as this person and his group is concerned, whoever they are. I have already been here for almost three full weeks and now suddenly he wants the weights – it must be for another reason – the weights are just a ruse. They have already discussed this and really intend something else. I will have to be very vigilant, but there aren't solutions for everything in prison, you are alone. If needs be I will defend myself against him and his group … rather than getting into trouble. Will never give up.

2. There are, dead simply, no warders in the prison. Everyone is off because it's payday. It is desperate times when the inmates complain about the staff not doing their work.

16 AUGUST

1. Flu very bad.

2. Gary and Alet [Wright] won't be able to visit on Sunday.

3. Discussed matter of the gang member with Nardies – told him it is about the theft of my computer and not about the weights.

4. Arranged for clothes to be made that fit.

5. Clear that some of the other white prisoners think their sentences will be reduced if I do something illegal that they can report – very irritating because I simply don't break the rules.

6. Received medication from the medical personnel at 14:30: Warfarin, Zokor and Adalat and Prexum.

7. A medical staff member brought it to my attention that the other inmates say I get preferential treatment – this matter is becoming boring because they do nothing for themselves, they are just lazy and useless and can't pull themselves together.

8. Walked a few laps – not too bad but I can feel my nose and throat are blocked – ears completely blocked too.

9. Strange how contact lenses degenerate after about the 10th to 12th day – probably from cleaning and protein build-up – also it is very dirty here and there is lots of dust. The chances of pulmonary tuberculosis, as miners get, is far greater here than in a mine from all the muck and disease in the air – a pigsty is healthier because there is better ventilation. The prison is generally on autopilot.

17 AUGUST

1. Spoke to Colette Dekker in connection with medical matters. There has clearly been NO progress – for whatever reason. I may need to think about getting another legal representative.

18 AUGUST

1. Flu is better but far from cured.

2. Have started devoting more time to studies – it has now become more bearable to learn and pay attention.

3. I hear they are confiscating computers and equipment from those who have unauthorised items

on their computers. I have nothing illegal on mine and thus fear nothing.

4. Almost no staff members today. Large numbers of prisoners are crowding at the gates waiting for someone to come past.

19 AUGUST

Consultation with Dr Verster. He is trying hard to get me to undergo narcoanalysis. Asked searching questions about Japie Maponya – who had shot him, also about the Nelspruit shooting. Maybe he wants to help, but I think it has more to do with his friendship with the judge who heard my case. I get the idea that he [Verster] is getting itchy because he can't dominate me. I asked him what it would achieve if we did the narcoanalysis – talking about things won't help, even less so if he can't treat me while I am in prison or even outside.

I get the idea he is eager for knowledge and might want to use the incident as case study material, to find out everything possible about the Generals (or anyone else who could be compromised). There is no doubt he thinks I am the most stupid, idiotic fucker who has ever breathed … he battles with the crimes committed by others that I tell him about …

15 SEPTEMBER

Got called to the head of the unit's office. He is very

full of himself and spiteful – I told him that my milk was not fit for drinking – he simply smiled complacently. The milk cartons are badly damaged and milk has leaked into the bag – some of the cartons are wet – looks as if there could be damaged packages [for medical reasons Eugene had permission to use fat-free milk].

The head talks the whole time about my 'preferential treatment'. Won't say who says so, could it just be him? I remember how he said to Clive Derby-Lewis that Derby-Lewis still needed to get to know him. He asked Derby-Lewis if he 'knew' him – suggesting trouble down the line. My milk had been there all morning – was lukewarm – had definitely been flung down with the aim to damage it. It looked as if someone had trampled on the bag, the plastic bag was very dirty – the head said that he would organise with BOSASA that I should get fat-free milk.

Asked if my contact lenses were cosmetic – he would talk to the doctor about them – said the whole time that I am getting preferential treatment. I asked for everyone to get the same preferential treatment – then they can also be thrown into C-Max and be treated just as I was.

16 September

Sent reports on: a) Spoiling of milk b) Report about spoiling by the Department of Correctional Services c) Application for contact lenses d) Application for milk e) Why there is constant reference to my receiving preferential treatment f) The handling of visitors and their being searched.

3 OCTOBER

Phoned H and thanked him for the visit. He says and confirms that he will come on the 14th – and then says that this is a Friday and that he will thus come on the 15th. I must just tell him whatever I need, no matter what it is. He says he will bring his daughter with him and asks whether I mind. I replied no, I don't mind, but I now know this visit and bringing his daughter with him is designed to 'soften' me. He and the others, and he in particular, thought nothing of destroying my family, stealing from me and bankrupting me. I told him I would phone again.

7 OCTOBER

1. Saw Advocate James Clark. Handed over more statements.

2. Talked to a woman in the passage at legal visits. Very friendly. After all the problems I had getting my computer, everyone is now so pleasant. What a bunch of sick buggers.

3. My fresh milk – 1 litre – fat-free is not available. They say there was a problem with the deliveries.

4. No Effexor [an antidepressant] since Monday. The first three nights the nightmares were terrible and unmanageable. Irritation level is high but controllable. Ringing in my ears and a sort of 'static' in my head is still very bad. Damage to my hearing and who knows what else. Nightmares are still very bad. So much so I feel as if I am being suffocated and almost fall off the bed to put an end to the nightmare. Luckily the cables I have strung [next to the bed] help me not to tumble down.

8 OCTOBER

1. Still no milk.

2. There was a problem at the telephone this afternoon. Prisoner in cell no. 17 tried to intimidate me by saying that he had to use the telephone before anyone else and that I was corrupting the telephone users. He didn't stand in the queue, went walking around, then wanted to push in at the front. I made it clear to him that I was not one of the useless whites who let themselves be intimidated, that numerous intimidators did not scare me in the least. I called staff member Brian Pedi who resolved the issue and let everyone go their separate ways without any trouble.

Surviving in Pretoria Central is a monotonous business. To stay occupied, Eugene took various courses, including one in journalism. This allowed him to have a computer in his cell. Later he started practising what he had learned by writing articles and book reviews for newspapers such as *Son* and *The New Age*.

For years he also worked in the prison's woodwork section. But his diary suggests that the constant uncertainty about his possible parole later overshadowed everything.

By mid-2014 Eugene had already been in prison for twenty years. Did his sentence bring about a change in the man who was once the assassin for the state?

In the most important ways, yes: he showed remorse for his actions, and appears to have gained true insight into the sorrow and grief his actions had caused others. He will never tread the path of violence again either.

Yet his resentment towards those who deserted him is a persistent theme. While I could understand the incredible bitterness he must once have felt, I had to ask him whether it wasn't time to let it go: bitterness, in my experience, is an all-consuming emotion that bars you from living a fulfilled, meaningful life.

I also felt that he could use his experiences in jail to inspire people on the outside. His penitence, resilience and will to survive could perhaps make people see their own lives differently.

'You have a chance to be human, to be normal again when you walk out of prison,' I said to him one day. 'No more war and death and bitterness. You can start working on a new legacy. After twenty years of purgatory, could you become a mentor and example for others?'

He looked at me closely.

'I don't know how to see myself. I don't feel like a mentor,' he answered. 'People can note my behaviour, and then disapprove or approve. I regard myself as just another life, no more important than anyone else … a minute speck in the universe, completely insignificant.'

He laughed. 'My father would have said: "Gene, you are so full of *kak*." So let me think about your question.'

I enquired about his solitary life in prison, the heartache, the grief.

'I allow myself just five minutes per day to torment myself or yearn for what I no longer have,' he replied. 'Then I let it go.'

'And how do you see life now, after everything that you – all of you – have done?'

'Let me explain it this way: in the book *Op soek na generaal Mannetjies Mentz*,[5] the daughter tells her father, who returns from exile to his devastated farm, that everything will be all right again, everything will be the same. To this, her father – who, meanwhile, has become such a "quiet man" – replies, "Nothing will ever be the same again."

'Whatever we do, we must shield those we love from hurt. And there must be no regrets ever for having known, cared for and for having loved one another. When I look behind me, all I see is shattered lives and places, the distance between each devastating event only a matter of time. I can never, ever go back into that desert. I won't. Nothing will ever be the same again.'

17

Light at the end of the tunnel

Like most prisoners, Eugene yearned constantly for freedom. His diaries show that, year after year, he focused all his energy on possible parole or a presidential pardon. The planning and work around this dominated his days.

In a letter to me in 2013 he described what he went through emotionally during an application for parole: 'For the past while I've slept too little and am tired all the time. It's not a "sick tired", if I can put it that way, but stress, and also the incarceration. I am a *veldmens* [nature lover], always will be – it's just how I am.'

Shortly after the dawn of the new millennium, Eugene made his first application for presidential pardon; since 2011 he has applied several times, unsuccessfully, for parole. In 2002 and 2003 he submitted requests for presidential pardon to former President Thabo Mbeki. Receipt of his requests was acknowledged, but there was no further reaction to them. In 2009, Eugene requested a meeting with President Jacob Zuma through Sarel Kruger. 'I met Sarel when he had a friend in the local prison. He was in the SAP. Armoury. After a while, we became friendly. In 2002 and 2003 he [Sarel] took my first request for presidential pardon to the president's office. He also facilitated the meeting with President Jacob Zuma. He arranged the first visit with Piet [Croucamp],' Eugene explained.

Zuma met Eugene in Pretoria Central shortly before the general election in April 2009, although the visit got no media attention until 2010. At the time, the Presidency would not divulge anything about the nature of the meeting. Later, Eugene said to me: 'The meeting with Jacob Zuma took place after Zuma became president of the ANC. The meeting was pleasant, relaxed, good-natured and friendly. I am sorry not to have met Jacob Zuma earlier, in the years 1990 to 1993. He was and is a strong leader.'

In 2010, political analyst and academic Piet Croucamp became part of Eugene's life when he wrote an article in Rapport called 'De Kock wás die apartheidstaat' ('De Kock was the apartheid state'). At that stage there was talk of Zuma granting political amnesty to selected prisoners. In his article, Croucamp suggested that as a 'political prisoner', and not 'merely a criminal', Eugene deserved to be freed. Croucamp continued: 'Up to and including the 1990s, there was no difference between what De Kock saw as his orders and what would have been required for maintaining an authoritarian security machine.'[1]

Once they had read the article, Eugene's aunt Naomi – and then Eugene himself – made contact with Croucamp, who eventually became the primary role-player in Eugene's parole applications. He also became one of Eugene's regular Pretoria Central visitors and the intermediary through whom I met Eugene.

A strange and – for many – unlikely bond grew between the two men.

Eugene applied for parole for the first time in 2011. Croucamp was involved. According to Eugene, the parole sitting on 15 December 2011 lasted for exactly one minute and 32 seconds. He also applied for parole in 2012, 2013 and 2014.

From my occasional contact with Croucamp over the past few years I gathered that the parole applications required a huge amount of work, and that the disappointment when yet another request was turned down, often for the strangest reasons, was crushing. For example, in 2014 the Minister of Correctional Services, Michael Masutha, maintained that the family members of Eugene's victims had not been consulted sufficiently.

This was despite the fact that Eugene asked many families personally for forgiveness and co-operated closely with both the Khulumani Support Group[2] and the National Prosecuting Authority's Missing Persons Task Team to help trace the remains of missing activists.

It was inevitable that Eugene's parole application would become a political point-scorer.

In July 2014 Masutha declared that Eugene de Kock would have to wait another year and consult with the families of the victims before his parole could be considered. Eventually, after a court hearing and much deliberation among legal advisors, it was agreed that the parole board would make a recommendation to the minister on 19 December, who would announce his decision on 31 January 2015. This was made an order of the court.

In an article published in July 2014, Croucamp wrote that the minister's refusal to grant parole was a 'bitter pill': 'In the past 20 years in at least 25 cases he [Eugene] has seen and entered into discussions with victims or their families. The minister's reasons for refusal to grant his parole – so that the families of the victims could be involved in the process – was like a kick in the stomach for me and De Kock. We'd been doing this for years.'[3]

He mentioned that not long before this, Eugene and some of his former colleagues had, through the National Prosecuting Authority's Missing Persons Task Team, brought an 84-year-old mother a degree of peace 'after she had searched for the remains of her child, a victim of apartheid, for almost three decades'.

One languid afternoon, a few days before Masutha's announce-ment, I waited for Croucamp at a Melville restaurant under the comforting shade of some trees. He arrived on his BMW motor-cycle, relaxed in shorts and his trademark dark-blue bandanna. Over a pizza and glasses of Sprite Zero we pondered his intense and committed involvement with Eugene over the past four years.

Croucamp explained that he had attended some of Eugene's court appearances as far back as 1996, taking careful note of how Eugene presented himself. 'He was always in the back of my mind,' said Croucamp. 'Then in 2010 the editor of *Rapport* asked me to write about him.'

Croucamp believes fairness should prevail in a democratic state and that, on this basis, Eugene deserved parole. According to him, their friendship initially had politics as a common denominator. 'I was also drawn to his extraordinary integrity,' he said. 'I developed compassion for him.'

Croucamp leaned forward, elbows on the table. 'It was a journey.'

He made it clear, however, that it had been worth the trouble in the end. 'The excellent relationship between me and Gene made it a natural process. Furthermore, politics is my natural habitat – and I wanted to see justice bear fruit.'

Shortly before his release, when I asked Eugene about his rela-tionship with Croucamp, he replied that the feeling was mutual and that he had learnt a great deal from the academic: 'While I developed slowly, Piet's IQ is sky high. Our friendship and con-versations also made me realise how much I had missed out on in my childhood,' he said. 'Just think what a difference committed teachers can make in leading children to 360-degree thinking!'

A small group of erstwhile comrades supported Eugene for the past 21 years, but along the way they were joined by a few others, such as Croucamp. He says the efforts by individuals such as Croucamp and others who tried to bring perspective to the debate around his case were of inestimable value. 'I was so bloody helpless and immature in my own life that I never would have been able to recognise the right advice. But I consciously decided to live – come hell or high water.'

Before Eugene's release, South Africans were divided about whether or not he should get parole. The Democratic Alliance (DA) was outspoken about its opposition to his release for some time. Many South Africans, such as Jane Quin, shared this sentiment. Vlakplaas operatives murdered Quin's sister Jacki and her husband on 19 December 1985 in an attack on their Lesotho home. Four ANC activists and three Lesotho civilians also died.[4]

In 2014 Quin wrote an emotional column in Daily Maverick entitled 'De Kock ordered my sister's killing – and no, his debt is not paid'.[5] While she believes he did not deserve to be released, she did find it unjust that he was the only one serving time for apartheid crimes.

She wrote about him in no uncertain terms: 'Let us not forget who De Kock is; what he has done. He was responsible for hundreds, if not thousands of deaths: sometimes indirectly through the provision of arms to Inkatha supporters, the Transkei coup plotters, tampered grenades, false information and through his activities with Koevoet outside the country. De Kock was directly responsible for multiple other murders, alone and/or with others …'

In her argument, Quin shows little or no forgiveness: 'If anyone seriously considers the possibility of parole for De Kock, at least ensure it is purposeful. Although any consideration would be over-compensatory to Prime Evil, at least ensure some material quid pro quo. For example, in this case, his possible release should depend on the successful conviction of the conspirators in command of the murder mission. Material from the Truth Commission cannot be used directly as evidence, but the testimony of De Kock can, with full transcripts of previous explanations available to assist his memory. Better yet, keep him inside as company to the other perpetrators when they come to join him.'

She ended by expressing the view that the Truth and Reconciliation Commission's valuable contribution to post-apartheid South Africa had been watered down: 'So it is less De Kock that I care about, one way or another, than it is the failure of the country to carry through the value and promise of the TRC.'

There was support for Eugene's parole application, however – including from clinical psychologist Pumla Gobodo-Madikizela, who conducted a number of interviews with Eugene in Pretoria Central in the 1990s. In 2013 her book, *A Human Being Died that Night*, was adapted for the stage and performed first in London, and then in Cape Town and Johannesburg, in 2014. It was also staged in New York in May 2015.

In March 2014 I attended a performance of the play at the Market Theatre. The stage, which depicted a jail cell, appeared grim and functional. Eugene was played by the British actor Matthew Marsh. In the opening scene he sat on a chair in ankle shackles that were bolted to a cement floor. At the beginning of the performance, Pumla – played by Noma Dumezweni, born in Swaziland but now a celebrated British actress – sat opposite him at a table, on a chair with castors so she could move away quickly should he become aggressive.

The two characters start off playing word games, and gradually progress to proper dialogue. Eugene's character eventually reveals his background, emotions and motives to Pumla. He also gives a penetrating and graphic description of the cruelty and murders he saw and took part in. The play does not spare the audience; it dredges up many gruesome recollections. But its message is ultimately one of hope and forgiveness, that honesty and open discussion can lead to us comprehend the full extent of our humanity. In her opening-night speech, Gobodo-Madikizela reiterated that forgiveness is the only marker on the road ahead for us South Africans: that our mission must be to rediscover and reclaim our humanity. The play, like the book, aims to promote healing and mutual understanding in a polarised society.

'I don't think Eugene de Kock is Prime Evil,' said Gobodo-Madikizela, concluding her speech. 'I think he represents the phenomena of a perpetrator.'

During our meeting in Melville, Piet Croucamp echoed this sentiment: 'The apartheid system was evil, but Eugene de Kock the man is not inherently evil. Remove the system and the person returns to normal.'

Eugene probably summed himself up best during one of his interviews with Pumla when he called himself 'apartheid's crusader.' 'That's how I saw myself. But at the end of the day, Pumla, all that I really am is a veteran of lost ideologies. Once you realise that, you lose your innocence.'[6]

After the performance I got talking to the two British actors and asked if they had ever met Eugene. Marsh and Dumezweni then seized the opportunity for a visit to Pretoria Central to meet him a few days before returning to Britain. They were deeply moved by the visit; on the way back, they expressed empathy with Eugene.

Gobodo-Madikizela mentioned in a subsequent telephonic conversation that she had seen the performance again the night after the two actors had met Eugene. She said even before they had told her about the visit, she could see in their acting that they had since met Eugene.

Marsh maintained contact, writing a few letters to Eugene. He also wrote an article about his meeting, which appeared in the British *The Guardian*. In it, he explained why he supported Eugene's release:

> Firstly, even though you can argue that his sentence – two life terms plus 212 years – was fully justified by his terrible crimes, I feel you have to place this in context: hundreds of people could have been charged with similar crimes, but he was one of only a handful put through that process. And of that handful, he is the only one still in prison …
>
> Secondly, I don't think prison should be solely for punishment, with no possibility of rehabilitation and for-giveness. Everything I have learned about De Kock has made me believe he has been on a profound moral journey, actively helping to locate missing persons from the years of apartheid, and also working to convert white suprema-cists in prison. I believe he has courageously acknowledged the evil he did and has worked hard to become a different man. He is not a monster. He is a man deserving of his freedom.
>
> In one of our after-show discussions – having played to an audience of psychologists, psychiatrists and psychother-apists – we heard from a black social worker helping people in Soweto deal with the wounds of the terrible ANC versus Inkatha violence of 1990–94. He recalled hearing an unre-pentant young man boasting about the thrill of slaughter. Strangely, the social worker still felt the urge to give that killer a hug, because he could see the damage within. When

Noma and I got up to say goodbye to De Kock, we hugged him, and he hugged us back. It felt like the right thing to do.[7]

In his foreword to Gobodo-Madikizela's book, former judge Albie Sachs writes that Eugene started to acknowledge the past, first tentatively and then more openly, on a factual as well as an emotional level. He writes that our image of the past is infinitely complicated by the way in which Eugene turned it on its head.

'He has become the accuser, not of those who denounce and convict him, but of those who initially extolled and rewarded his services. The same sharp intelligence and vivid perceptions that he once used as head of the assassination unit, he now employs to expose his former masters. With a formidable capacity to analyse his own conduct, he reflects on the wicked activities of his generation and exposes the far from banal evil he had contributed towards.'[8]

Sachs also says, though, that he doubts whether Eugene has revealed himself fully: 'At the same time, it is also undeniable that he has a highly organised and creative mind, a great facility with language, and a well-developed capacity to read others reading him. What is the truth about the truth about the truth?'[9]

Will we ever know?

'As I understand it, you would have been sentenced to death under the previous dispensation?' I asked Eugene in my very last visit to Kgosi Mampuru II on 24 January 2015 – his eldest son's 28th birthday, coincidentally.[10]

'Yes, I would have,' he replied. 'And I wouldn't have opposed it. I would, however, have wanted to stipulate the execution method. It would have to be a firing squad of my friends and family, especially those from the defence force and the SAP. They would do it. I would definitely not want to be executed by the "enemy".'

I nearly choked on my flavoured prison water.

British actors Noma Dumezweni and Matthew Marsh who played Pumla Gobodo-Madikizela and Eugene de Kock in the theatre production *A Human Being Died That Night*. Here they are at the Koevoet Wall of Remembrance at the Voortrekker Monument in Pretoria.

While in jail Eugene has been contacted about matters relating to the past, including weapons supplied to the IFP or missing ANC and PAC members. The ANC keeps a list of missing persons – all the names of comrades who have not been accounted for and whom they suspect the security forces murdered. The search for their remains is ongoing and Eugene is committed to righting the injustices of the past.

The National Prosecuting Authority's Missing Persons Task Team (MPTT)[11] oversees this search and has asked Eugene to help.

During our last conversation in Melville, Croucamp mentioned the persistent and unfailing involvement of Madeleine Fullard, head of the MPTT, as well as the quality of the reports she had sent to the government about Eugene's assistance played a decisive role in his eventual parole. Her reports emphasise his dedication to help find the remains of former freedom fighters.

For example, on 3 September 2013 Eugene was taken under heavy guard to Croucamp's guesthouse in Melville for discussions with Fullard and other apartheid-era role-players, among them former cadres from the liberation movements and some of Eugene's former colleagues. The goal was to assist the ANC with its list of missing persons from the apartheid era and, possibly, to point out where bodies had been buried. Eugene told me in a letter how he experienced the day:

> The day started early. There were many guards with me. I was not used to all that space. And luckily I had not eaten that morning – I started feeling carsick – almost like feeling seasick – from all the rocking and back and forth and up and down in the car on the way to the meeting.
>
> I managed to persuade some of the guys [former Security Branch members and a few former defence force members] to help – the guys were not there themselves, but all the middlemen were. They would talk to the perpetrators and help [to provide information about where bodies had been buried] from there. That was the promise.
>
> What was good was that the people could look one another in the eye and see whether someone was lying or being false, or had been false. In that respect the whole exercise was worth the effort. We also made progress in various other respects. We met some of the MK veterans.

We could talk, at least, and there was good interaction as veterans and former opponents. So, we'll see what comes of it.

I just hope that the people of the NPA are satisfied because it took persuasion to get and keep that group of people [former operatives] together. They would not have been there if not to help me.

Piet Croucamp was satisfied but visibly relieved when we left, I think. Some of the neighbours from across the road, and others driving past, were rather interested to know what was up. Piet handled everything with humour, so I told him he should simply tell them that old skeletons belonging to us [Vlakplaas] had been found in his garden. He was not amused! But progress was definitely made, in my opinion.

Madeleine Fullard sat today with people whose faces are angelic but who are, in truth, as hard as granite.

They bought Nando's for me for lunch. It was beyond okay and I packed away three Magnum ice creams. What a pleasure!

Eugene told me, later, that the MK veterans keep a comprehensive record of every person for whom they are still searching. According to him, on that day in September 2013 he helped them in four cases with the names of those who had abducted and killed their comrades.

Croucamp's eyes crinkled at the corners when he started reminiscing about how impatient Eugene got, and how he fixated on small details to the detriment of the bigger picture, while working with the Missing Persons Task Team. 'He's his own worst enemy sometimes. I had to keep reminding him to stay focused on the light at the end of the tunnel.'

The freedom that beckoned after 21 years must have been difficult for Eugene to truly comprehend.

He often said to Croucamp of this process: 'I must just not incur a penalty kick in injury time.'

Eugene told me, also, that searching for the missing veterans' remains was a fascinating process. 'The body has to be exhumed with absolute precision in accordance with prescriptions, a process the forensic archaeologist [Eugene calls her 'the Argentine'] controls. She can establish with a high degree of certainty which blows were inflicted and which blow or wound probably caused the person's death.'

As I see it, through Eugene's involvement with the work done by Fullard and the Missing Persons Task Team he could slowly but surely start to recreate his identity. This team achieved great success thanks to his contributions and in this way he became an active helper or aide during his last years in prison. His contribution in this regard builds on his testimony at the TRC and the prosecuting authority in the 1990s, as well as his assistance to the Khulumani Group. Letters from the family members of apartheid victims who, with his help, had found a measure of peace, as well as the positive reaction by former MK members, all contributed to his successful parole application.

However, it also meant that with his last, successful parole application, Eugene was especially exposed and vulnerable in terms of the feedback given by the Missing Persons Task Team to the parole board. From our conversations I realised he often still struggled to trust them. The man who seldom trusted others and who had always worked on the principle of divide and rule remains ever suspicious. Once you have descended into the underworld of covert action, it is very difficult to accept people and things at face value again.

Eugene remains a complex, enigmatic figure. Even after twenty years in prison, the last chapters of his personal narrative – the story he tells to others and to himself – has not been written yet. Exciting new chapters await – the first year of his parole which he'll spend in a safe house, under the strictest imaginable conditions. Then, possibly, a new career and continued involvement with the Missing Persons Task Team. The chance to reunite with his children.

But the way I see it, living an ordinary and normal life might never be part of his reality.

18

Afrikaner fado

'That we remain alive is our guilt.'

This quote by German psychologist and philosopher Karl Jaspers on a Facebook page came to mind when I recently went to see a movie at The Bioscope, a theatre in Fox Street in Johannesburg's trendy Maboneng Precinct. The evening's film was a surprise: *The Terminator* (1984), starring Arnold Schwarzenegger.

But when the scenes of fire, death and destruction started, waves of nausea washed over me. The film cut too close to the bone after all the stories I had heard over the past few years. The scene of a woman burned to a skeleton triggered images of Vlakplaas torture victims.

It felt as if an unbearable weight was pressing down on my Afrikaner chest. It was a wake-up call: I had strayed too close to the abyss.

On one hand I realised that if I had not climbed into the heart of the whore, as Dirk Coetzee put it, I would not have gained insight into Eugene the person, the soldier, the assassin for the state. I had to dive in head-first to complete a book about Eugene and the madness of the Vlakplaas era. On the other hand I felt I knew too much.

I needed to get out.

After three years on the trail documenting Eugene's life, I think differently about many things. Nothing will ever be the same again.

I view men – especially those who were in the SAP and the SADF in the apartheid era – with empathy and greater understanding. I am reminded of something I read in Antjie Krog's *Country of My Skull*: 'And suddenly I know: I have more in common with the Vlakplaas five than with this man [FW de Klerk]. Because they have walked a road, and through them some of us have walked a road. And hundreds of Afrikaners are walking this road – on their own with their own fears and shame and guilt. And some say it, most just live it. We are so utterly sorry. We are deeply ashamed and gripped with remorse.'[1]

I have listened to the stories of many former Security Branch members. Their brutal actions can never be euphemised. But once upon a time they were simply youthful foot soldiers of the government of the day, young men who believed they were fighting a just war. The apartheid system dehumanised the victims of atrocities as well as the transgressors who committed these crimes.

They lived a unique kind of hell, as Nick Howarth, a former sergeant in the East Rand riot unit described it: 'For the riot policeman on the ground it was hell on earth. They were given the task of curbing the violence which entailed putting their bodies in the line of fire, loading many hundreds of corpses for the morgue (victims of township violence) and placing their own family lives on the sacrificial altar of duty. They were the only barrier between peace and an all-out civil war. They were shot at, spat at, blamed, maimed, killed, divorced and driven crazy by being exposed to the horror reality of non-stop violence.'[2]

In our polarised society today, it is more critical than ever for the recollections and voices of war veterans and former armed forces members to be heard. Former members need to talk to their loved ones about their experiences (as Eugene de Kock was able to in court and during his TRC amnesty hearing) – even if it is shocking to listen to their wild, primitive side that caused such damage and destruction. Marlantes says society must give former members and war veterans space to express all aspects of their experiences: the guilt, the sadness and the pride.[3]

Being an Afrikaner is a complex thing; for many years I felt ambiguous about it. As sweetly familiar my mother-tongue Afrikaans is, as culturally foreign some fellow Afrikaners are to me. I wanted nothing to do with their blinkered outlook, stubbornness and conservative culture. Yes, this is a gross generalisation. But try as I might to prove the opposite – we are by no means all the same – we still have the same blood flowing through our veins. We differ as widely as the heavens yet share an umbilical cord.

This is one of the most important insights I've come to. By squarely facing the past, I have learnt how, as an Afrikaner woman, I can face the future without guilt but with a heightened sense of responsibility, insight and respect. It took this revisiting and reassessing of the past to become a whole person, a whole Afrikaner, again. This time, for the first time, without any ignorance or pretence.

'Afrikaner history embodies simultaneously a fatalistic anticipation of unavoidable collective loss and a mysterious vitality,' writes historian Hermann Giliomee in his book *The Afrikaners: Biography of a People.*[4]

I hear the *saudade,* the call in which yesterday, today and tomorrow are united for us; our insignificance on the African continent as opposed to a fate that sways over everything. This is the Afrikaner fado that will echo in this wide and complex country until all eternity.

On 30 January 2015, a day after Eugene's 66th birthday, Masutha announced that Eugene would be released on parole. At the media conference the minister began by thanking President Jacob Zuma for his advice and assistance. He stumbled slightly over his words and the microphone buzzed before he went on to say that he had taken cognisance of the various positive reports that had been submitted; Eugene's continuous attempts to improve his skills; the assistance he had given to the Missing Persons Task Team and the National Prosecuting Authority; and the fact that Eugene had consulted fully with the family members of the victims.

At last, Eugene was on parole.

It's over.

I walk around in Bedford Shopping Centre, looking for the linen and towels Eugene has requested for his room in the safe house that will be his home for the next year. Down pillows and a duvet, two sets of single bedsheets – everything cotton, in dove grey or dark blue. Two sets of towels. My small contribution to his first steps to freedom.

In a letter dated December 2012, Eugene outlined his wishes for the future.

> What will life be like if I get out? I want to live simply and quietly and with as much dignity as possible.
>
> To thank the people who stood by me through the years and even just yesterday and today. Everyone, each individual, has played a part in my survival, in maintaining my spirit, humanity, soul and body.
>
> I will look around for something to do, and work. Must support myself at all costs.
>
> I will even approach the press for difficult assignments they don't want, or that others won't do. The more dangerous the better, like second-by-second reporting from

the very first vehicle on the frontline in Libya. I am not on a self-destruction mission, but don't want to be idle and my experience can surely be put to use. Makes no difference what the salary is.

Simplicity will be the philosophy. A glass of good red wine, a light cheese, plenty of fresh, raw vegetables, a good, fresh slice of bread, nothing rich.

My clothes ordinary, serviceable, neat, workman/ outdoor type, a pair of good Hi-Tec boots, etc. Nothing opulent or expensive; just good quality that lasts and lasts, but as little of it as possible. Have never been a man for jewellery etc.

Live simply, so if you get somewhere and want to stay there, you don't have to go back to collect anything.

Good company, laughter, space, fresh air. I have always been like this. Not a person for crowds or being surrounded by people.

Walk, exercise, but the most enjoyable is always the simplest, nature; there from whence we all came.

And then write and write. Read what I could not get here [in prison]; lap up the good DVDs [movies]. Put up a bird feeder, not just for seed-eaters, but also put fruit out for the fruit-eaters. The fruit in turn attracts insects, so the insect-eaters come too.

I want to watch *Scent of a Woman* with Al Pacino, my favourite, six or ten times. The story, the depth of it and the never-give-up factor is really palpable. See it if you haven't yet – you'll be the richer for it. It is deeply human and authentic.

I want to see my two sons. Thank their mother for how well she has brought them up, and apologise for all her suffering, loneliness, hardship and isolation from all that was familiar once. They have made history in their own way; a deep story in itself.

There'll be no celebrating, revelry or excess.

My time, biologically, is short, relative to those who are younger, and I want what I have left to be quality time. If possible I want to thank everyone who has helped and supported me personally with a handshake. There is only one way to do this properly and that is to look the person in the eye.

Then I must see to my health. I have arranged with Dr Wouter Basson for all medical tests and whatever else needs doing. I will also ask his advice about other aspects, because although I am advanced in years I do not plan to go celibate to my grave. I don't believe in that. Not at all! My role model is the late Dr Chris Barnard.

Walk through flea markets. Visit bookshops. Drink a cappuccino. Meander through art galleries and lose myself there.

See a Nataniël performance.

Sit in the pouring rain of a summer thunderstorm while the wind gusts and the thunder and lightning shake and light up the heavens.

Go walking with dogs, and hug them sometimes. Laugh at their tricks and attention-seeking.

Join a nature conservation project for a threatened species.

Answer honestly when people ask questions about the past.

Withhold answers about personal matters, past or present.

I can't believe I ever took up a weapon for this *Vervloekte land* [cursed country], one book that FA Venter never wrote. There was *Geknelde land, Offerland, Beloofde land* – I'm not even sure any more. He forgot about this cursed fucking country when he wrote *Die keer toe ek my naam vergeet.*

I will never pick up a weapon for any country again. Never!

Early in the morning, four o'clock, just to go and sit quietly with my coffee and hear which bird starts chirping first. All the other birds then start, here and there. It's never the same kind of bird, never in the same place. In the bush or the city, the birds are the same: they wait for one to start chirping first. Almost as if they're reluctant to disturb the others, and wait, rather, for one to break the rule.

I want to sit quietly beside a stream and watch how the insects fall into the water and count the seconds down for a fish to take them from below.

Everything that made me a good hunter. Not of animals.

Endnotes

Chapter 1

1   Van Niekerk, Dolf. 1972. *Die son struikel.* Johannesburg: Perskor Publishers.

Chapter 2

1   Wilkens, I. & Strydom, H. 2012. *The Super Afrikaners: Inside the Afrikaner Broederbond.* Johannesburg and Cape Town: Jonathan Ball. Foreword by Max du Preez.

2   The report was written in Afrikaans and has been translated here into English.

3   Until Standard 4 (Grade 6) Eugene attended Laerskool Christiaan Beyers in Springs and for his Standard 5 year he went to Baanbreker Laerskool in Boksburg.

4   This political and cultural organisation was in favour of replacing the Union with an Afrikaner republic and was against South Africa's participation in the Second World War. In the 1940s, when it became increasingly paramilitary, the Ossewabrandwag was banned.

5   Initially called *Nongqai* now *Servamus*.

6   Compiled from: De Kock, E.A. Handwritten report for the Unisa criminologist, Prof. A. van der Hoven, as part of her evaluation for mitigation of sentence in *State vs Eugene Alexander de Kock*, 1996. Supplemented with information from my personal discussions with De Kock.

7   De Kock, E.A. Handwritten report for the Unisa criminologist, Prof. A. van der Hoven, as part of her evaluation for mitigation of sentence in *State vs Eugene Alexander de Kock*, 1996. Supplemented with information from my personal discussions with De Kock.

8   Compiled from: De Kock, E.A. Handwritten report for Prof. A. van der Hoven, as part of her evaluation for mitigation of sentence in *State vs Eugene Alexander de Kock*, 1996. Supplemented with information from my personal discussions with De Kock.

9   Compiled from: De Kock, E.A. Handwritten report for Prof. A. van der Hoven, as part of her evaluation for mitigation of sentence in *State vs Eugene Alexander de Kock*, 1996.

10   Van der Hoven, A. Evaluation report re mitigation of sentence in *State vs Eugene Alexander de Kock*, Case No. CC 266/94. At the time, Van der Hoven was with Unisa's Department of Criminology and testified on behalf of De Kock for mitigation of punishment.

Chapter 3

1   From August 1967 military service was obligatory for all white South African men above the age of 16 years.

2   De Kock, E. & Gordin, J. 1998. *A Long Night's Damage: Working for the Apartheid State.* Saxonwold: Contra Press.

3   De Kock, E. & Gordin, J. 1998. *A Long Night's Damage: Working for the Apartheid State.* Saxonwold: Contra Press.

4   De Kock, E.A. Handwritten report for criminologist Prof. A. Van der Hoven as part of her evaluation report in mitigation of sentence in *State vs Eugene Alexander de Kock*, 1996.

5   Ibid.

6   Sergeant Johan Kuhn, Constable Robert Swart, Constable Erhard Strydom, Constable Donnie Hough and Constable Willem Conradie were captured on 8 March 1974 while they were swimming in the Zambezi River.

7   De Kock, E.A. Handwritten report for criminologist Prof. A. van der Hoven, as part of her evaluation report in mitigation of sentence in *State vs Eugene Alexander de Kock*, 1996.

8   Henderson, J.L. 1990. Heroes and Hero Makers. In C. Jung et al. *Man and His Symbols.* London: Penguin Arkana.

9   Van der Hoven, A. 1996. Evaluation report in *State vs Eugene Alexander de Kock*, Case No. CC 266/94.

Chapter 4

1   Jansen, A. 2012. Eenheid 6: Die Oosrand brand. *e-Nongqai* 3(7), July 2012.

2   Scholtz, L. 2013. *Die SAW in die Grensoorlog, 1966–1989*. Cape Town: Tafelberg.

3   De Kock, E.A. Handwritten report for criminologist Prof. A. van der Hoven as part of her evaluation report for mitigation of sentence in *State vs Eugene Alexander de Kock*, 1996.

4   From special Operation Koevoet, later called Ops K and then simply Koevoet (Crowbar).

5   Compiled from: De Kock, E.A. Handwritten report for criminologist Prof. A. van der Hoven as part of her evaluation report for mitigation of sentence in *State vs Eugene Alexander de Kock*, 1996; and De Kock, E.A. 'Red Horse War', Unpublished manuscript.

Chapter 5

1   De Kock, E. & Gordin, J. 1998. *A Long Night's Damage: Working for the Apartheid State*. Saxonwold: Contra Press.

2   Pittaway, J. *Koevoet: The Men Speak*. Unpublished manuscript.

3   Stiff, P. 2004. *The Covert War: Koevoet Operations Namibia 1979–1989*. Alberton: Galago Publishing.

4   Baker, D. Unpublished manuscript, copy in author's possession. According to Baker, Derrick Botha handled administration. Interpretation of intelligence and interaction with 5 Recce was carried out by Jan Potgieter and Andy van der Walt. Investigation was Coetzee Els and Eric Winter's responsibility. The operational investigation teams were divided as follows: Z4 under Sakkie du Plessis and André Erwee; Z6 under Diempie du Plessis and Timol Coetzee (at Ombalantu); and Z8 under Joos Engelbrecht (at Oganjera). Willem Botha and Okkie Marais handled Oshivelo. Sakkie van der Merwe and Dicks Dietrichsen were stationed at Onaimwandi, where captured SWAPO soldiers were held. At the fighting groups' base, George Steyn and Chris Nell were responsible for recruitment, training, salaries, logistics and the welfare of the special constables.

5   Feinstein, A. 2011. *Battle Scarred: Hidden Costs of the Border War*. Cape Town: Tafelberg.

6   De Kock, E.A. Handwritten report for criminologist Prof. A. van der Hoven as part of her evaluation for mitigation of sentence in *State vs Eugene Alexander de Kock*, 1996. Translated here into English.

7   De Kock, E. 'Red Horse War'. Unpublished manuscript, copy in author's possession.

8   Bradley died tragically on 31 March 2013, the night before he was due to leave his home in Durban to attend the unveiling of the Koevoet Wall of Remembrance at the Voortrekker Monument. He was attacked by robbers in his home and shot dead.
9   Hattingh, Dawid. Unpublished manuscript, copy in author's possession.
10 Ibid.
11 Marlantes, Karl. 2011. *What it is Like to Go to War.* London: Corvus.

Chapter 6

1   Marlantes, K. 2011. *What it is Like to Go to War.* London: Corvus.
2   Junger, S. 'Why Veterans Miss War'. TED conference, January 2014. Available at www.ted.com/talkssebastian_junger_why_veterans_miss_war.
3   Spaarwater, M. 2012. *A Spook's Progress: From Making War to Making Peace.* Cape Town: Zebra Press.
4   Hanton, L. As quoted in in *Koevoet – The Men Speak.* Unpublished manuscript by Jonathan Pittaway.
5   De Kock, E.A. Handwritten report for criminologist Prof. A. van der Hoven as part of her evaluation for mitigation of sentence in *State vs Eugene Alexander de Kock,* 1996.
6   De Kock, E.A. 'Red Horse War', Unpublished manuscript.
7   Letter from E. de Kock to P. Stiff. Copy in author's possession.
8   De Kock, E.A. Handwritten report for criminologist Prof. A. van der Hoven as part of her evaluation for mitigation of sentence in *State vs Eugene Alexander de Kock,* 1996.
9   Ibid.
10 De Kock, E. 'Application for presidential pardon: Mr Eugene Alexander de Kock', 11 June 2002.
11 Ibid.

Chapter 7

1   De Kock, E. 'Application for presidential pardon: Mr Eugene Alexander de Kock', 11 June 2002.
2   Van der Hoven, Anna. Evaluation report for mitigation of sentence in *State vs Eugene Alexander de Kock,* 1996. Translated here into English.
3   Ibid.
4   Ibid.

5   Craig Michael Williamson is a former policeman who was unmasked as a spy in 1980. He received amnesty from the TRC for the murders of Jeanette and Katryn Schoon and Ruth First (Joe Slovo's wife).

6   Anonymous: 'Bomb blast at ANC London office', *The Guardian*, 14 March 1982.

7   Drogin, Bob. 'Apartheid spy tied to '86 assassination of Sweden's Palme' in the *Los Angeles Times*, 27 September 1996, see http://articles.latimes. com/1996-09-27/news/mn-48144_1_apartheid-spy.

8   Klein Angola was a residential area in a cul-de-sac behind the Oshakati General Hospital. People of different nationalities, including German and Angolan-Portuguese residents, as well as the Koevoet loners, lived there. Four houses on both sides of the dirt road were used as barracks for the Alpha and Bravo groups.

9   De Kock, E.A. Handwritten report for criminologist Prof. A. van der Hoven as part of her evaluation for mitigation of sentence in *State vs Eugene Alexander de Kock*, 1996.

10   De Kock, E.A. Handwritten report for criminologist Prof. A. van der Hoven as part of her evaluation for mitigation of sentence in *State vs Eugene Alexander de Kock*, 1996.

11   De Kock, E.A. 'Red Horse War'. Unpublished manuscript.

Chapter 8

1   De Kock, E. 'Application for presidential pardon: Mr Eugene Alexander de Kock', 11 June 2002.

2   Johan Coetzee. 'Die stigting van Vlakplaas en die Teen-Terroriste Eenheid'. Undated and unsigned. Memorandum in the possession of Hennie Heymans.

3   Coetzee was commissioner of police from 1 June 1983 to 30 June 1987.

4   De Kock, E. 'Application for presidential pardon: Mr Eugene Alexander de Kock', 11 June 2002. Additional information has been taken from our numerous discussions.

5   Johan Coetzee. 'Die stigting van Vlakplaas en die Teen-Terroriste Eenheid'. Undated and unsigned. Memorandum in the possession of Hennie Heymans.

6   De Kock, E. 'Application for presidential pardon: Mr Eugene Alexander de Kock', 11 June 2002.

7   De Kock, E. 'Application for presidential pardon: Mr Eugene Alexander de Kock', 11 June 2002.

8   The SOE decoration was awarded between 1979 and 2004. Recipients are entitled to the post-nominal letters SOE, which stands for the latin *Stella Officii Egregii*. See http://en.wikipedia.org/wiki/South_African_Police_Star_for_Outstanding_Service

9   See http://www.thecradockfour.co.za/Home.html.

10   See http://www.justice.gov.za/trc/media/pr/1999/p990618a.htm.

11   De Kock, E. & Gordin, J. 1998. *A Long Night's Damage: Working for the Apartheid State*. Saxonwold: Contra Press, p. 135.

12   Ibid, p. 134.

13   On 14 August 1986 the alleged MK operators Mbongeni Kone (MK Bernard), Shadrack Msolwa Sithole, Assen Jeremia Thimula (MK Tallman) and Mzwandile Hadebe (MK Zandile) were shot dead in an ambush near the Swaziland border on the Nerston–Amsterdam road.

14   Four members of the Chesterville Youth Organisation, namely Russell Mngomezulu, Muntuwenkosi Dlamini, Russell Mthembu and Sandile Khawula, were murdered during an operation in May/June 1986 by Vlakplaas askaris. See http://sabctrc.saha.org.za/reports/volume3/chapter3/subsection20.htm?t=%2BVlakplaas&tab=report.

15   See http://www.sabctrc.saha.org.za/reports/volume2/chapter2/subsection29.htm and https://web.stanford.edu/class/history48q/Documents/EMBARGO/2chap2.htm.

16   See http://sabctrc.saha.org.za/reports/volume6/section3/chapter1/subsection13.htm?t=%2BVlakplaas&tab=report

17   Report of the Truth and Reconciliation Commission, Volume 2. See http://www.justice.gov.za/trc/report/finalreport/Volume%202.pdf.

18   See http://sabctrc.saha.org.za/reports/volume1/chapter5/subsection13.htm?t=%2BVlakplaas&tab=report.

19   De Kock, E. & Gordin, J. *A Long Night's Damage: Working for the Apartheid State*. Saxonwold: Contra Press.

20   Laurence, P. 1990. *Death squads: Apartheid's Secret Weapon*. London: Penguin Forum Series.

21   Ibid.

22   De Kock, E. 'Application for presidential pardon: Mr Eugene Alexander de Kock', 11 June 2002.

23   Ibid.

24 De Kock, E. & Gordin, J. 1998. *A Long Night's Damage: Working for the Apartheid State*. Saxonwold: Contra Press, p. 139.

25 Marlantes, K. 2011 *What it is Like to Go to War*. London: Corvus.

26 https://www.nelsonmandela.org/omalley/index.php/site/q/03lv02167/04lv 02264/05lv02335/06lv02357/07

27 De Kock, E. 'Application for presidential pardon: Mr Eugene Alexander de Kock', 11 June 2002.

28 Ibid. After Vlakplaas's activities came to light in 1989, Eugene was warned by a general that the media planned to visit the farm and he was asked to 'clean up' the place. According to him, the weapons were first moved to the police farm called Daisy and later to a police training centre at Maleoskop before they were taken to the Police College in Pretoria.

29 De Kock, E. 'Application for presidential pardon: Mr Eugene Alexander de Kock', 11 June 2002.

30 Ibid.

31 Ibid.

32 Klatzow, D. 2011. *Steeped in Blood: The Life and Times of a Forensic Scientist*. Cape Town: Zebra Press, p. 94.

33 In January 1991, on orders from Eugene de Kock, Sikhakhane was kidnapped and murdered by Vlakplaas operators in Greytown. He was dissatisfied that he had not been permanently appointed by the police and threatened to return to the ANC. Vlakplaas operator Willie Nortjé gave evidence before the TRC that he took Sikhakhane into the bush near Greytown, shot him with an AK-47, and left the body for the wildlife to consume. Evidence was presented that the police had a problem with Sikhakhane and had called in the help of Vlakplaas. De Kock received amnesty for the murder of Sikhakhane. See http://m24arg02.naspers.com/ argief/berigte/dieburger/1996/03/29/12/18.html and http://sabctrc.saha. org.za/documents/amntrans/pietermaritzburg/53696.htm.

34 According to De Kock, Lieutenant-General Johan le Roux, former head of the West Rand security police, told him that he never wanted to see Japie Maponya again in Krugersdorp. De Kock understood that this meant Maponya had to be murdered. De Kock said that Maponya was captured and taken to Vlakplaas were he was interrogated about his brother Odirile, who was an MK member. Maponya was tortured and the next day De Kock took him to Swaziland where he was to be murdered. He was accompanied by David van der Walt, Willie Nortjé and Eugene Fourie. They collected a variety of garden tools from Freek Pienaar of Piet Retief

and went to a plantation just this side of the Swaziland border. Nortjé shot Maponya in the head with a 9 mm pistol and De Kock then stood above the dead man and hit the corpse with a spade over the head. Sapa, 'De Kock hit victim with spade to ensure death', 13 July 1999; see also http://www.justice.gov.za/trc/media%5C1999%5C9907/p990713c.htm.

35 De Kock, E. 'Application for presidential pardon: Mr Eugene Alexander de Kock', 11 June 2002.

36 The Sanhedrin was the highest court in ancient Israel. In the New Testament the Sanhedrin held the series of mock trials that eventually led to the crucifixion of Jesus. See www.gotquestions.org/Sanhedrin.html

37 De Kock, E. 'Application for presidential pardon: Mr Eugene Alexander de Kock', 11 June 2002.

38 Ibid.

39 De Kock, E. 'Application for presidential pardon: Mr Eugene Alexander de Kock', 11 June 2002.

40 De Kock, E. & Gordin, J. 1998. *A Long Night's Damage: Working for the Apartheid State*. Saxonwold: Contra Press.

41 Open letter from Eugene de Kock to Jacques Pauw, July 2014. In author's possession. Translated from the Afrikaans.

42 Van der Merwe, J. 'Ope brief aan Helen Zille oor Eugene de Kock', 13 July 2014. See http://praag.co.za/?p=25772.

43 Van der Merwe, J. 'A Crying Shame that Colonel De Kock has not been Pardoned,' 13 July 2014. See http://praag.org/?p=14695.

44 Open letter from Eugene de Kock to Jacques Pauw, July 2014. In the author's possession.

Chapter 9

1 Dlamini, J. 2014. *Askari*. Auckland Park: Jacana Media.

2 De Kock, E. 'Application for presidential pardon: Mr Eugene Alexander de Kock', 11 June 2002.

3 TRC: Final report, volume 2, chapter 3, section 66: see http://sabctrc.saha.org.za/reports/volume2/chapter3/subsection66.htm&tab=report.

4 Dlamini, Jacob. *Askari*. Auckland Park: Jacana Media, 2014.

5 De Kock, E. 'Application for presidential pardon: Mr Eugene Alexander de Kock', 11 June 2002.

6 Ibid.

7 Ibid.

8 Dlamini, J. 2014. *Askari*. Auckland Park: Jacana Media.

9 De Kock, E. 'Application for presidential pardon: Mr Eugene Alexander de Kock', 11 June 2002.

10 Ibid.

11 Dlamini, J. 2014. *Askari*. Auckland Park: Jacana Media.

12 De Kock, E. 'Application for presidential pardon: Mr Eugene Alexander de Kock', 11 June 2002.

13 Ibid.

14 Dlamini, J. 2014. *Askari*. Auckland Park: Jacana Media.

15 Ibid.

16 De Kock, E. 'Application for presidential pardon: Mr Eugene Alexander de Kock', 11 June 2002.

17 De Kock, E. 'Application for presidential pardon: Mr Eugene Alexander de Kock', 11 June 2002.

18 De Kock, E.A. 'The Betrayal of Glory Sedibe – Combat name: MK September', 5 September 2011, abridged. Copy in author's possession.

19 Donaldson, A. 'Glory Sedibe and the Boers', 3 December 2014. See http://www.politicsweb.co.za/politicsweb/view/politicsweb/en/page71619?oid=847294&sn=Detail

20 De Kock, E.A. 'The Betrayal of Glory Sedibe – Combat name: MK September', 5 September 2011, abridged. Copy in author's possession.

21 Ibid.

22 Dlamini, J. 2014. *Askari*. Auckland Park: Jacana Media; see also Rebecca Davis, 'Betrayal Chronicles: The Agonising Case of Apartheid's Black Collaborators', Daily Maverick, 5 December 2014.

Chapter 10

1 Van der Hoven, A. 'Evaluation report in the case *State vs Eugene Alexander de Kock*', case number CC 266/94.

2 'Investigative inquiry: Wilhelm Riaan Bellingan', Truth and Reconciliation Commission, 12 February 1997, pp. 35-64, translated.

3 Ibid.

4 Van der Hoven, A. 'Evaluation report in the case *State vs Eugene Alexander de Kock*', case number CC 266/94.

5 This act was revoked on 31 March 1993. See the submission of General Krappies Engelbrecht to the TRC on 24 October 1996.

6   De Kock, E. 'Application for presidential pardon: Mr Eugene Alexander de Kock', 11 June 2002.
7   Ibid.
8   Ibid.

Chapter 11

1   Laurence, P. 1990. *Death Squads: Apartheid's Secret Weapon*. London: Penguin Forum Series.
2   Ibid.
3   Human Rights Watch. 1991. 'The Killings in South Africa: The Role of the State Security Forces and the Response of the State', at http://www.hrw. org/reports/1991/southafrica1/5.htm#_ftn17. See also Harms Commission of Inquiry Records 1990, Historical Papers, William Cullen Library, University of the Witwatersrand, at http://www.historicalpapers.wits.ac.za/ inventory.php?iid=8255; and Laurence, P. 1990. *Death Squads: Apartheid's Secret Weapon*. London: Penguin Forum Series.
4   De Kock, E. 'Application for presidential pardon: Mr Eugene Alexander de Kock', 11 June 2002.
5   See http://www.justice.gov.za/trc/amntrans%5C1999/99081631_ pre_990823pt.htm, 'On resumption: 23 August 1999 – Day 5'.
6   Human Rights Watch. 1991. 'The killings in South Africa: The role of the State Security Forces and the Response of the State', at http://www.hrw.org/ reports/1991/southafrica1/5.htm#_ftn17.
7   The operatives at Vlakplaas were Dave Baker, Riaan Bellingan and Martiens Ras.
8   The operatives at Midrand were Paul van Dyk, Louw van Niekerk and Wouter Mentz.
9   The operatives in Waterkloof were Eugene de Kock, Willie Nortjé, Dawid Brits, Snor Vermeulen and Lionel Snyman.
10 De Kock, E. 'Application for presidential pardon: Mr Eugene Alexander de Kock', 11 June 2002.
11 See http://www.justice.gov.za/trc/amntrans%5C1999/99081631_ pre_990823pt.htm, 'On resumption: 23 August 1999 – Day 5'.
12 See www.justice.gov.za/trc/amntrans/1999/99081631_pre_990819pt.htm. According to the transcript, Operation Excalibur led to the tracing of a large number of weapons that had been smuggled illegally into South Africa.

13 Among other things, Operation Vula enabled Nelson Mandela (still in jail at the time) to make contact with Oliver Tambo (then ANC president in exile). Padraig O'Malley writes in *Shades of Difference: Mac Maharaj and the Struggle for South Africa* that Operation Vula was centralised mainly in Natal and that between 1988 and 1990 large quantities of weapons were brought into, and hidden in, South Africa. Operation Vula is described as one of the ANC's most successful operations. See http://www.armsdeal-vpo.co.za/articles10/vula.html.

14 De Kock, E. 'Application for presidential pardon: Mr Eugene Alexander de Kock', 11 June 2002.

15 The Goldstone Commission, officially known as the Commission of Inquiry Regarding the Prevention of Public Violence and Intimidation, was appointed to investigate the political violence and intimidation that took place between July 1991 and April 1994. The chairman was Judge Richard Goldstone. See http://www.anc.org.za/themes.php?t= Goldstone%20Commission&y=1992.

16 O'Mally, P. 'Provision of weapons to the IFP', see https://www.nelsonmandela.org/omalley/index.php/site/q/03lv02167/04lv02264/05lv02335/06lv02357/07l; and http://sabctrc.saha.org.za/originals/finalreport/volume2/html/BMvolume2_s1ch7_pg23.htm.

17 O'Mally, P. 'Provision of weapons to the IFP', see https://www.nelsonmandela.org/omalley/index.php/site/q/03lv02167/04lv02264/05lv02335/06lv02357/07l.

18 Potgieter, De Wet. 'Eugene de Kock's Explosive 64-tonne Question'. Daily Maverick, 27 March 2013.

19 O'Malley, P. 'Political Violence in the Era of Negotiations and Transition, 1990-1994', see https://www.nelsonmandela.org/omalley/index.php/site/q/03lv02167/04lv02264/05lv02335/06lv02357/07lv02372/08lv02379.htm.

20 O'Malley, P. 'Political Violence in the Era of Negotiations and Transition, 1990-1994', see https://www.nelsonmandela.org/omalley/index.php/site/q/03lv02167/04lv02264/05lv02335/06lv02357/07lv02372/08lv02379.htm.

21 Novello, A. Handwritten notes compiled during the court case, dated 17 September 1996.

22 De Kock, E. & Gordin, J. 1998. *A Long Night's Damage: Working for the Apartheid State*. Saxonwold: Contra Press.

23 De Beer, F. 'Vlakplaas-base wis glo van gru-moord', 28 January 1995, at http://152.111.1.87/argief/berigte/dieburger/1995/01/28/5/2.html

24 De Kock, E. 'Application for presidential pardon: Mr Eugene Alexander de Kock', 11 June 2002.

25 See http://www.justice.gov.za/trc/decisions%5C2001/ac21141.htm.

26 Open letter from Eugene de Kock to Jacques Pauw, July 2014. In author's possession. Translated from the Afrikaans.

27 De Kock, E. & Gordin, J. 1988. *A Long Night's Damage: Working for the Apartheid State.* Saxonwold: Contra Press.

28 Ibid.

29 Open letter from Eugene de Kock to Jacques Pauw, July 2014. In author's possession.

30 According to Hennie Heymans, this was the covert collection unit of military intelligence, with Brigadier 'Tolletjie' Botha in command.

31 Eugene maintained that all declarations for the various commissions of enquiry – particularly the Harms Commission – were drawn up by General [then Brigadier] Krappies Engelbrecht. 'We just had to sign. We did not make any declarations ourselves. The police could not risk letting us draw up our own submissions. Claims registers, travel and accommodation registers, documents such as security reports and all possible proof was traced and removed or destroyed. In this way we wiped out all records and any proof that might [later] have exonerated us.'

A former police officer, Marius Morland, explained that in about March 1994 an order was issued to the police to destroy all secret documentation. A second order was sent out in August 1994 that under no circumstances were any documents in police possession to be destroyed, not even dossiers. That order still stands today. (Information provided by Hennie Heymans.)

32 De Kock, E. 'Application for presidential pardon: Mr Eugene Alexander de Kock', 11 June 2002.

33 Novello, A. Handwritten notes made during the court case, dated 17 September 1996. She also mentions that Eugene feared for the safety of his wife and children and said he would not be able to testify if they were still in the country.

34 De Kock, E.A. 'Application to take an early pension', 1993; 'Settlement agreement between the SAP and E.A. de Kock', 1993.

Chapter 12

1 The IPA is the biggest police organisation in the world and there is no

discrimination of any kind among members on grounds of rank, gender, race, colour, language or religion.

2   De Kock, E. & Gordin, J. 1998. *A Long Night's Damage: Working for the Apartheid State*. Saxonwold: Contra Press.

3   De Kock, E. 'Application for presidential pardon: Mr Eugene Alexander de Kock', 11 June 2002.

4   Ibid.

5   Ibid.

6   Gideon Nieuwoudt (1951–2005), a former member of the Security Branch, was involved in many incidents of torture and the murders of anti-apartheid activists including Steve Biko, the Cradock Four and the Pebco Three. He was a deeply feared policeman: his interrrogation methods involved wet sacks, poison and torture instruments. He had more than five sittings before the TRC. SABC, 'Truth Commission: Special Report', Episode 68, Section 2. See http://sabctrc.saha.org.za/tvseries/episode68/section2/transcript1.htm?t=%2BMotherwell+%2Bcar+%2Bbomb&tab=tv.

7   SABC, 'Truth Commission: Special Report', Episode 68, Section 2. See http://sabctrc.saha.org.za/tvseries/episode68/section2/transcript1.htm?t=%2BMotherwell+%2Bcar+%2Bbomb&tab=tv.

8   According to De Kock, they included Herman Barend du Plessis, Johannes Martin Van Zyl, Marthinus Ras and Wybrand du Toit.

9   De Kock, E. 'Application for presidential pardon: Mr Eugene Alexander de Kock', 11 June 2002.

10 Ibid.

11 Minister Adriaan Vlok and General Johan van der Merwe also admitted guilt in 2007 in a criminal hearing on the charge of Rev. Frank Chikane's attempted murder. They received suspended sentences. See Wanneburg, G. 2007. 'Adriaan Vlok spared jail', *Mail & Guardian*, 17 August 2007, at http://mg.co.za/article/2007-08-17-adriaan-vlok-spared-jail.

12 Van der Hoven, A. 'Evaluation report in the matter of *State vs Eugene Alexander de Kock*', case number CC 266/94.

13 Ibid.

14 Ibid.

15 Van der Merwe, J. 2010. *Trou tot die dood toe: Die Suid-Afrikaanse Polisiemag*. Johannesburg: Praag.

16 Acccording to Hennie Heymans, General Johan van der Merwe told him Eugene had specifically asked to be placed at Vlakplaas.

17 Truth and Reconciliation Commission: Investigation section 29-19,

November 1996. Questions and answers with Brigadier Willem Frederick Schoon, pp. 22–23.

18 Ibid., pp. 67–73.
19 Van der Merwe, J. 2010. *Trou tot die dood toe: Die Suid-Afrikaanse Polisiemag.* Johannesburg: Praag, p. 402. Quotations translated from the original Afrikaans.
20 Ibid., p. 402.
21 Kotzé, J. 2012. *Mean Streets: Life in the Apartheid Police.* Bloemfontein: Smashwords.
22 Giliomee, H. 2003. *The Afrikaners: Biography of a People.* Cape Town: Tafelberg, pp. 641–642.
23 Heunis, J. 2007. *Die Binnekring: Terugblikke op die Laaste Dae van Blanke Regering.* Johannesburg and Cape Town: Jonathan Ball Publishers. Quotation translated from the original Afrikaans.
24 De Kock, E. & Gordin, J. 1998. *A Long Night's Damage: Working for the Apartheid State.* Saxonwold: Contra Press.
25 Ibid.
26 Junger, S. 'Why Veterans Miss War'. TED talk presented in January 2014. See www.ted.com/talks/sebastian_junger_why_veterans_miss_war
27 Van der Hoven, A. 'Evaluation report in the matter of *State vs Eugene Alexander de Kock*', case number CC 266/94.
28 Bing, E. 2013. *Unmaking of the Torturer.* Pretoria: Lapa.
29 Marlantes, K. 2011. *What it is Like to Go to War.* London: Corvus.

Chapter 13

1 Van der Merwe, J. Abridged version of the sentencing proceedings in the matter of *State v Eugene Alexander de Kock,* case number CC 266/94, 1996.
2 Ibid.
3 Van der Hoven, A. 'Evaluation report in the matter of *State vs Eugene Alexander de Kock*', case number CC 266/94.
4 Eugene de Kock as quoted in Van der Hoven, A. 'Evaluation report in the matter of *State vs Eugene Alexander de Kock*', case number CC 266/94.
5 Van der Hoven, A. 'Evaluation report in the matter of *State vs Eugene Alexander de Kock*', case number CC 266/94.
6 Ibid.
7 Van der Merwe, J. Abridged version of the sentencing proceedings in the matter of *State v Eugene Alexander de Kock,* case number CC 266/94, 1996.

8   Van der Hoven, A. 'Evaluation report in the matter of *State vs Eugene Alexander de Kock*', case number CC 266/94, p. 29.

9   Van der Merwe, J. Abridged version of the sentencing proceedings in the matter of *State v Eugene Alexander de Kock,* case number CC 266/94, 1996.

Chapter 14

1   Bizos, G. 2000. *No One to Blame? In Pursuit of Justice in South Africa.* Cape Town: David Philip, p. 236.

2   De Kock, E. 'Application for presidential pardon: Mr Eugene Alexander de Kock', 11 June 2002.

3   As quoted in De Kock, E. 'Application for presidential pardon: Mr Eugene Alexander de Kock', 11 June 2002.

4   De Kock, E. 'Application for presidential pardon: Mr Eugene Alexander de Kock', 11 June 2002.

5   As quoted in De Kock, E. 'Application for presidential pardon: Mr Eugene Alexander de Kock', 11 June 2002.

6   De Kock, E. 'Application for presidential pardon: Mr Eugene Alexander de Kock', 11 June 2002.

7   Ibid.

8   Gobodo-Madikizela, P. 2004. *A Human Being Died that Night.* Cape Town: David Philip.

9   See http://www.faithandleadership.com/multimedia/pumla-gobodo-madikizela-forgiveness-possible.

10 'Pumla Gobodo-Madikizela, Review: Dare We Hope? Facing our Past to Find a New Future', at http://karinamagdalena.com/tag/pumla-gobodo-madikizela/.

11 See http://en.wikipedia.org/wiki/King_Leopold%27s_Ghost.

12 As quoted in De Kock, E. 'Application for presidential pardon: Mr Eugene Alexander de Kock', 11 June 2002.

13 Novello, A. Handwritten notes made during the court case, dated 17 September 1996.

14 As quoted in De Kock, E. 'Application for presidential pardon: Mr Eugene Alexander de Kock', 11 June 2002. See also attachment to De Kock's application: Affidavit by Felicia Mathe (previously Dlodlo), sworn and signed at Johannesburg on this 3rd day of June 2002.

Chapter 15

1 See http://en.wikipedia.org/wiki/C_Max.
2 Verster, JP, Report to Pieter Botha, attorney, regarding the prisoner Eugene Alexander de Kock, 30 July 2009. Copy in possession of author. Original document in Afrikaans.
3 Compiled from Verster, JP, Report to Pieter Botha, attorney, regarding the prisoner Eugene Alexander de Kock, 30 July 2009. Copy in author's possession.
4 Ibid.
5 Turner, Jann. 'Eugene: From Apocalypse now to Scotland the Brave', *The Weekly Mail & Guardian*, 28 May 1999. Copy in author's possession.
6 Ibid.
7 Ibid.
8 De Kock, L, 'Psychological Report: Eugene de Kock', 20 May 2002. Copy in author's possession.
9 Du Toit, HG [chief social worker: Pretoria Local Prison], 'Social Work Report: Eugene de Kock', 20 May 2002. Copy in author's possession.
10 Ibid.
11 Geldenhuys, M., Coetzee, J. & Van der Merwe, J., 'Representations regarding presidential pardon or reprieve in terms of Section 84 of the Constitution of South Africa with regard to convictions and/or terms of imprisonment: Colonel de Kock', 18 May 2002. Copy in author's possession.

Chapter 16

1 Brink, A.P. 1970. *Fado*. Cape Town: Human & Rousseau. Quotation freely translated from the original Afrikaans.
2 Rex, T. 2012. *6 Ster: Binne die ingewande van Pretoria-Sentraal*. Pretoria: Lapa.
3 Ibid. Quotations translated from the original Afrikaans.
4 The diary entries are translated from the original Afrikaans.
5 Coetzee, C. 1998. *Op soek na generaal Mannetjies Mentz*. Cape Town: Tafelberg.

Chapter 17

1 Croucamp, P. 'De Kock wás die apartheidstaat', *Rapport*, 10 January
2010, at http://152.111.1.87/argief/berigte/rapport/2010/01/12/RH/17/
PietDeKock.html. Quotation translated from the original Afrikaans.

2 Nearly 85 000 survivors of apartheid-related human-rights violations are
members of the Khulumani Support Group, which was started by survivors who testified at the Truth and Reconciliation Commission. See http://
www.khulumani.net/reconciliation/item/986-free-de-kock-as-tribute-to-
legacy-of-mandela.html.

3 Croucamp, P. 'Vyande sal De Kock laat gaan', *Netwerk24*, 22 July 2014, at
http://www.netwerk24.com/stemme/2014-07-22-vyande-sal-de-kock-laat-
gaan. Quotation translated from the original Afrikaans.

4 See http://www.polity.org.za/polity/govdocs/pr/2000/pr0531b.html for
more information.

5 Quinn, J. 'De Kock ordered my sister's killing – and no, his debt is not
paid', 24 June 2014, at http://www.dailymaverick.co.za/article/2014-06-27-
op-ed-de-kock-ordered-my-sisters-killing-and-no-his-debt-is-not-paid/#.
VMDanNKUeSo.

6 Gobodo-Madikizela, P. 2003. *A Human Being Died that Night.* Cape Town:
David Philip.

7 Marsh, M. 'The Day I Hugged Prime Evil', *The Guardian*, 9 June 2014.

8 Gobodo-Madikizela, P. 2003. *A Human Being Died that Night.* Cape Town:
David Philip.

9 *Ibid.*

10 In June 1995 the Constitutional Court abolished the death penalty
after the president at the time, FW de Klerk, had placed a morato-
rium on it in 1990. See http://www.sahistory.org.za/dated-event/
sa-constitutional-court-abolishes-death-penalty-0.

11 By 2014 the Missing Persons Task Team had exhumed and recovered the remains of 97 activists, returned them to their families and
facilitated reburial arrangements. See http://www.justice.gov.za/
events/2014events/20140816-trc.html.

Chapter 18

1 Krog, A. 1998. *Country of My Skull.* Johannesburg: Random House.

2 Howarth, N. 2012. *War in Peace.* Alberton: Galago Publishing.

3   Marlantes, K. 2011. *What it is Like to Go to War.* London: Corvus.
4   Giliomee, H. 2003. *The Afrikaners: Biography of a People.* Cape Town: Tafelberg.

Bibliography

Allen, R. (SAP Special Task Force). Written contributions, 2014.

Arendt, H. 1964. *Eichmann in Jerusalem: A Report on the Banality of Evil.* New York: The Viking Press.

Baker, D. 2014. (Koevoet and Vlakplaas). Use of material from an unpublished Koevoet manuscript.

Blake, A. 2013. *Moord-en-roof: Die lewe van 'n baasspeurder.* Cape Town: Tafelberg.

Bezuidenhout, L. & Kamongo, S. 2012. *Skadu's in die sand.* Johannesburg: 30 Degrees South Publishers.

Bing, E. 2013. *Unmaking of the Torturer.* Pretoria: Lapa.

Bing, E. 2009. 'Unmaking the torturer: Re-establishing meaning and identity after committing atrocities', at http://hdl.handle.net/10500/2744.

Botha, P.H. 2008. 'Petition for a Presidential Pardon in Terms of the Provisions of Section 84(2)(j) of the Constitution of the Republic of South Africa (Receipt of previously dated application 2002-06-11)'.

Brink, André P. 1970. *Fado.* Cape Town: Human & Rousseau.

Coetzee, C. 1998. *Op soek na generaal Mannetjies Mentz.* Cape Town: Tafelberg.

Coetzee, J., Geldenhuys, M. & Van der Merwe, J. 2002. 'Representations Regarding Presidential Pardoning or Reprieve in Terms of Section 84 of the Constitution of South Africa with Regard to Convictions and/or Terms of Imprisonment: Colonel Eugene de Kock', 18 May 2002.

De Kock, E & Gordin, J. 1998. *A Long Night's Damage: Working for the Apartheid State.* Saxonwold: Contra Press.

De Kock, E.A. 2002. 'Application for Presidential Pardon: Mr Eugene Alexander De Kock'.

De Kock, E.A. 1996. Handwritten report for criminologist Prof. A. van der Hoven for use in her submission for mitigation of sentence.

De Kock, E.A. 'Red Horse War', unpublished manuscript. Copy in author's possession.

De Kock, E.A. 'The Betrayal of Glory Sedibe – Combat Name: MK September', 5 September 2011.

De Kock, E.A. Discussions, correspondence, provision of his personal computer, documents, personal photographic material; also psychological reports from the time of imposition of sentence to the present, 2011–2014.

De Kock, E.A. Personal diary, 2005, Pretoria Central. Copy in author's possession.

De Kock, E.A. Personal diary 2006, Pretoria Central. Copy in author's possession.

De Kock, E.A. Personal diary 2007, Pretoria Central. Copy in author's possession.

De Kock, L. 'Psychological Report: Eugene de Kock', 20 May 2002.

De Kock, E.A. 'Luister nou, Generaal, onthou u die keer toe …' *Rapport*, 20 July 2014, p. 6.

Dlamini, J. 2014. *Askari*. Auckland Park: Jacana Media.

Durand, A. 2011. *Zulu Zulu Golf*. Cape Town: Zebra Press.

Durand, A. 2012. *Zulu Zulu Foxtrot*. Cape Town: Zebra Press.

Du Toit, H.G. 2002. (Chief social worker: Pretoria Local Prison). 'Social Work Report: Eugene de Kock'.

Elsdon, A.D. 2009. *Die lang generaal: Die duistere politieke sluipmoorde van die ou Suid-Afrika*. Cape Town: Umuzi.

Feinstein, A. 2011. *Battle Scarred: Hidden costs of the Border War*. Cape Town: Tafelberg.

Finkel, D. 2013. *Thank you for your Service*. New York: Sarah Crichton Books.

Giliomee, H. 2003. *The Afrikaners: Biography of a People*. Cape Town: Tafelberg.

Gobodo-Madikizela, P. 2003. *A Human Being Died that Night*. Cape Town: David Philip.

Herbstein, D. & Evenson, J. 1989. *The Devils are Among Us: The War for Namibia*. London: Zed Books.

Heunis, J. 2007. *Die binnekring: Terugblikke op die laaste dae van blanke regering*. Johannesburg and Cape Town: Jonathan Ball Publishers.

Hooper, J. 2012. *Koevoet! Experiencing South Africa's Deadly Bush War*. Warwickshire: GG Books.

Howarth, N. 2012. *War in Peace*. Alberton: Galago Publishing.

Jansen, A. 2014. *Glipstroom*. Cape Town: Human & Rousseau.

Jung, C.G. 1990. *Man and his Symbols*. London: Penguin.

Junger, S. 'Why veterans miss war', TED Talk, January 2014, at www.ted.com/talks/ sebastian_junger_why_veterans_miss_war.

Karsten, C. 2013. *'n Man van min belang*. Cape Town: Human & Rousseau.

Klatzow, D. 2010. *Steeped in Blood: The Life and Times of a Forensic Scientist*. Cape Town: Zebra Press.

Korff, G. 2009. *19 with a Bullet: A South African Paratrooper in Angola*. Johannesburg: 30 Degrees South Publishers.

Kotzé, J. 2012. *Mean Streets: Life in the Apartheid Police*. Bloemfontein: Smashwords.

Krog, A. 1998. *Country of My Skull*. Johannesburg: Random House.

Krog, A. 2009. *A Change of Tongue*. Cape Town: Zebra Press.

Laurence, P. 1990. *Death Squads: Apartheid's Secret Weapon*. London: Penguin Forum Series.

Lemon, D. 2006. *Never Quite a Soldier: A Rhodesian Policeman's War 1971–1982*. Alberton: Galago Publishing.

Lubbe, L. 2014. *Van Ovamboland tot Masjonaland*. Pretoria: Self-published.

Madikizela-Mandela, W. 2013. *491 Days: Prisoner Number 1323/69*. Johannesburg: Picador Africa.

Mandela, N. 1994. *Long Walk to Freedom*. Randburg: Macdonald Purnell.

Marlantes, K. 2011. *What it is Like to Go to War*. London: Corvus.

Marlantes, K. 2010. *Matterhorn: A Novel of the Vietnam War*. New York: Atlantic Monthly Press.

Marsh, Matthew. 'The Day I Hugged Apartheid's Prime Evil', *The Guardian*, 9 June 2014.

Mathe, F. In the Application of Eugene Alexander de Kock and The President of the Republic of South Africa: Affidavit by Felicia Mathe (previously Dlodlo), sworn and signed at Johannesburg on this 3rd day of June 2002. (Copy of this document attached as part of 'Eugene Alexander de Kock: Application for Presidential Pardon', 2002.)

Motau, C.M. Affidavit in the application of Eugene Alexander de Kock (Applicant) and The President of the Republic of South Africa (Respondent): 3 June 2002.

Napier, V, et al. *Risk Homeostasis: A Case Study of the Adoption of a Safety Innovation on the Level of Perceived risk*. Doctoral study, 2014, Pima Community College. (Secondary source: reference provided by Jim Hooper in an e-mail to the author.)

Nortje, P. 2003. *32 Battalion: The inside Story of South Africa's Elite Fighting Unit*. Cape Town: Zebra Press.

Novello, A. Evaluation report: Mr E.A. de Kock, Clinical impressions, 1996.

Novello, A. Handwritten notes taken during court case, dated 17 September 1996.

Pauw, J. 2006. *Dances with Devils: A Journalist's Search for Truth*. Cape Town: Zebra Press.

Pauw, J. 2012. *Little Ice Cream Boy*. Johannesburg: Penguin Books.

Pauw, J. 1992. Violence: The Role of the Security Forces. Paper presented at the Centre for the Study of Violence and Reconciliation, Seminar No. 4, 27 May 1992.

Pittaway, J. 2014. *Koevoet: The Men Speak*. Unpublished manuscript, permission granted for the use of certain parts of the manuscript.

Popham, P. 'Eugene de Kock: Apartheid's Sadistic Killer who his Country cannot Bring itself to Forgive', at http://www.independent.co.uk/news/world/africa/eugene-de-kock-apartheids-sadistic-killer-that-his-country-cannot-bring-itself-to-forgive-9631936.html, 28 July 2014.

Potgieter, D. 2007. *Totale aanslag: Apartheid se vuil truuks onthul*. Cape Town: Zebra Press.

Quinn, J. 2014. 'De Kock ordered my sister's killing – and no, his debt is not paid' in *Daily Maverick*, 27 June 2014.

Retief, H. 2011. *Byleveld: Dossier van 'n baasspeurder*. Cape Town: Umuzi.

Rex, T. 2012. *6 Ster: Binne die ingewande van Pretoria-Sentraal*. Pretoria: Lapa.

SAP, Confidential. 13 November 1963. *Veiligheidskeurings: Handleiding vir veldwerkers*.

Sereny, G. 1998. *Cries Unheard: The Story of Mary Bell*. London: Macmillan.

Scholtz, L. 2013. *The SADF in the Border War, 1966–1989*. Cape Town: Tafelberg.

Spaarwater, M. 2012. *A Spook's Progress: From Making War to Making Peace*. Cape Town: Zebra Press.

Stiff, P. 2004. *The Covert War: Koevoet Operations, Namibia 1979–1989*. Alberton: Galago Publishing.

Strachan, A. 1984. *'n Wêreld sonder grense*. Cape Town: Tafelberg.

Taljaard, J. 'Boyish Killer with an Itchy Trigger Finger', in *Mail & Guardian*, 10 March 1995.

Truth and Reconciliation Commission: Inquiry – Section 29, 19 November 1996, Questions and Answers: Brigadier Willem Frederick Schoon.

Truth and Reconciliation Commission: 12 February 1997, Investigative Inquiry: Wilhelm Riaan Bellingan.

Truth and Reconciliation Commission: Day 1 – 2 December 1996, Investigative Inquiry: Joe Mamasela.

Truth and Reconciliation Commission: Day 1 – 24 October 1996, Submission: General Krappies Engelbrecht.

Truth and Reconciliation Commission: Inquiry – Section 29, Day 2 – 25 October 1996, Submissions, questions and answers: General Basie Smit.

Truth and Reconciliation Commission: 29 October 1996, Submission: Johan Hendrik le Roux.

Truth and Reconciliation Commission: Inquiry in terms of Section 29 held at Durban on 16 July 1997, Major-General Jacobus Buchner. In camera.

Turner, J. 'Eugene: From Apocalypse Now to Scotland the Brave', in *Mail & Guardian*, 28 May 1999.

Van der Hoven, A. 2006. Application for Condonation for the Lapsed Period Regarding the Lodging of an Appeal against Two Lifelong Sentences.

Van der Hoven, A. 1996. Evaluation Report in the case *State vs Eugene Alexander de Kock* (Case No. CC 266/94).

Van der Merwe, J. 2010. *Trou tot die dood toe: Die Suid-Afrikaanse Polisiemag*. Praag Publishers.

Van der Merwe, J. 'Geen greintjie waarheid'. *Rapport Weekliks*, 27 July 2014.

Van der Merwe, J. 2014. The Conflict of the Past: A Factual Review, 2014, at http://www.enongqaipublications.com/blog/the-conflict-of-the-past-a-factual-review.

Van der Merwe, J. 'Ek het De Kock nie in die steek gelaat', in *Beeld*, 24 July 2014.

Van der Merwe, W. 1996. Abridged version of sentencing proceedings in *State vs Eugene Alexander de Kock* (original in Afrikaans).

Van Niekerk, D. 1972. *Die son struikel*. Johannesburg: Perskor.

Van der Spuy, C. 2012. *Mens of monster: Die psige van 'n misdadiger*. Pretoria: Lapa.

Van Rooyen, P. 2012. *Rodriguez*. Cape Town: Quellerie.

Verster, JP. 2011. Addendum to reports (originals in Afrikaans) submitted to Pieter Botha, attorney, dated 22 July 2005 and 31 July 2006.

Verster, JP. Report (original in Afrikaans) to Pieter Botha, attorney, regarding prisoner Eugene Alexander de Kock, 30 July 2009.

Verster, JP. Report (original in Afrikaans) to Pieter Botha, attorney, regarding Mr Eugene Alexander de Kock, July 2005.

Verster, JP. Correspondence to Pieter Botha, attorney, regarding Eugene Alexander de Kock, December 2006.

Van Reybrouck, D. 2003. *Die plaag: Die stil geknaag van skrywers, termiete en Suid-Afrika*. Pretoria: Protea Bookhouse.

Vlok, A. 'Representations on Behalf of Colonel Eugene de Kock with Reference to an Official Presidential Pardon in Terms of Section 84 of the Constitution of The Republic of South Africa', 22 May 2002.

Wilkens, I. & Strydom, H. 2012. (Foreword by Max du Preez). *The Super Afrikaners: Inside the Afrikaner Broederbond*. Johannesburg and Cape Town: Jonathan Ball Publishers.

Woods, Kevin. 2007. *The Kevin Woods Story: In the Shadows of Mugabe's Gallows*. Johannesburg: 30 Degrees South.

INTERVIEWS

Airola, Katia. Discussions, written contributions and photographic material, 2012-2014.

Archer, George. Discussion, 2013.

Baker, Dave. Discussions and editing of parts of this manuscript, 2014.

Bellingan, Riaan. Discussion, 2014.

Benninghof, Dieter. Discussions, 2013.

Bezuidenhout, Leon. Discussion, 2013.

Bing, Elaine. Discussion, March 2014.

Bradley, Rodney. Discussion and written contributions, December 2012.

Brits, Koos. Discussions and written contributions, 2012.

Brüwer, Gerrit. Discussions and photographic material, 2012-2013.

Costa, Jorge. E-mail correspondence, 2014.

Croucamp, Piet. Discussions, 2011-2015.

Crouse, Deon. Discussions, June 2014.

De Kock, Elmarie. Discussions, 2014.

De Kock, Rita. Discussions, 2013.

De Kock, Vos. Discussions and photographic material, 2012–2013.

Dietrichsen, Dicks. Discussion, 2013.

Dreyer, Hans, General. Discussions and photographic material, 2012–2013.

Dumezweni, Noma. Discussion, 2014.

Du Toit, Daan. Discussion, 2013.

Eloff, Karin. Discussion, 2011 and 2014.

Fouchè, Paul. Discussions and perusal of his Compensation Commission report re
   PTSD, 2012–2013.

Fullard, Madeleine. Telephonic communication, 2015.

Gobodo-Madikizela, Pumla. Discussions, 2014.

Goosen, Thys. Discussion, 2014.

Gumbi, Kwanele. Discussion, 2014.

Hanton, Larry J. Discussions, photographic material and assistance while conducting
   interviews and during the writing process, 2011–2014.

Hattingh, Dawid. Discussions, 2014, and permission to use parts of his unpublished
   Koevoet manuscript, 2014.

Heymans, Hennie. Discussions, written contributions, assistance during the writing process and photographic material, 2012–2015.

Hooper, Jim. Photos and written contributions, 2014.

Horne, Christie (nèe De Villiers). Discussion, March 2014.

Howarth, Nick. Discussion, December 2013.

Kamongo, Shorty. Discussions, 2012.

Kariuke, F. Discussion, 2014.

Kilian, Hein. Discussions, 2013.

Kilino, Tony and Eugene. Discussion, 2013.

Koevoetbond vir Veterane [Society of Koevoet Veterans]. Discussions and contributions,
   2012 to 2014.

Liebenberg, John. Discussion, 2013.

Lourentz, George. Discussions, 2013.

Lotriet, Johan. Discussions and photo, 2013.

Mama, Candice. Discussions, 2014.

Marsh, Matthew. Discussions, 2014.

Matthews, Russell. Discussion, 2013.

Nel, Nella. Discussions, 2014.

Nortjé, Willie. Discussions and photos, as well as editing of parts of this manuscript, 2014.

Pienaar, Pine. Photos and discussions, 2013–2014.

Pittaway, Jonathan. Discussions and photos, 2013–2015.

Pigou, Piers. Telephonic communication and providing transcriptions, 2013.

Pretorius, Roelf. Discussion, 2013.

Roeland, Paula. Discussion, 2013.

Snyman, Lionel. Discussion, 2014.

Stoltz, Conrad. Visit to Eugene, 2014.

Van der Merwe, Izak. Discussions, 2013.

Van Etten, Naomi. Discussion, 2013.

Van Rensburg, Kobie. Discussion, 2014.

Vermeulen, Denise. Discussions, 2014.

Vermeulen, Nick. Discussions and illustrative material, 2012–2014.

Vingerkraal, group of former black Koevoet members. Interviews and photographic material, 2012.

Viktor, J General. Telephonic discussion, 2014.

Winter, Eric. Discussion, June 2014.

Woods, Kevin. Discussion, 2014.

Wright, Alet. Discussion, 2013.

Acknowledgements

My thanks to Larry Hanton who dedicated a few years of his life to accompanying me to countless meetings; Hennie Heymans who made an enormous contribution; Nicole Cronjé who made the manuscript a reality with her graphic expertise; Lorinda Nel, Amanda Geyer and Towes Pierce for reading sections of the manuscript; and to Marie Nel for her translations of parts of the manuscript.

Thank you so much to my family: Chris, Rohan, Christian and Carina for their patience and encouragement; also to all those who were prepared to talk to me and make photos available; and to Anne-Marie Mischke for her perceptive observations and comments. A special word of thanks goes to David (pseudonym). Above all I wish to thank my editor, Annie Olivier, for her close involvement in every aspect of this book this past year; for her unerring hand at the helm, her input, her honing and shaping, and her boundless energy. This book is her book too.

Lightning Source UK Ltd.
Milton Keynes UK
UKOW03f0928240316

270797UK00005B/181/P